Fresh Ways with
Vegetarian Dishes

TIME-LIFE BOOKS

EUROPEAN EDITOR: Ellen Phillips
Design Director: Ed Skyner
Director of Editorial Resources: Louise Tulip
Chief Sub-Editor: Ilse Gray

New edition © 1995 Time-Life Books Inc. All rights reserved.
This edition published 1995 by Brockhampton Press, a member of Hodder Headline PLC.
First published 1989 by Time-Life Books Inc,

No part of this book may be reproduced in any form or by any electronic or mechanical means, including information storage and retrieval devices or systems, without prior written permission from the publisher, except that brief passages may be quoted for review.

ISBN 1 86019 046 4
TIME-LIFE is a trademark of Time Warner Inc. U.S.A.

HEALTHY HOME COOKING

SERIES EDITOR: Jackie Matthews
Studio Stylist: Liz Hodgson

Editorial Staff for *Fresh Ways with Vegetarian Dishes:*
Editor: Frances Dixon
Researcher: Eva Reynolds
Designer: Paul Reeves
Sub-Editors: Christine Noble, Eugénie Romer

PICTURE DEPARTMENT:
Administrator: Patricia Murray
Picture Co-ordinator: Amanda Hindley

EDITORIAL PRODUCTION:
Chief: Maureen Kelly
Assistant: Samantha Hill
Editorial Department: Theresa John, Debra Lelliott

THE CONTRIBUTORS

SILVIJA DAVIDSON studied at Leith's School of Food and Wine and specializes in the development of recipes from Latvia and other international cuisines.

JOANNA FARROW, a home economist and recipe writer who contributes regularly to food magazines, is especially interested in decorative presentation of food. Her books include *Creative Cake Decorating* and *Novelty Cakes for Children.*

ANTHONY KWOK, originally a fashion designer from Hong Kong, has won several awards for his Orient-inspired style of cooking and was the *London Standard* Gastronomic Seafish Cook of 1986.

COLIN SPENCER, a well-known author on vegetarian cuisine, writes a regular column for *The Guardian* newspaper. He has published 12 cookery books in as many years, including *Gourmet Cooking for Vegetarians, Cordon Vert* and *The New Vegetarian.*

JANE SUTHERING is a cookery writer and home economist who has concentrated on the development of wholefood and vegetarian dishes. She is consultant to Cranks, a major health-food restaurant chain, and has created the recipes for all eight of their cookery books.

The following also contributed recipes to this volume: Pat Alburey, Cordelia Banks, Joanna Blythman, Maddalena Bonino, Jo Chalmers, Gail Duff, Anne Gains, Yvonne Hamlett, Carole Handslip, Cristine MacKie, Roselyne Masselin, Susie Theodorou, Nicole Veillard, Rosemary Wadey, Steven Wheeler.

THE COOKS

The recipes in this book were cooked for photography by Pat Alburey, Jacki Baxter, Allyson Birch, Jane Bird, Jill Eggleton, Joanna Farrow, Anne Gains, Carole Handslip, Antony Kwok, Lesley Sendall. Jane Suthering, Rosemary Wadey, Steven Wheeler. *Studio Assistant:* Rita Walters.

CONSULTANT

PAT ALBUREY is a home economist with a wide experience of preparing foods for photography, teaching cookery and creating recipes. She has written a number of cookery books and she was the studio consultant for the Time-Life series *The Good Cook.* In addition to acting as the general consultant on this volume, she created a number of the recipes.

NUTRITION CONSULTANT

PATRICIA JUDD trained as a dietician and worked in hospital practice before returning to university to obtain her MSc and PhD degrees. Since then she has lectured in Nutrition and Dietetics at London University.

Nutritional analyses for *Fresh Ways with Vegetarian Dishes* were derived from McCance and Widdowson's *The Composition of Food* by A. A. Paul and D. A. T. Southgate, and other current data.

This volume is one of a series of illustrated cookery books that emphasize the preparation of healthy dishes for today's weight-conscious, nutrition-minded eaters.

Fresh Ways with Vegetarian Dishes

BY

THE EDITORS OF TIME-LIFE BOOKS

BROCKHAMPTON PRESS

Contents

Asparagus Mousse with Goat Cheese Sauce

Polenta Pizza

Butter Bean Succotash

3 *A Sustaining Trio* 91

Goat Cheese and Parsley Ravioli

Fennel, Broccoli and Okra Croustades

4 *Microwaving Vegetarian Dishes* 123

The Vegetarian Alternative

In the prosperous West, where meat and fish have long been the cornerstones of a privileged diet, a significant change is under way. While entrenched carnivores continue to insist that a meal without animal flesh is not a true meal at all, a growing number of people are beginning to discover that meatless meals are not only possible, but are positively enjoyable. They also discover the paradox of vegetarian cooking: instead of less choice, there somehow seems to be more. Vegetables emerge from supporting roles on side dishes, challenging the imagination of a creative cook with their dazzling variety. Pasta and bread, no longer regarded as mere fillers, prove capable of the most sophisticated variations, while humble pulses and grains — so long dismissed as the poor man's food — become the respected, nutritious staples of the vegetarian alternative.

This book explores the wide world of cooking without meat, from simple suppertime bakes of vegetables or pulses to festive centrepieces for the dinner party. As with other volumes in the Healthy Home Cooking series, all of these dishes keep within low levels of sodium, cholesterol and saturated fat. In adhering to these guidelines, Time-Life's cooks have been assisted by the ingredients themselves, for vegetables and grains are naturally low in these substances. The result is a revelatory anthology of original vegetarian dishes.

A wealth of nutrients

Enjoying a meatless meal requires no elaborate justification. The food is quite simply delicious. It is also very good for you. A mere glance at the nutritional charts on pages 136 to 139 offers reassurance to the novice in vegetarian cookery. Grains, pulses (the group including dried beans, lentils and peas), nuts, eggs and cheese are all packed with proteins. Many of the green vegetables, including cabbage, broccoli and asparagus, are also valuable sources of this body-building nutrient. A single sweet green pepper contains approximately three times the recommended daily minimum intake of vitamin C; two carrots a day provide more than enough vitamin A. Spinach is a storehouse of calcium and iron — along with a whole alphabet of vitamins — while the lowly potato is not only high in vitamins B_3 and B_6, but surprisingly low in calories too.

Less familiar nutrients, all of them equally essential to good health, are also amply represented by vegetarian ingredients. Peanuts, vegetable oils and egg yolk are among foods rich in vitamin E, necessary for healthy cells and the healing of wounds. Cabbage, lettuce and cauliflower all contain vitamin K, which enables the blood to clot. Wheat bran, a major component of wholemeal flour, is rich in magnesium, potassium, zinc and copper.

Of all the essential nutrients, carbohydrates are the least appreciated. Our principal source of energy, they include sugars and starches. While sugars convert readily into energy but contain few nutrients, starches are a much misrepresented food group. Traditional slimming diets have frightened people away from starchy foods such as potatoes, bread and pasta. Yet these satisfying staples are not in themselves particularly fattening. A potato, for instance, contains fewer calories than an equal weight of lean steak. It is the topping traditionally associated with starchy foods — the butter, soured cream or rich sauce — that does the damage. What is more, carbohydrates are naturally full of proteins, vitamins and minerals. When prepared with discretion, they can be eaten with a clear conscience.

Any vegetarian dish made with whole, unrefined ingredients has the added benefit of a high fibre content. Dietary fibre is itself indigestible, yet it assists the digestion of food and bulks out waste material, thus speeding up its passage through the intestines. Extravagant health claims have been made for this improbable nutritional hero, but it is likely that fibre helps prevent diseases of the bowel — possibly including cancer — and reduces the body's absorption of cholesterol. Whole grain cereals are a major source of dietary fibre, but so too are nuts and pulses, as well as fresh vegetables such as celery, cabbage, spinach, broccoli, peas and potatoes eaten in their skins.

A meatless way of life

There are many reasons for adopting a vegetarian diet. For some it is simply a matter of a distaste for meat and fish; others may be attracted by the relatively low price of meatless meals; yet others find a persuasive moral justification for becoming vegetarians. Whatever the motivation, those reducing or abandoning meat in their diet must look closely at what they eat. In giving up meat they are abandoning a rich source of nutrients, especially of protein. In a diet that includes meat and fish, protein deficiency is very rare; just 125 g (4 oz) of beef, for instance, supplies half of the recommended daily intake of protein for an adult man. When meat is absent from the diet, eggs and cheese loom large as key sources of protein. Eggs are 12 per cent protein and hard cheeses about 25 per cent, compared with 20 to 30 per cent in meat and about 20 per cent in fish. Increasing one's intake of eggs and cheese to compensate for lost meat and fish protein, however, is not an ideal solution. Egg yolks are high in cholesterol and many cheeses are full of saturated fat, which increases the level of cholesterol in the blood. Although some cholesterol is necessary to the proper functioning of the body, a diet high in cholesterol and saturated fat can lead to arterial disease and the danger of strokes. Thus the wise vegetarian gains the bulk of his or her protein from grains — 6 to 13 per cent protein — and pulses — about 20 per cent.

But percentages do not tell the whole story. Of the 20 amino acids that are the building blocks of proteins, 12 can be synthesized within the body; the other eight, known as "essential" amino acids, must be obtained from food. Meat, fish, eggs and dairy products are the only foods that have all eight of these essential acids in almost exactly the right proportion for the body's needs. Grains, pulses, nuts and seeds each contain only some of these eight acids. Thus to complete the protein jigsaw vegetarians must be sure to eat a variety of foods. Pulses cooked with grains or with nuts and seeds supplement each other to create a balanced amino acid intake.

Many traditional vegetarian diets strike just this balance. A poor Jamaican may cook no more than a dish of rice and peas for his main meal; a poor Indian eats his lentils with a wholemeal chappati. Lacking any precise nutritional knowledge, these two diverse cultures, like many others, have devised ways of providing a balanced supply of protein from vegetarian sources.

Variety is the key not just to consuming the right mix of amino acids but also to gaining a good supply of all vitamins and minerals. Vegetarians must make a point of choosing widely from the vast range of vegetables, fruits, grains, pulses, nuts and seeds available. Provided they do so, and also eat modest quantities of eggs and cheese, they have no need of food supplements. Only vegans, who reject animal products entirely, must supplement their diets with vitamin B_{12}. Small amounts of this nutrient are essential to human life but only significantly present in animal sources. It is readily available, however, in tablets or in fortified vegetarian foods such as yeast extracts.

Choosing and storing vegetarian ingredients

Few modern convenience foods are more truly convenient than grains, nuts, seeds and pulses. Supermarkets increasingly stock supplies of these ingredients, but many are still only available from wholefood shops. Choose an outlet with a rapid turnover to ensure that the stock is fresh. It is not easy to guess the age of most dry ingredients. Beans with wrinkled skins, however, have almost certainly spent too long on the shelf.

Kept cool, dark and dry in airtight containers, whole grains such as rice and millet will keep virtually for ever. Under the same conditions, beans, peas and lentils have a shelf life of up to six months. If they are kept beyond this time, they require more cooking, until finally they reach an age when they will not become tender with boiling at all.

Unshelled nuts also keep fresh-tasting for six months or more. Shelled whole nuts, which are more convenient for cooking, remain fresh for about three months when stored in airtight containers. Nut fragments or ground nuts go stale more quickly and should be used within six weeks.

Shopping for fresh ingredients is more of a challenge. It is important to buy vegetables that are as fresh as possible, choosing those with crisp leaves and stalks or firm skins. Avoid limp, pale-coloured specimens; deep oranges, yellows and greens promise a rich supply of vitamin A.

Vegetables are best not stored at all but eaten straight from the shop or — better still — the garden. Green vegetables such as celery, lettuce, spinach and broccoli are particularly affected by light and warmth, losing nutrients even while on display in a shop. A shop-tired cabbage may have lost half of its vitamin C by the time it reaches home. If they must be stored, perishable vegetables keep best in the refrigerator at a temperature of between 2° and 5°C (35° and 40°F). Root vegetables are more durable. Stored in a dark, airy place at a temperature of about 10°C (50°F) — a basement or a cool cupboard is ideal — carrots and onions will remain fresh for several weeks. Potatoes can last throughout the winter in these conditions, though they will inevitably lose some of their vitamin C if stored for long periods.

The best cooking methods

Much of the art in preparing nutritious vegetarian food lies in cooking vegetables so that they do not lose their goodness. However carefully fresh ingredients have been selected and

The Key to Better Eating

Healthy Home Cooking addresses the concerns of today's weight-conscious, health-minded cooks with recipes developed within strict nutritional guidelines.

The chart on the right gives dietary guidelines for healthy men, women and children. Recommended figures vary from country to country, but the principles are the same everywhere. The average daily amounts of calories and protein shown here are taken from a report by the U.K. Department of Health and Social Security; the maximum advisable daily intake of fat is based on guidelines given by the National Advisory Committee on Nutrition Education (NACNE); those for cholesterol and sodium are based on upper limits suggested by the World Health Organization.

The volumes in the Healthy Home Cooking series do not purport to be diet books, nor do they focus on health foods. Rather, the books express a commonsense approach to cooking that uses salt, sugar, cream, butter and oil in moderation while including other ingredients that also contribute flavour and provide satisfaction.

The recipes in this volume make few unusual demands. Naturally they call for fresh ingredients, offering substitutes should these be unavailable. (Only the original ingredient is calculated in the nutrient analysis, however.) Most of the ingredients can be found in any well-stocked supermarket; the occasional exceptions can be bought in speciality or ethnic food shops.

Recommended Dietary Guidelines

		Average Daily Intake		Maximum Daily Intake			
		CALORIES	PROTEIN _grams_	CHOLESTEROL _milligrams_	TOTAL FAT _grams_	SATURATED FAT _grams_	SODIUM _milligrams_
Females	7-8	1900	47	300	80	32	2000*
	9-11	2050	51	300	77	35	2000
	12-17	2150	53	300	81	36	2000
	18-53	2150	54	300	81	36	2000
	54-74	1900	47	300	72	32	2000
Males	7-8	1980	49	300	80	33	2000
	9-11	2280	57	300	77	38	2000
	12-14	2640	66	300	99	44	2000
	15-17	2880	72	300	108	48	2000
	18-34	2900	72	300	109	48	2000
	35-64	2750	69	300	104	35	2000
	65-74	2400	60	300	91	40	2000

*(or 5g salt)

About cooking times

To help the cook plan ahead effectively, Healthy Home Cooking takes time into account in all its recipes. While recognizing that everyone cooks at a different speed, and that stoves and ovens may differ somewhat in their temperatures, the series provides approximate "working" and "total" times for every dish. Working time stands for the minutes actively spent on preparation; total time includes unattended cooking time, as well as time devoted to marinating, steeping or soaking various ingredients. Because the recipes emphasize fresh foods, the dishes may take a bit longer to prepare than those that call for canned or packaged products, but the difference in flavour, and often in added nutritional value, should compensate for the little extra time involved.

stored, careless cooking can undo their nutritional value in a matter of minutes. Boiling — traditionally the most popular way of preparing vegetables — can also be the most destructive to nutrients. Prolonged exposure to boiling water leaches out B vitamins and some minerals, while destroying up to 80 per cent of vitamin C. Ironically, the nutritious cooking liquid is then drained away, while the nutritionally decimated vegetable is respectfully consumed at table.

For quickly cooked green vegetables, however, boiling is a very acceptable method. Plunged into a large open pan of rapidly boiling water, vegetables such as Brussels sprouts and French beans cook swiftly, and so retain a major part of their colour, flavour and nutrients.

Steaming, a gentler process than boiling, suits vegetables that require a longer cooking time. Cauliflower and roots — which take time to tenderize — lose less nutritive value in the steamer than by lengthy boiling in water. Various types of steamer are commercially available, including adjustable steel baskets and multi-tiered steamers for cooking several vegetables at once. Lacking a purpose-made steamer, use a colander or a chip basket; provided that the vegetables do not touch the water, and that the saucepan can be tightly covered, an improvised steamer serves just as well. And remember that, whether steamed or boiled, vegetables cooked in their skins suffer less nutritional decimation than those that are first peeled and sliced.

Stir-frying, a technique borrowed from Oriental cookery, is another successful way of preserving a vegetable's volatile nutrients. Rapidly heated and continually turned in a wok or frying pan, finely cut vegetables have time to cook through, yet retain their colours and suffer only an insignificant loss in vitamins and minerals.

About this book

Many of the recipes in this book include modest amounts of eggs and cheese, for these versatile, flavourful and highly nutritious foods greatly extend the possibilities of vegetarian cookery. However, the chefs and nutritionists at Time-Life Books have resisted the temptation to give them the major role that they occupy in many vegetarian cookery books. This has enabled levels of saturated fat, cholesterol and sodium to be kept within acceptable limits, while also ensuring that pulses, grains and vegetables assume a central importance.

This volume will appeal to many non-vegetarians who simply enjoy having some meals without meat. But the recipes have been devised to be acceptable to strict vegetarians. Thus gelatine, which is obtained from animal bones, makes no appearance. Instead the recipes make use of agar, a setting agent prepared from seaweed that is available either in flakes or in powder. Similarly, vegetable stock *(recipe, right)* is used in place of meat stock. Vegetable suet replaces beef suet in pastry, and vegetable extract, a concentrated source of protein and B vitamins, is employed as an alternative to beef extract. And, although vegetarian cheeses are not called for in the ingredients lists, they may easily be purchased by those who prefer not to consume cheese set with animal rennet.

This volume divides the vast realm of vegetarian cookery into four chapters. The first chapter, quite properly, is devoted to vegetables themselves. Chapter 2 explores the grains and pulses — crops as old as civilization — which have potential both to nourish and to delight in a beguiling variety of combinations. Chapter 3 contains a collection of recipes based upon pasta, pastry and bread: in essence no more than flour and water, this international trio proves capable of the most bewildering and sophisticated of disguises. The concluding chapter is not about a type of food, but a method of cooking. The microwave oven, which is now an established part of the modern kitchen, is singularly suited to the preparation of vegetarian meals, preserving not just the freshness, flavour and colour of the ingredients but their wholesomeness as well.

Fresh Ways with Vegetarian Dishes serves as no more than an introduction to a healthy alternative way of eating. But whether you are a dedicated vegetarian, someone who likes to enjoy the occasional meatless meal, or perhaps someone who cooks for a vegetarian friend or member of the family, these recipes will furnish you with a multitude of fresh flavours and new ideas to enhance your diet.

Vegetable Stock

Makes about 1 ½ litres (2 ½ pints)
Working time: about 25 minutes
Total time: about 1 hour and 30 minutes

3	sticks celery with leaves, finely chopped	3
3	carrots, scrubbed, sliced into 3 mm ⅛inch rounds	3
3	large onions (about 750 g/1 ½ lb), coarsely chopped	3
2	large broccoli stems, coarsely chopped (optional)	2
1	medium turnip, peeled and cut into 1 cm (½ inch) cubes	1
5	garlic cloves, coarsely chopped	5
20 g	parsley (with stems), coarsely chopped	¾ oz
10	black peppercorns	10
2	fresh tyme sprigs, or 1 tsp dried thyme	2
2	bay leaves	2

Put the celery, carrots, onions, broccoli if you are using it, turnip, garlic, parsley and peppercorns in a heavy stock-pot. Pour in enough water to cover them by 5 cm (2 inches). Slowly bring the liquid to the boil over medium heat, skimming off any scum that rises to the surface. When the liquid reaches the boil, add the thyme and bay leaves. Stir the stock once and reduce the heat to low; cover the pot, leaving the lid slightly ajar. Let the stock simmer undisturbed for 1 hour

Strain the stock into a large bowl, pressing down lightly on the vegetables to extract all their liquid. Discard the vegetables. Allow the stock to stand until it is tepid, then refrigerate or freeze it.

Tightly covered and refrigerated, the stock may safely be kept for five to six days. Stored in small, lightly covered freezer containers and frozen, the stock may be kept for as long as six months.

*1*Crammed with vitamins, minerals and flavour, fresh vegetables lie ready for the cook's attention.

A Wealth of Vegetables

For their versatility and nutritional value, their wealth of flavours and sheer good looks, vegetables are in a class by themselves. Roots, stems, seeds, flowers, leaves — sometimes entire plants, sometimes only tiny parts of them — this vast family of food naturally provides the low-fat, low-sodium, high-fibre diet that nutritionists now urge us to eat. When prepared with protein-rich pulses and grains, or small quantities of eggs and cheese, vegetables need not be relegated to side dishes — the lowly accompaniment to meat: they increasingly take pride of place as a main course.

Nutritional awareness alone does not explain the vegetable's new-found prestige. Improved transport and storage, combined with a growing taste for international cuisine, have stocked greengrocers and supermarkets with a rainbow of vegetable ingredients. In addition to familiar favourites such as cabbage, cauliflower and root vegetables, aubergines, sweet peppers, tomatoes and courgettes routinely bring year-round Mediterranean warmth to northern climes.

Some, admittedly, still require a little searching for. Scorzonera, a thin, white-fleshed root with a flavour said to resemble oysters, is not in every high street. The slim, green okra and the bulky, misshapen yam — mainstays of Afro-Carribean cookery — still involve a short voyage of discovery to suppliers of ethnic food, where they will be found alongside the sweet potato, an excellent source of vitamin A. But wild and exotic mushrooms such as ceps, morels and shiitake — formerly only found dried in Oriental groceries can now be purchased fresh from specialist greengrocers and some large supermarkets.

With the move from side dish to centre-table, even the most ordinary vegetable assumes new forms to suit its new station. Potatoes can be stewed with saffron *(page 38)*, swedes curried and served as a soup *(page 43)*. Layered with pine-nuts and cheese *(page 30)*, spinach proves to be one of the most socially mobile of vegetables, while the pumpkin becomes a delicate Cinderella of a dish in the soufflé on page 19.

For maximum flavour and goodness, vegetables should be as fresh as possible when cooked. Even the freshest home-grown ingredients, however, will lose nutrients if not prepared with care. As a general rule, the less chopping and paring the better. Whenever possible, cook and eat vegetables in their skins. When peeling is absolutely necessary, remove only a thin outer layer. Work with a light hand when trimming leaf vegetables: the outer leaves of a cabbage, for instance, contain many of its nutrients. Finally, prepare vegetables just before cooking and avoid soaking them, especially if they are peeled and chopped, as some vitamins and minerals leach out in water.

Courgette Tian

THIS PROVENÇAL VEGETABLE GRATIN TAKES ITS NAME
FROM THE HEAVY EARTHENWARE POT IN WHICH IT IS
TRADITIONALLY COOKED.

Serves 4
Working time: about 45 minutes
Total time: about 1 hour and 15 minutes

Calories **190**
Protein **8g**
Cholesterol **100mg**
Total fat **9g**
Saturated fat **3g**
Sodium **195mg**

750 g	courgettes, trimmed and finely sliced	1 ½ lb
3 tsp	virgin olive oil	3 tsp
60 g	brown rice	2 oz
1	garlic clove	1
¼ tsp	salt	¼ tsp
3	shallots, finely chopped	3
2	small eggs, beaten	2
2 tbsp	freshly grated Parmesan cheese	2 tbsp
1 tbsp	shredded fresh rocket leaves	1 tbsp
1 tbsp	shredded fresh basil leaves	1 tbsp
1 tbsp	finely chopped flat-leaf parsley	1 tbsp
⅛ tsp	white pepper	⅛ tsp

Place the courgettes in a heavy-bottomed saucepan with 2 teaspoons of the oil and cook them gently over low heat, covered, until they are just tender — about 10 minutes. Stir from time to time to prevent the courgettes from sticking.

Meanwhile, rinse the brown rice under cold running water and place it in a small, heavy-bottomed saucepan with 30 cl (½ pint) of water. Bring the water to the boil, then reduce the heat, cover the pan and simmer for 15 minutes. Drain the rice well and set it aside, covered.

Preheat the oven to 180°C (350°F or Mark 4). Crush the garlic with the salt. Heat the remaining teaspoon of oil in a small, heavy-bottomed saucepan, add the shallots and garlic, and soften them over very low heat, covered, for about 5 minutes.

Lightly grease a wide, shallow gratin dish. In a large mixing bowl, stir together the courgettes, rice, shallots and garlic; add the eggs and half of the Parmesan. Stir well, then mix in the rocket, basil, parsley and pepper. Transfer the mixture to the prepared dish, levelling the courgette slices so that they lie flat, and sprinkle on the remaining Parmesan.

Bake the tian in the oven, uncovered, for 20 minutes, then increase the oven temperature to 220°C (425°F or Mark 7) and bake it for a further 10 to 15 minutes, until a crust has formed. Serve hot or warm.

SUGGESTED ACCOMPANIMENTS: *mixed salad of radicchio, curly endive, lamb's lettuce and escarole; crusty French bread.*

Spanish Omelette

Serves 4
Working time: about 20 minutes
Total time: about 35 minutes

Calories **190**
Protein **7g**
Cholesterol **110mg**
Total fat **10g**
Saturated fat **2g**
Sodium **260mg**

2 tbsp	virgin olive oil	2 tbsp
1	onion, chopped	1
2	garlic cloves, chopped	2
2	small courgettes (about 125 g/4 oz), trimmed and thinly sliced	2
2	eggs	2
2	egg whites	2
½ tsp	salt	½ tsp
	freshly ground black pepper	
1	large potato (about 300 g/10 oz), peeled, cooked in boiling water for 25 to 30 minutes, drained and coarsely chopped	1
125 g	French beans, trimmed, cooked in boiling water for 5 minutes, drained, refreshed under cold running water and cut into 2.5 cm (1 inch) lengths	4 oz
2	tomatoes (about 175 g/6 oz), skinned, seeded (page 14) and chopped	2
½ tbsp	chopped fresh oregano, or ½ tsp dried oregano	½ tbsp

Heat 1½ tablespoons of the oil in a heavy frying pan over medium heat. Add the onion and fry until it is soft — about 3 minutes. Add the garlic and courgettes, cover the pan and cook the vegetables gently for 10 minutes, stirring them occasionally. Remove the pan from the heat.

In a large bowl, beat together the eggs and egg whites, the salt and some black pepper. Add the fried vegetables, the potato, beans, tomatoes and oregano, and stir gently to mix the ingredients.

Heat the remaining oil in a 25 cm (10 inch) non-stick frying pan and pour in the egg mixture. Cook the omelette gently over medium heat for 3 to 4 minutes, until the underside is pale golden. Place the frying pan under a preheated medium-hot grill and cook the omelette for a further 2 to 3 minutes, or until it is lightly set. Cut it into quarters and serve.

SUGGESTED ACCOMPANIMENT: *mixed salad.*

To prepare the filling, heat the olive oil in a heavy-bottomed saucepan and add the onion, sweet peppers and the courgette trimmings. Cover the pan and soften the vegetables over gentle heat for 6 to 8 minutes. Add the aubergine, oregano, coriander and tomato paste, stir well and cook for a further 25 minutes. Stir in the tomatoes and agar flakes and simmer for a final 5 minutes. Season with some black pepper. Transfer the ratatouille to the lined tin and smooth the top. Allow the terrine to cool, then chill it for at least 3 hours.

Trim the courgette slices level with the rim of the tin, then turn the terrine out on to a plate. Remove the plastic film and slice the terrine with a serrated knife.

SUGGESTED ACCOMPANIMENTS: *hot herbed garlic bread; crisp green salad.*

Ratatouille Terrine

Serves 4
Working time: about 1 hour
Total time: about 4 hours and 30 minutes (includes chilling)

Calories **120**
Protein **3g**
Cholesterol **0mg**
Total fat **8g**
Saturated fat **1g**
Sodium **10mg**

250 g	aubergine, diced	8 oz
2 tsp	salt	2 tsp
350 g	courgettes, trimmed	12 oz
2 tbsp	virgin olive oil	2 tbsp
150 g	onion, coarsely chopped	5 oz
150 g	sweet red pepper, seeded, deribbed and coarsely chopped	5 oz
150 g	sweet green pepper, seeded, deribbed and coarsely chopped	5 oz
1 tsp	dried oregano or marjoram	1 tsp
½ tsp	ground coriander	½ tsp
1 tbsp	tomato paste	1 tbsp
250 g	tomatoes, skinned, seeded (box, right) and coarsely chopped	8 oz
1 ½ tbsp	agar flakes	1 ½ tbsp
	freshly ground black pepper	

In a bowl, toss the aubergine with the salt. Place the aubergine in a colander and weight it down with a small plate. Let the aubergine drain for 30 minutes, then rinse it under cold running water to rid it of the salt. Drain it well.

Meanwhile, slice the courgettes lengthwise using a vegetable slicer; chop and reserve any uneven pieces and trimmings. Blanch the strips in boiling salted water for 3 minutes, then refresh them under cold running water. Drain them well.

Line a 22 by 10 by 7.5 cm (9 by 4 by 3 inch) loaf tin with plasticizer-free film. Lay two strips of courgette lengthwise down the centre of the tin, then completely line the long sides of the tin with the remaining strips, placing one end of each strip on the centre seam of courgettes and overlapping the strips slightly.

Skinning and Seeding a Tomato

1 *SKINNING THE TOMATO. Core the tomato by cutting a conical plug from its stem end. Cut a shallow cross in the base. Immerse the tomato in boiling water for 10 to 30 seconds, then plunge it into cold water. When the tomato has cooled, peel the skin away from the cross in sections.*

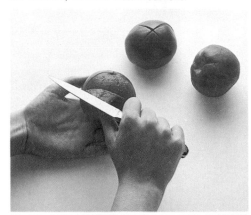

2 *SEEDING THE TOMATO. Halve the skinned tomato. Gently squeeze one of the halves, forcing out its seeds and juice. Rotate the tomato 90 degrees and squeeze once more. Dislodge any seeds from the inner chambers. Repeat the process with the other half.*

Aubergine and Mozzarella Ramekins

Serves 6
Working time: about 1 hour and 30 minutes
Total time: about 2 hours

Calories **275**
Protein **19g**
Cholesterol **35mg**
Total fat **13g**
Saturated fat **6g**
Sodium **385mg**

3	large aubergines (about 500 g/1 lb each), sliced into 5 mm (¼ inch) rounds	3
1 tsp	salt	1 tsp
2 tbsp	virgin olive oil	2 tbsp
350 g	low-fat mozzarella cheese, grated	12 oz
2 tbsp	chopped fresh oregano	2 tbsp
100 g	thick Greek yogurt	3½ oz
15 cl	plain low-fat yogurt	¼ pint
1 tbsp	cut chives	1 tbsp
Tomato coulis		
750 g	ripe tomatoes, skinned, seeded (box, left) and chopped, or 400 g (14 oz) canned tomatoes, with their juice, chopped	1½ lb
1	carrot, finely chopped	1
1	small onion, finely chopped	1
1	stick celery, trimmed and finely chopped	1
1	bay leaf	1
1	fresh red chili pepper, seeded and finely chopped (caution, page 25)	1
¼ tsp	salt	¼ tsp

First, prepare the tomato coulis. Place all the ingredients in a heavy-bottomed non-reactive saucepan with 8 cl (3 fl oz) of water. Bring the ingredients to the boil, then reduce the heat to low, cover the pan and simmer for 45 minutes. Discard the bay leaf and pro-cess the coulis in a food processor for 2 minutes. Strain the coulis back into the pan and keep it warm.

While the coulis is cooking, prepare the aubergines. Arrange the slices on a wire rack set over a tray, and sprinkle them with ½ teaspoon of the salt. Allow them to drain for 15 minutes, then turn them over and repeat the process with the remaining salt. At the end of the second draining period, rinse the slices well under cold running water. Pat them dry on paper towels.

Preheat the oven to 190°C (375°F or Mark 5). Lightly grease six 8 cl (3 fl oz) ramekins measuring about 7.5 cm (3 inches) in diameter.

Preheat the grill to hot and lightly brush the aubergine slices on one side only with the oil. Grill the oiled side of the slices for 3 to 4 minutes, until they are lightly coloured. Line the bottom of each ramekin with two or three slices of grilled aubergine, grilled side down, then sprinkle on a little grated mozzarella and chopped oregano. Continue adding layers of aubergine, mozzarella and oregano until the ramekins are full, finishing with a layer of aubergine.

Stand the ramekins on a baking sheet and bake them in the oven for 20 minutes. Meanwhile, place the yogurts in a food processor or blender with the chives and process for 1 minute, until smooth.

Remove the ramekins from the oven and leave them to stand for 2 to 3 minutes. Carefully run a small metal spatula or knife round the inside of each one and invert the contents on to individual serving plates. Serve the unmoulded aubergine ramekins with the tomato coulis and yogurt sauce.

SUGGESTED ACCOMPANIMENTS: *crusty bread rolls; broccoli and broad beans.*

Aubergine Rolls with a Ricotta-Raisin Filling

Serves 4
Working time: about 45 minutes
Total time: about 1 hour and 15 minutes

Calories **270**	4	long aubergines (about 250 g/8 oz each)	4
Protein **14g**	2 tsp	virgin olive oil	2 tsp
Cholesterol **15mg**	250 g	low-fat ricotta cheese	8 oz
Total fat **13g**	60 g	raisins, chopped	2 oz
Saturated fat **5g**	30 g	pine-nuts, toasted	1 oz
Sodium **275mg**	2 tbsp	freshly grated Parmesan cheese	2 tbsp
	¼ tsp	salt	¼ tsp
		freshly ground black pepper	
	60 g	dry-packed sun-dried tomatoes, soaked for 10 minutes in 15 cl (¼ pint) boiling water	2 oz
	1 tbsp	balsamic, or red wine vinegar	1 tbsp
	2 tbsp	fresh wholemeal breadcrumbs	2 tbsp
	1 tsp	arrowroot	1 tsp
	2 tbsp	tomato paste	2 tbsp

Preheat the oven to 220°C (425°F or Mark 7). Oil a 35 by 25 cm (14 by 10 inch) baking sheet.

Cut off and discard a little of the stem end and base of the aubergines. Remove a wide strip of skin from two opposite sides of each one, then cut the trimmed aubergines lengthwise into six equal slices, so that each slice has a border of skin at the sides. Lay the aubergine slices close together on the baking sheet. Using a wide pastry brush, quickly brush the exposed surfaces of the slices with the olive oil. Cover the baking sheet loosely with foil and roast the aubergine slices in the oven for about 10 minutes, until they are sufficiently soft to be rolled but are not browned. Remove them from the oven and reduce the oven temperature to 180°C (350°F or Mark 4).

Meanwhile, put the ricotta in a bowl and beat in the raisins, pine-nuts, half the Parmesan, the salt and some pepper. Drain the tomatoes well, reserving the soaking liquid, then chop them finely and stir them into the ricotta mixture.

Lay the aubergine slices on the work surface and place a heaped teaspoonful of the filling near one end of each slice. Roll up the slices round the filling. Pack all 24 aubergine rolls into a shallow baking dish.

Blend the vinegar with 2 tablespoons of the reserved tomato-soaking liquid and pour this round the aubergine rolls. Grind black pepper generously over the top, and sprinkle the rolls with the breadcrumbs and the remaining Parmesan. Cover the dish with foil and bake the rolls for 30 minutes, until they are tender. Remove the dish from the oven and, lifting one end, tilt it carefully and spoon out the juices into a measuring jug — there should be about a tablespoonful. Cover the dish again with the foil and set it aside in a warm place while you prepare the sauce.

Make up the cooking juices from the rolls to 30 cl (½ pint) with the reserved tomato-soaking liquid and water. Dissolve the arrowroot in 2 tablespoons of this mixture in a small bowl, then stir the arrowroot solution into the liquid in the jug. Transfer the contents of the jug to a small saucepan and bring it to the boil, stirring continuously. Reduce the heat and simmer the sauce for a few seconds, until it is clear and thick. Remove the pan from the heat, stir in the tomato paste, and pour the sauce round the aubergine rolls.

Crisp the surface of the rolls by placing the dish under a hot grill for 5 minutes.

SUGGESTED ACCOMPANIMENT: *saffron rice.*

EDITOR'S NOTE: *To toast pine-nuts, place them in a small, heavy frying pan over medium-high heat and cook them for 1 to 2 minutes, stirring constantly, until they are golden-brown and release their aroma.*

Aubergine Fans

Serves 4
Working time: about 45 minutes
Total time: about 3 hours

Calories **275** Protein **20g** Cholesterol **60mg** Total fat **14g** Saturated fat **6g** Sodium **350mg**		

4	aubergines (about 250 g/8 oz each), washed and dried	4
4	garlic cloves, quartered lengthwise	4
4	large, firm beef tomatoes, cut lengthwise into 1 cm (½ inch) slices	4
175 g	low-fat mozzarella cheese, cut into thin slices	6 oz
	freshly ground black pepper	
60 g	fine fresh wholemeal breadcrumbs	2 oz
1	small egg, beaten	1
1 tbsp	grated Parmesan cheese	1 tbsp
Basil spread		
30 g	fresh basil leaves, very finely chopped	1 oz
1 tbsp	extra virgin olive oil	1 tbsp
60 g	thick Greek yogurt	2 oz
1 tbsp	grated Parmesan cheese	1 tbsp
½ tsp	dry mustard	½ tsp

Preheat the oven to 180°C (350°F or Mark 4).

Cut the stems off the aubergines. Cutting from near the stem end of each aubergine, slice them lengthwise, making cuts about 1 cm (½ inch) apart and leaving the slices joined by 3 to 4 cm (1¼ to 1½ inches) at the stem end. With the tip of a sharp knife, make four small cuts into the unsliced stem end of each aubergine. Press a slice of garlic into each of these cuts.

To make the basil spread, combine the chopped basil leaves with the oil in a small basin. Add the yogurt, Parmesan and mustard, and stir until they are evenly mixed. Divide the basil spread among the aubergines, spreading a little over each cut surface.

Sprinkle the slices of tomato and mozzarella with plenty of freshly ground black pepper. Place a slice or two of each between the segments of aubergine: the mozzarella will probably sit more easily near the stem end, the tomato near the thicker end. Cut any remaining tomato and mozzarella into smaller pieces and insert them between the aubergine slices wherever there is a space to fill.

Select a baking dish wide enough to take all four aubergines, packed close together. Brush the base of the dish lightly with olive oil and sprinkle it with 1 to 2 teaspoons of the breadcrumbs to absorb the juices produced during cooking. Use a pastry brush to paint a little beaten egg over the sides and top of each aubergine, then sprinkle on the remaining breadcrumbs, pressing them down lightly to keep them in place. Arrange the aubergines in the oiled baking dish, pressing down on the upper surface of each to fan out the slices a little. Sprinkle the grated Parmesan cheese over the fans.

Cover the dish with foil, and bake the aubergines for 2 to 2½ hours, or until a thin skewer inserted at the stem end meets with little resistance. Remove the foil, increase the oven temperature to the maximum setting and continue to cook the fans for 10 to 15 minutes, until the topping is crisp.

SUGGESTED ACCOMPANIMENT: *fresh crusty bread.*

EDITOR'S NOTE: *For best results, select elongated aubergines for this recipe.*

Pumpkin Soufflé

Serves 4
Working time: about 30 minutes
Total time: about 2 hours and 45 minutes

Calories **200**
Protein **11g**
Cholesterol **85mg**
Total fat **12g**
Saturated fat **6g**
Sodium **300mg**

750 g	slice of pumpkin, seeds removed	1 ½ lb
2 tbsp	dry breadcrumbs	2 tbsp
30 g	unsalted butter	1 oz
2 tbsp	plain flour	2 tbsp
12.5 cl	skimmed milk	4 fl oz
1	egg yolk	1
¼ tsp	salt	¼ tsp
1 tsp	ground cinnamon	1 tsp
3 tbsp	freshly grated Parmesan cheese	3 tbsp
5	egg whites	5

Preheat the oven to 190°C (375°F or Mark 5).

Wrap the pumpkin in a sheet of foil and place it on a baking sheet. Bake it in the oven for about 1 hour, until it is soft. Check the pumpkin after this time; if it is still hard, return it to the oven for a further 20 minutes to cook it through. When the pumpkin is ready, remove it from the oven and set it aside to cool, uncovered.

Meanwhile, grease a 90 cl (1 ½ pint) soufflé dish and dust the base and sides with the breadcrumbs. Re-duce the oven temperature to 200°C (400°F or Mark 6).

Using a metal spoon, scoop all the pumpkin pulp from the skin and pass the pulp through a nylon sieve; there should be about 350 g (12 oz) of sieved pumpkin. Put the pumpkin in a saucepan and, stirring continuously, dry out the pulp over medium heat until it becomes fairly dense and is no longer wet — about 10 minutes. Set the pumpkin aside.

In a small, heavy-bottomed saucepan, melt the butter over gentle heat. Remove the pan from the heat. Using a wooden spoon, stir in the flour, then stir in the milk a little at a time. Return the pan to the heat and cook the mixture for about 30 seconds, stirring constantly, until it thickens. Take the pan off the heat again and stir in the egg yolk, followed by the pumpkin, salt, cinnamon and 2 tablespoons of the Parmesan. Set the mixture aside.

Whisk the egg whites until they hold their shape; using a metal spoon, fold them gently into the pumpkin mixture. Turn the mixture into the prepared soufflé dish and sprinkle it with the remaining Parmesan.

Bake the soufflé in the oven for about 40 minutes, until it is well risen and set. Serve immediately.

SUGGESTED ACCOMPANIMENT: *salad of mixed green leaves, fennel and avocado.*

Spring Vegetables in Watercress Crêpes

Serves 4
Working (and total) time: about 1 hour

Calories **200**
Protein **13g**
Cholesterol **55mg**
Total fat **10g**
Saturated fat **3g**
Sodium **300mg**

1	egg	1
¼ tsp	salt	¼ tsp
60 g	plain flour	2 oz
12.5 cl	skimmed milk	4 fl oz
2 tsp	safflower oil	2 tsp
2	shallots	2
45 g	watercress leaves	1½ oz
500 g	asparagus spears, trimmed and peeled	1 lb
150 g	baby sweetcorn, trimmed if necessary	5 oz
200 g	baby carrots, trimmed	7 oz
125 g	low-fat fromage frais	4 oz
	Sweet pepper sauces	
175 g	sweet red pepper, grilled and peeled (opposite), coarsely chopped	6 oz
175 g	sweet yellow pepper, grilled and peeled (opposite), coarsely chopped	6 oz
4	shallots, finely chopped	4
1 tsp	finely chopped fresh thyme	1 tsp
17.5 cl	unsalted vegetable stock (recipe, page 9)	6 fl oz
4 tsp	fresh lemon juice	4 tsp

First make the crêpe batter. Put the egg and ⅛ teaspoon of the salt into a food processor or blender and blend them well. Add the flour, skimmed milk, half the oil and the shallots. Blend the mixture again until the shallots are very finely chopped, then add the watercress leaves and blend once more. Transfer the batter to a measuring jug and place it in the refrigerator

to chill for 30 minutes while you prepare the vegetables and sauces.

Cut each asparagus spear into two or three pieces approximately 5 cm (2 inches) long. Bring a large saucepan of water to the boil. Add the sweetcorn then, after 1 minute, add the carrots. After a further minute, add the asparagus pieces; boil the vegetables for 3 minutes until they are cooked but still crisp. Drain them and refresh them under cold running water, then drain them again and set them aside.

To make the two sweet pepper sauces, put the red pepper in one small saucepan and the yellow pepper in another. Divide the shallots, thyme and stock equally between the two pans and bring both to the boil. Reduce the heat under the pans and simmer the ingredients until the peppers are soft — about 5 minutes. Purée the two sauces separately in a food processor or blender; sieve them both and return them to separate pans. Season each sauce with 2 teaspoons of the lemon juice, then cover the pans and set the sauces aside while you cook the crêpes.

Heat a 15 cm (6 inch) crêpe pan or non-stick frying pan over low heat and brush a little of the remaining oil over the surface of the pan using a paper towel. Stir the batter well; if it has thickened, stir in 1 tablespoon of water to restore it to its former consistency. Pour one eighth of the batter into the crêpe pan. Swirl the pan to coat the bottom with an even layer of batter and cook until the top side of the crêpe becomes firm and starts to bubble — about 1 minute. Using a spatula, carefully turn the crêpe over and cook it for a further 15 to 30 seconds, until it is very lightly browned on the second side. Slide the crêpe on to a piece of greaseproof paper and set it aside. Cook seven more crêpes in the same way, brushing a little more oil over the pan as necessary and stacking the cooked crêpes between sheets of greaseproof paper.

Preheat the oven to 170°C (325°F or Mark 3). Stir the remaining ⅛ teaspoon of salt into the *fromage frais*. Fold each crêpe in half, then in half again, creating pockets between the layers. Place the folded crêpes in pairs on top of one another on the work surface. Divide the cooked vegetables into four portions, and decoratively arrange one portion in the pockets of each pair of crêpes; leave room in the top pocket of each pair for the *fromage frais*.

Carefully arrange the eight crêpes, still in their pairs, in a gratin dish. Spoon a quarter of the *fromage frais* into the top pocket of the four upper crêpes and cover the dish loosely with foil. Bake the crêpes in the oven for about 10 minutes, until they are heated through. Meanwhile, gently reheat the sweet pepper sauces.

Place a pair of crêpes on each of four warmed serving plates and spoon round them a little of each sauce.

SUGGESTED ACCOMPANIMENT: *grissini (breadsticks)*.

Peeling Sweet Peppers

1 *LOOSENING THE SKIN. Place the peppers about 5 cm (2 inches) below a medium grill. Turn the peppers as their sides become slightly scorched, until their skin has blistered on all sides. Transfer the peppers to a bowl and cover it with plastic film, or put them in a paper bag and fold it shut; the trapped steam will make the peppers limp and loosen their skins.*

2 *REMOVING THE SKIN. When the peppers are cool enough to handle, use a paring knife to peel off a pepper's skin in sections, working from top to bottom. Repeat the process to skin the other peppers. The peppers may then be seeded and deribbed.*

Asparagus Mousse with Goat Cheese Sauce

Serves 4
Working time: about 30 minutes
Total time: about 1 hour and 40 minutes

Calories **195**
Protein **17g**
Cholesterol **90mg**
Total fat **10g**
Saturated fat **5g**
Sodium **470mg**

750 g	large asparagus spears, trimmed and peeled	1 ½ lb
15 g	unsalted butter	½ oz
1	onion, chopped	1
2 tsp	cornflour	2 tsp
15 cl	skimmed milk	¼ pint
¼ tsp	salt	¼ tsp
	freshly ground black pepper	
¼ tsp	freshly grated nutmeg	¼ tsp
1 tbsp	chopped flat-leaf parsley	1 tbsp
1	egg yolk	1
3	egg whites	3
	flat-leaf parsley sprigs, for garnish	
	Goat cheese sauce	
1 tsp	cornflour	1 tsp
4 tbsp	white wine	4 tbsp
1	garlic clove, crushed	1
	freshly ground black pepper	
125 g	soft goat cheese, rind removed, cubed	4 oz ▶

Preheat the oven to 180°C (350°F or Mark 4). Lightly grease four ¼ litre (8 fl oz) level ring moulds or individual ramekins.

To make the mousse, cut off the asparagus tips about 1 cm (½ inch) below the buds, and cut the remaining stalks in half. Cook the stalks in a little boiling water for 2 minutes. Add the tips and cook for a further minute, then drain the asparagus pieces and refresh them under cold running water. Cut the tips in half lengthwise and reserve them for garnish.

Melt the butter in a small saucepan. Add the onion, cover the pan, and cook it over high heat for about 3 minutes, stirring occasionally, until it is soft. In a small bowl, blend the cornflour with 2 tablespoons of the milk. Stir in the remaining milk, then add this to the pan with the salt, some pepper and the nutmeg. Bring the mixture to the boil and cook it, stirring constantly, for 2 minutes, until it forms a smooth sauce.

In a food processor or blender, process the asparagus stalks, onion sauce, chopped parsley, egg yolk and whites for about a minute, until completely smooth. Turn the mixture into the prepared moulds. Cover each mould with lightly greased foil and place them in a baking dish; pour boiling water into the dish to a depth of 1 cm (½ inch). Bake the moulds for about 1 hour, or until the mousse is just firm.

Meanwhile, make the goat cheese sauce. In a small saucepan, blend the cornflour with a little of the wine. Stir in the remaining wine, the garlic and some pepper. Bring the mixture to the boil, stirring, then remove the pan from the heat and add the cheese. Stir until the cheese has melted. Keep the sauce warm.

Remove the moulds from the baking dish and leave them to stand for 10 minutes. Using a small metal spatula or round-bladed knife, loosen the edges and invert each mousse on to a warmed serving plate. Divide the asparagus tips among the centres of the mousses and garnish each one with a sprig of parsley. Spoon the sauce over and around the mousses and serve them immediately.

SUGGESTED ACCOMPANIMENT: *new potatoes*.

Fennel Baked in a Roquefort Sauce

Serves 4
Working time: about 35 minutes
Total time: about 1 hour

Calories **165**
Protein **113g**
Cholesterol **10mg**
Total fat **8g**
Saturated fat **3g**
Sodium **530mg**

4	fennel bulbs (about 200 g/7 oz each), trimmed and halved lengthwise	4
175 g	low-fat cottage cheese	6 oz
60 g	Roquefort cheese	2 oz
	freshly ground black pepper	
30 g	fresh wholemeal breadcrumbs	1 oz
1 tsp	safflower oil	1 tsp
30 g	watercress leaves	1 oz
1 tsp	cornflour	1 tsp
12.5 cl	skimmed milk	4 fl oz
2 tbsp	dry vermouth	2 tbsp

Blanch the fennel bulbs in a large saucepan of boiling water for about 5 minutes, until the layers have separated and softened slightly. Drain and set them aside.

Press the cottage cheese through a nylon sieve into a bowl. Crumble the Roquefort into the bowl, add some black pepper, and beat well. In another bowl, blend the breadcrumbs with the oil.

Preheat the oven to 180°C (350°F or Mark 4). Open out the layers of the halved fennel bulbs. Set one third of the cheese mixture aside in a separate bowl. Spread each layer of one of the halved fennel bulbs with some of the remaining cheese mixture and tuck in a few of the watercress leaves. Repeat with the other bulbs. Place two half bulbs, cut sides down, in each of four individual gratin dishes, or place all the fennel in a large, shallow ovenproof dish.

In a small saucepan, blend the cornflour with 3 tablespoons of the milk. Add the remaining milk, then cook over medium heat, whisking continuously, until the sauce has thickened slightly. Remove the pan from the heat and stir in the vermouth and the reserved cheese mixture. Spoon the sauce over the fennel and sprinkle on the oiled breadcrumbs.

Bake the fennel in the oven for about 20 minutes, until the breadcrumbs are golden, and serve hot.

SUGGESTED ACCOMPANIMENTS: *oven-baked chips; mashed potatoes and swedes, sprinkled with chopped parsley.*

Chicory Baked with Pistachio-Stuffed Tomatoes

Serves 4
Working time: about 30 minutes
Total time: about 45 minutes

Calories **200**
Protein **9g**
Cholesterol **10mg**
Total fat **14g**
Saturated fat **3g**
Sodium **90mg**

4	chicory heads (about 125 g/4 oz each)	4
8	firm small tomatoes	8
1 tbsp	virgin olive oil	1 tbsp
60 g	shelled pistachio nuts, skinned and coarsely chopped	2 oz
3	garlic cloves, finely chopped	3
15 g	dry wholemeal breadcrumbs	½ oz
30 g	Parmesan cheese, grated	1 oz
1	lemon, cut into wedges, for garnish	1

Preheat the oven to 220°C (425°F or Mark 7).

Trim the chicory and slice each head lengthwise into four. Blanch the cut chicory in boiling water for 30 seconds. Drain and refresh the chicory under cold running water, and set it aside. Slice off and discard the tops of the tomatoes. Using a teaspoon, hollow out and discard the insides of the tomatoes, then turn them upside down on paper towels to drain.

Heat the olive oil in a frying pan and sauté the pistachio nuts for about 2 minutes, until crisp. Add the garlic and sauté for another 1 to 2 minutes, until the garlic has softened. Remove the pan from the heat.

Lay the chicory slices in diagonal lines across the base of a rectangular baking dish, alternating these with lines of hollowed-out tomatoes. Fill the tomatoes with the garlic and pistachio mixture, spooning any extra neatly round them in the dish. Brush the olive oil from the frying pan over the chicory. Mix the breadcrumbs with the Parmesan cheese and sprinkle this mixture over the chicory. Bake for 15 minutes, or until the chicory and tomatoes are tender.

Serve hot, garnished with the lemon wedges.

SUGGESTED ACCOMPANIMENT: *crusty bread.*

EDITOR'S NOTE: *To skin pistachio nuts, drop them into boiling water and simmer them for 1 minute. Drain them thoroughly, wrap them in a towel and rub them briskly until they have shed their skins.*

Stuffed Leeks with a Gruyère Sauce

Serves 4
Working time: about 1 hour
Total time: about 1 hour and 30 minutes

Calories **250**
Protein **10g**
Cholesterol **25mg**
Total fat **9g**
Saturated fat **3g**
Sodium **330mg**

90 cl	unsalted vegetable stock (recipe, page 9)	1½ pints
20 g	dried ceps	¾ oz
600 g	leeks, tough outer leaves discarded, washed thoroughly to remove all grit, trimmed to 10 cm (4 inch) lengths	1¼ lb
125 g	buckwheat groats (kasha), rinsed well under cold running water	.4 oz
15 g	unsalted butter	½ oz
200 g	mushrooms, 150 g (5 oz) finely diced, 50 g (2 oz) finely sliced and tossed in 1 tbsp fresh lemon juice	7 oz
125 g	sweet yellow or red pepper, seeded, deribbed and finely chopped	4 oz
¼ tsp	salt	¼ tsp
2 tbsp	fresh breadcrumbs	2 tbsp
Gruyère sauce		
250 g	low-fat fromage frais	8 oz
60 g	Gruyère cheese, grated	2 oz
⅛ tsp	grated nutmeg	⅛ tsp

Heat the stock in a saucepan over medium heat until it is hot but not boiling. Place the ceps in a heatproof bowl. Pour the stock over the ceps and leave them to soak for 10 to 15 minutes.

Meanwhile, separate 26 outer leaves from the leeks. Blanch them in a saucepan of boiling water for 1 minute, then refresh them under cold running water. Drain the leaves and set them aside to dry flat on several layers of paper towels. Chop the remaining inner parts of the leeks finely and set them aside. You should have about 125 g (4 oz) of chopped leeks.

Remove the ceps from the stock. Squeeze them dry, then chop them finely and set them aside. Strain ½ litre (16 fl oz) of the vegetable stock through a piece of muslin, and reserve it.

Put the buckwheat in a saucepan, add the reserved strained stock and bring the liquid to the boil. Reduce the heat, cover the pan and simmer the buckwheat for 15 minutes. Remove the pan from the heat and leave the buckwheat to rest, covered, for another 10 minutes. At the end of this time all the cooking liquid will have been absorbed.

Melt one third of the butter in a heavy or non-stick frying pan over low heat. Gently sauté the chopped leeks, diced mushrooms and finely chopped ceps until they are lightly browned — about 7 minutes. Remove the frying pan from the heat, stir in the chopped sweet pepper and the buckwheat, and season the mixture with the salt.

Preheat the oven to 200°C (400°F or Mark 6). Divide the buckwheat mixture into 12 equal portions. Cut two of the blanched leek leaves lengthwise into six ribbons each. Lay two of the remaining whole leaves next to one another on the work surface and overlap two adjacent long edges by about 4 cm (1½ inches). Spoon a portion of the buckwheat mixture along one of the remaining, outer long edges, then roll up the leaves round the filling and tie the roll with a leek ribbon. Repeat this process to make 12 rolls in all, and arrange the rolls side by side, in a single layer, in a large, rectangular gratin dish.

In a bowl, blend together the ingredients for the Gruyère sauce. Place the gratin dish in a large, deep roasting pan and pour boiling water into the tin to reach two thirds of the way up the sides of the gratin dish. Pour the sauce over both ends of the leeks, leaving the middles uncovered. Melt half of the remaining butter and brush it over the middles of the leeks. Cover the dish loosely with foil and bake the leeks in the oven for 25 minutes.

Preheat the grill to medium hot. Remove the gratin dish from the oven and discard the foil. Sprinkle the breadcrumbs over the sauce, cover the unsauced middles of the leeks with a strip of foil, and place the dish under the grill for 5 to 7 minutes, until the breadcrumbs are golden-brown.

Meanwhile, melt the remaining butter in a non-stick frying pan and gently sauté the sliced mushrooms for 2 to 3 minutes. Divide the stuffed leeks among four individual plates, allowing three rolls per portion, and serve garnished with the sautéed mushrooms.

Spicy Mould of Courgettes, Cabbage and Leeks

Serves 6
Working time: about 30 minutes
Total time: about 14 hours and 30 minutes (includes chilling)

Calories **295**
Protein **5g**
Cholesterol **0mg**
Total fat **10g**
Saturated fat **2g**
Sodium **220mg**

500 g	courgettes, trimmed and coarsely grated	1 lb
500 g	Savoy cabbage, trimmed and very finely shredded	1 lb
500 g	leeks, trimmed, washed thoroughly to remove all grit, sliced into very fine rings	1 lb
¾ tsp	salt	¾ tsp
4 tbsp	virgin olive oil	4 tbsp
5 cm	piece fresh ginger root, grated	2 inch
1	dried hot red chili pepper, crushed (caution, below, right)	1
2	garlic cloves, crushed	2
1 tbsp	coriander seeds, crushed	1 tbsp
2 tsp	curry powder	2 tsp
1 tbsp	low-sodium soy sauce or shoyu	1 tbsp
5	sheets nori seaweed, each about 20 cm (8 inches) square	5

Place the grated courgettes, shredded cabbage and sliced leeks in separate bowls. Sprinkle ¼ teaspoon of salt over each vegetable and leave them to drain for 1 hour, to rid them of their bitter juices. At the end of this time, squeeze out each vegetable very thoroughly in a piece of muslin. Once more place the vegetables in separate bowls.

Heat 2 tablespoons of the oil in a heavy frying pan over medium heat. Add the ginger, chili and garlic to the pan and fry, stirring frequently, for about 1 minute. Pour the contents of the pan over the leeks and toss them in the flavoured oil. Heat the remaining 2 tablespoons of oil in a clean pan and fry the coriander and curry powder for 1 minute. Pour the spiced oil over the shredded cabbage and toss it thoroughly. Leave both bowls for 1 hour, to allow the flavours to develop.

Meanwhile, in a large, square shallow dish, mix the soy sauce with 2 tablespoons of water. Moisten the sheets of nori in the solution and leave them in the dish for 5 minutes, then remove them and, using a sharp knife, cut each sheet diagonally into two triangles. Lay all the triangles out on the work surface facing the same way. Line a 1.25 litre (2 pint) bowl or mould with the triangles, placing them in the mould one at a time and overlapping them; one 45-degree corner should be placed in the bottom of the bowl and the other should overhang the rim at the top.

Place the cabbage mixture in the bottom of the mould, pressing it down firmly. Follow with the courgettes, then the leeks. Fold over the overhanging sheets of nori to enclose the filling. Set a small plate or board on top of the mould and place a heavy weight on top. Refrigerate the mould for at least 12 hours.

To serve, turn out the mould on to a plate and slice it into wedges using a sharp knife.

SUGGESTED ACCOMPANIMENTS: *radicchio salad; potato gratin.*

EDITOR'S NOTE: *Nori, paper-like dark green or black sheets of dried seaweed, can be purchased from health food shops and Oriental food shops. If nori is unavailable, spinach leaves, blanched in boiling water for 30 seconds, may be used to line the mould instead.*

Chili Peppers—a Cautionary Note

Both dried and fresh hot chili peppers should be handled with care. Their flesh and seeds contain volatile oils that can make skin tingle and cause eyes to burn. Rubber gloves offer protection — but the cook should still be careful not to touch the face, lips or eyes when working with chilies.

Soaking fresh chilies in cold, salted water for an hour will remove some of their fire. If canned chilies are substituted for fresh ones, they should be rinsed in cold water in order to eliminate as much of the brine used to preserve them as possible.

Chestnuts and Brussels Sprouts with Red Cabbage and Caraway Potatoes

Serves 8
Working time: about 45 minutes
Total time: about 1 hour

Calories **245**
Protein **7g**
Cholesterol **10mg**
Total fat **5g**
Saturated fat **2g**
Sodium **155mg**

2 tbsp	caraway seeds	2 tbsp
8	potatoes, scrubbed and halved	8
½ tsp	salt	½ tsp
1 tsp	virgin olive oil	1 tsp
1	onion, sliced	1
1 kg	red cabbage, shredded	2 lb
20 cl	red wine	7 fl oz
2 tbsp	red wine vinegar	2 tbsp
1	bay leaf	1
1	cooking apple, peeled, cored and chopped	1
½	orange, grated rind and juice only	½
1	garlic clove	1
1	large parsley sprig	1
30 g	unsalted butter	1 oz
2 tsp	sugar	2 tsp
500 g	fresh chestnuts, peeled (page 37)	1 lb
2 tbsp	unsalted vegetable stock (recipe, page 9) or water	2 tbsp
500 g	Brussels sprouts, trimmed, halved if large	1 lb

Preheat the oven to 200°C (400°F or Mark 6). Place the caraway seeds on a small plate. Press the potato halves into the seeds, so that an even layer adheres to each cut surface. Place the potatoes, seeded side up,

on a baking sheet and sprinkle them with half of the salt. Bake the potatoes for 45 minutes, or until the flesh feels soft when pierced with a skewer.

Meanwhile, heat the olive oil in a very large, heavy-bottomed saucepan over medium heat. Add the onion and sauté it for about 5 minutes, until it has softened and is lightly browned. Add the shredded red cabbage to the pan and stir-fry it for 2 minutes. Mix in the wine, vinegar, bay leaf, apple, orange rind and juice, the garlic clove, the remaining salt and the parsley sprig. Bring the contents of the pan to the boil, then reduce the heat, cover the pan, and simmer for 35 to 40 minutes, or until the cabbage is tender. Remove and discard the bay leaf, garlic clove and parsley sprig.

Meanwhile, prepare the chestnuts and Brussels sprouts. In a heavy frying pan set over medium heat, stir the butter and sugar together until melted — about 2 minutes. Add the peeled chestnuts and glaze them by stirring them in the butter and sugar mixture for about 3 minutes. Add the stock, cover the pan tightly and reduce the heat to low. Simmer the chestnuts until they are soft — about 20 minutes. Towards the end of this time, place the Brussels sprouts in a steamer set over a pan of simmering water and steam them for about 5 minutes, until they, too, are tender. Add the sprouts to the pan with the chestnuts and mix both together thoroughly.

Transfer the baked potato halves, red cabbage, and chestnuts and Brussels sprouts to hot serving dishes.

Spiced Red Cabbage

Serves 6
Working time: about 20 minutes
Total time: about 1 hour and 50 minutes

Calories **330**
Protein **15g**
Cholesterol **20mg**
Total fat **13g**
Saturated fat **4g**
Sodium **390mg**

1 tbsp	juniper berries	1 tbsp
1 tbsp	coriander seeds	1 tbsp
2 tbsp	virgin olive oil	2 tbsp
5	garlic cloves, sliced	5
1	large red cabbage (about 2.25 kg/ 4½ lb), trimmed and sliced	1
30 cl	dry cider	½ pint
	freshly ground black pepper	
3	large green cooking apples (about 750 g/1 ½ lb), cored, peeled, halved and placed in acidulated water	3
90 g	matured Edam cheese, thinly sliced	3 oz

Preheat the oven to 180°C (350°F or Mark 4). Crush the juniper berries and coriander seeds using a mortar and pestle.

Heat the oil over medium heat in a 7 litre (12 pint) fireproof casserole. Add the garlic and crushed spices and stir-fry them briefly, then add the red cabbage and stir-fry for 3 to 4 minutes. Remove the casserole from the heat. Pour the cider over the cabbage and season it with black pepper. Cover the casserole and cook the cabbage in the oven for 1 hour.

Stir the cabbage and transfer it to a 3.5 litre (6 pint) ovenproof casserole — the cabbage will have halved in volume by this stage. Drain the apple halves, pat them dry on paper towels and lay them on top of the cabbage. Cover the casserole and return the cabbage to the oven for a further 30 minutes.

Preheat the grill to medium. Remove the casserole from the oven, take off the lid and, without stirring the contents, lay the slices of cheese over the apples. Put the casserole under the grill for about 5 minutes, until the cheese has melted and begun to brown. Serve the cabbage at once.

SUGGESTED ACCOMPANIMENT: *buckwheat, burghul, couscous or millet.*

Lacy Pancakes with a Spinach Filling

Serves 4
Working time: about 45 minutes
Total time: about 1 hour

Calories **410**
Protein **18g**
Cholesterol **25mg**
Total fat **16g**
Saturated fat **5g**
Sodium **360mg**

1 kg	spinach, washed and stemmed	2 lb
15 g	unsalted butter	½ oz
1	onion, chopped	1
2	garlic cloves, crushed	2
1	sweet red pepper, seeded, deribbed and cut into 2.5 cm (1 inch) strips	1
300 g	potatoes, peeled and grated	10 oz
	freshly ground black pepper	
125 g	rice flour	4 oz
⅛ tsp	salt	⅛ tsp
2	egg whites, made up to 30 cl (½ pint) with water	2
2 tbsp	safflower oil	2 tbsp
125 g	low-fat mozzarella cheese, thinly sliced	4 oz

Blanch the spinach in a saucepan of boiling water for 1 minute, then drain it and refresh it under cold running water. Drain the spinach again thoroughly, then squeeze it dry and chop it.

Melt the butter in a large, non-stick frying pan over low heat. Add the onion and garlic and cook for 2 minutes. Mix in the red pepper strips and grated potatoes and cook, stirring frequently, for 20 minutes, until the potatoes are cooked through. Remove the pan from the heat and stir in the spinach and some black pepper. Cover the pan and set it aside while you make the pancakes.

Put the rice flour and salt into a bowl and gradually beat in the egg whites and water to make a batter. Heat a 15 cm (6 inch) crêpe pan or non-stick frying pan over medium-high heat, then spread a little of the oil over the entire surface of the pan with a paper towel. Pour in about 2 tablespoons of batter and immediately swirl the pan to coat the bottom with a thin, even layer. Cook the pancake until it is firm — about 1 minute — then lift the edge with a spatula and turn the pancake over. Cook the second side until it is dry — about 30 seconds. Slide the pancake on to a plate. Make seven more pancakes in this way, spreading a little oil over the pan as necessary. Stack the cooked pancakes on top of one another.

Preheat the oven to 190°C (375°F or Mark 5). Lay each pancake in turn out flat on the work surface and spoon an eighth of the spinach mixture down the centre. Roll up the pancake to enclose the filling, then transfer it to a lightly oiled, shallow ovenproof dish. Lay the cheese slices evenly over the pancakes and bake them in the oven for about 15 minutes, until the filling has heated through and the cheese has melted and is beginning to brown. Serve at once.

SUGGESTED ACCOMPANIMENT: *tomato salad*.

Spinach, Stilton and Tomato Roulade

Serves 4
Working time: about 40 minutes
Total time: about 55 minutes

Calories **200**	500 g	spinach, washed, stems removed	1 lb
Protein **18g**	2	egg yolks	2
Cholesterol **115mg**	¼ tsp	grated nutmeg	¼ tsp
Total fat **10g**	30 g	fresh wholemeal breadcrumbs	1 oz
Saturated fat **5g**	¼ tsp	salt	¼ tsp
Sodium **410mg**		freshly ground black pepper	
	4	egg whites	4
	Stilton and tomato filling		
	175 g	low-fat soft cheese	6 oz
	45 g	Stilton cheese, rind removed, mashed	1 ½ oz
	2 tbsp	finely cut chives	2 tbsp
	4	tomatoes, skinned, deseeded (page 14) and chopped	4
		freshly ground black pepper	

Preheat the oven to 200°C (400°F or Mark 6). Line the bottom and sides of a 30 by 20 cm (12 by 8 inch) Swiss roll tin with non-stick parchment paper.

Cook the spinach in a saucepan of boiling water for 2 to 3 minutes, until it has wilted. Drain the spinach in a colander, refresh it under cold running water, then place it in a piece of muslin and squeeze out all the liquid. Purée the spinach in a food processor.

In a mixing bowl, stir together the puréed spinach, the egg yolks, nutmeg, breadcrumbs, salt and some black pepper. Whisk the egg whites until they are fairly stiff. Using a metal tablespoon, fold 1 tablespoon of the whites into the spinach mixture, then carefully fold in the remainder. Spread the roulade mixture evenly in the prepared Swiss roll tin and smooth the surface. Bake the mixture for 10 to 15 minutes, until it is firm to the touch, then remove it from the oven, cover it with a clean tea towel and set it aside to cool.

To make the filling, blend the soft cheese and the mashed Stilton together in a bowl. Mix in the cut chives, chopped tomatoes and some freshly ground black pepper. Turn the baked spinach rectangle out on to a sheet of greaseproof paper and carefully peel off the lining paper. Spread the filling over the surface of the rectangle. Starting from one of the short sides, roll the base and filling into a cylinder: lift one end of the underlying greaseproof paper to start the roulade off, and nudge it along by gradually lifting the rest of the paper. Serve the roulade cut into slices.

SUGGESTED ACCOMPANIMENTS: *hot herbed bread; watercress and apple salad.*

Spinach and Pine-Nut Layered Terrine

Serves 4
Working time: about 45 minutes
Total time: about 1 hour and 40 minutes

Calories **295**	1 kg	spinach, washed, stems removed	2½ lb
Protein **25g**	175 g	low-fat ricotta cheese	6 oz
Cholesterol **75mg**	60 g	low-fat cottage cheese	2 oz
Total fat **13g**	30 g	Parmesan cheese, freshly grated	1 oz
Saturated fat **5g**	30 g	pine-nuts, toasted	1 oz
Sodium **530mg**	1	egg, separated	1
	1	egg white	1
		freshly ground black pepper	
	Red pepper sauce		
	2	sweet red peppers, seeded, deribbed and sliced	2
	1	onion, sliced	1
	2	garlic cloves, crushed	2
	¼ litre	unsalted vegetable stock (recipe, page 9)	8 fl oz
	60 g	fresh wholemeal breadcrumbs	2 oz
	⅛ tsp	salt	⅛ tsp
		freshly ground black pepper	

Select 12 medium-sized spinach leaves for lining the terrine. Blanch them in a saucepan of boiling water for 30 seconds, then drain them and refresh them under cold running water. Drain the leaves again and lay them out to dry on paper towels. Place the rest of the spinach, with water still clinging to the leaves, in a large, heavy-bottomed saucepan. Cover the pan and cook the spinach over low heat until it has wilted and reduced in volume by a third — 2 to 3 minutes. Drain the spinach, squeeze out any excess moisture in a piece of muslin, and chop the spinach roughly. Place the chopped spinach in a bowl. Preheat the oven to 200°C (400°F or Mark 6).

Line a 1 litre (1¾ pint) rectangular terrine mould, measuring about 18 by 7.5 by 7.5 cm (7 by 3 by 3 inches), with the blanched spinach leaves, leaving enough overhanging the rim of the mould to fold over the top of the terrine. Combine the ricotta, cottage and Parmesan cheeses in a bowl with the toasted pine-nuts and the egg yolk. Whisk the egg whites until they are stiff but not dry, then fold them gently into the chopped spinach. Layer the prepared mould with a third of the spinach and egg white mixture, then half of the cheese mixture, another third of the spinach, the remaining cheese mixture, and a final layer of spinach; smooth each layer with a rubber spatula before adding the next. Fold the spinach leaves over the top of the terrine.

Cover the mould with buttered greaseproof paper, then place it in a deep baking dish and pour enough water into the dish to come two thirds of the way up the sides of the mould. Bake the terrine until the top feels firm to the touch — about 45 minutes.

While the terrine is cooking, prepare the red pepper sauce. Put the sweet red peppers, onion, garlic and stock in a saucepan and bring the liquid to the boil. Cover the pan, reduce the heat and simmer gently for about 20 minutes, until the peppers and onion are soft. Stir in the breadcrumbs, salt and some black pepper. Purée the mixture in a food processor or blender and return it to the saucepan.

Remove the terrine from the oven and let it rest for 5 minutes while you gently reheat the pepper sauce. Turn out the terrine on to a warmed serving dish and serve it cut into slices. Spoon a little of the red pepper sauce round each portion and serve the remaining sauce separately.

SUGGESTED ACCOMPANIMENT: *Melba toast.*

EDITOR'S NOTE: *To toast pine-nuts, place them in a small, heavy frying pan over medium-high heat, and cook them for 1 to 2 minutes, stirring constantly, until they are golden-brown and release their aroma.*

Kohlrabi and Courgette Gratin

Serves 4
Working time: about 35 minutes
Total time: about 1 hour and 10 minutes

Calories **145**	750 g	kohlrabi, leaves and stems removed, unpeeled if young	1 ½ lb
Protein **8g**			
Cholesterol **15mg**	250 g	courgettes, trimmed	8 oz
Total fat **7g**	30 g	unsalted butter	1 oz
Saturated fat **4g**	500 g	tomatoes, skinned, seeded (page 14) and chopped	1 lb
Sodium **415mg**			
	2 tbsp	finely chopped parsley	2 tbsp
	2	garlic cloves, crushed	2
	⅛ tsp	cayenne pepper	⅛ tsp
	½ tsp	salt	½ tsp
		freshly ground black pepper	
	30 g	fresh wholemeal breadcrumbs	1 oz

Using a sharp knife or a mandolin, cut the kohlrabi horizontally into very thin, even slices. Cut the courgettes lengthwise into equally thin slices. Put the kohlrabi slices in a steamer set over a pan of boiling water and steam for 15 minutes, then add the courgette slices to the steamer. Keep the two vegetables separate. Continue to cook the vegetables until both are just tender — another 5 to 10 minutes.

Meanwhile, melt the butter in a heavy-bottomed saucepan over low heat. Add the tomatoes, parsley and garlic, and season the mixture with the cayenne pepper, salt and some black pepper. Stir the ingredients well and cook them over medium heat for 10 to 15 minutes, stirring occasionally, until the tomatoes have reduced to a fairly thick, dry purée.

Preheat the oven to 180°C (350°F or Mark 4). Grease a round or oval gratin dish.

Drain the kohlrabi and courgette slices and pat them dry with paper towels. Arrange alternate layers of kohlrabi and courgette slices in the prepared gratin dish. Spoon the tomato purée over the top and sprinkle on the breadcrumbs. Put the dish in the oven and bake the gratin for 20 to 30 minutes, until the topping is crisp and lightly browned.

SUGGESTED ACCOMPANIMENT: *mashed potatoes with chives.*

Stuffed Mushroom Caps

Serves 6
Working time: about 35 minutes
Total time: about 1 hour and 10 minutes

Calories **185**
Protein **7g**
Cholesterol **15mg**
Total fat **6g**
Saturated fat **3g**
Sodium **260mg**

6	large field, or open cup, mushrooms, wiped clean, stalks removed and finely chopped	6
½ tsp	salt	½ tsp
	freshly ground black pepper	
1 tbsp	virgin olive oil	1 tbsp
1	onion, finely chopped	1
1	small sweet red pepper, seeded, deribbed and finely chopped	1
125 g	Italian round-grain rice	4 oz
2	garlic cloves, crushed	2
30 g	pine-nuts	1 oz
35 cl	unsalted vegetable stock (recipe, page 9)	12 fl oz
2 tbsp	shredded fresh basil leaves	2 tbsp
125 g	low-fat mozzarella cheese, diced	4 oz
30 g	fresh wholemeal breadcrumbs	1 oz
1 tbsp	chopped parsley	1 tbsp

Preheat the oven to 200°C (400°F or Mark 6).

Place the mushroom caps in a shallow ovenproof dish with 2 tablespoons of cold water. Season the mushrooms with a little of the salt and some freshly ground black pepper. Cover the dish with a lid or aluminium foil, and set it aside.

Heat the oil in a large, heavy-bottomed saucepan over medium heat. Add the onion and red pepper and cook gently for 6 to 8 minutes, until soft. Stir in the chopped mushroom stalks, the rice, garlic and pine-nuts, and cook for 5 minutes, stirring occasionally, until the rice is very lightly browned. Add the stock, basil, the remaining salt, and some pepper. Bring to the boil, then reduce the heat to low and cover the pan tightly. Cook gently for 20 to 25 minutes, until the rice is cooked and the stock has been absorbed. Meanwhile, put the mushrooms in the oven to cook for 20 minutes, until they are almost soft.

Remove the rice mixture from the heat and stir in the diced mozzarella cheese, then divide the mixture evenly among the mushrooms, mounding it neatly on top of each one. Sprinkle on the wholemeal bread-crumbs and return the mushrooms to the oven for another 10 minutes, or until the mozzarella cheese begins to melt. Serve the mushrooms sprinkled with the chopped parsley.

SUGGESTED ACCOMPANIMENT: *French beans.*

Celeriac Rolls with Mustard Sauce

Serves 4
Working time: about 1 hour and 15 minutes
Total time: about 2 hours and 15 minutes

Calories **260**
Protein **15g**
Cholesterol **15mg**
Total fat **9g**
Saturated fat **4g**
Sodium **320mg**

1 tbsp	virgin olive oil	1 tbsp
1	garlic clove, crushed	1
1	small onion, finely chopped	1
250 g	tomatoes, skinned, seeded (page 14) and chopped	8 oz
1 tbsp	tomato paste	1 tbsp
½ tsp	dried mixed herbs	½ tsp
	freshly ground black pepper	
4	young leeks (about 125 g/4 oz each), trimmed, washed thoroughly to remove all grit	4
60 cl	unsalted vegetable stock (recipe, page 9)	1 pint
2	celeriac roots (about 1 kg/2 ½ lb each), scrubbed	2
1 tbsp	fresh lemon juice	1 tbsp
2 tbsp	dry wholemeal breadcrumbs	2 tbsp
Mustard sauce		
2 tbsp	cornflour	2 tbsp
¼ tsp	grated nutmeg	¼ tsp
60 cl	skimmed milk	1 pint
½	bay leaf	½
3 tbsp	grainy mustard	3 tbsp
60 g	Cheddar cheese, grated	2 oz
⅛ tsp	salt	⅛ tsp
	freshly ground black pepper	

Heat the oil in a heavy-bottomed saucepan and sauté the garlic and onion over medium heat for 3 to 4 minutes, until the onion is transparent. Stir in the tomatoes, tomato paste and dried mixed herbs, and season generously with black pepper. Simmer the mixture for 15 minutes, stirring frequently, until it is very thick. Leave it to cool.

While the tomato mixture cools, simmer the leeks, whole, in the vegetable stock, until they are just tender — about 7 minutes. Allow them to cool in the stock while you prepare the celeriac slices.

Peel the celeriac roots. Using a mandolin or a very sharp knife, cut 12 horizontal slices about 3 mm (⅛ inch) thick from each one; take the slices from the widest part of each root. Drop the slices into acidulated water as you work, together with the unused top and bottom sections; the latter may be reserved for another use.

Bring a large saucepan of water to the boil and add the lemon juice. Cook the celeriac slices in the water for 3 to 4 minutes, until they are just tender and pliable. Drain them in a colander and place them in a bowl of iced water to cool.

Drain the leeks thoroughly and squeeze out as much moisture as possible using paper towels. Cut each leek in half lengthwise, then cut each half crosswise into three, to give a total of 24 pieces. Drain the celeriac slices and dry them thoroughly on paper towels. Preheat the oven to 200°C (400°F or Mark 6). Lightly grease a large, rectangular baking dish.

To assemble the celeriac rolls, put about 1 teaspoonful of the tomato mixture on one half of each slice of celeriac. Top the tomato with a piece of leek and roll up each slice carefully, and quite tightly. Arrange the celeriac rolls, seam side down, in a single layer in the prepared dish.

For the mustard sauce, place the cornflour and nutmeg in a large bowl and stir in 15 cl (¼ pint) of the milk until smoothly blended. Bring the rest of the milk to the boil, in a heavy-bottomed saucepan, with the bay leaf. Pour the milk into the bowl, stirring constantly, and return the mixture to the saucepan. Bring the sauce back to the boil, still stirring. Cook it over high heat for about 2 minutes, until it has thickened slightly. Take the pan off the heat, discard the bay leaf and stir in the mustard, cheese, salt and plenty of pepper.

Pour the mustard sauce over the celeriac rolls and sprinkle the breadcrumbs over the top. Bake the rolls for 30 minutes, until the surface is bubbling and golden-brown. Serve hot.

Scorzonera with Pepper and Onion Relish

Serves 6
Working (and total) time: about 45 minutes

Calories **190**
Protein **7g**
Cholesterol **0mg**
Total fat **5g**
Saturated fat **1g**
Sodium **140mg**

1 kg	scorzonera, scrubbed well	2 ½ lb
1	large sweet red pepper, seeded, deribbed and coarsely chopped	1
9	pickled mild green chili peppers, finely chopped	9
1	red onion, finely chopped	1
6	spring onions, trimmed, white bottoms sliced, green tops coarsely sliced	6
4	tomatoes, skinned and seeded (page 14), finely chopped	4
½	cucumber, peeled and diced	½
1 ½ tbsp	capers	1 ½ tbsp
6 tbsp	coarsely chopped flat-leaf parsley	6 tbsp
1 tbsp	virgin olive oil	1 tbsp
1	lime, juice only	1
⅛ tsp	cayenne pepper	⅛ tsp
3	black olives, stoned and sliced	3
	lamb's lettuce, for garnish	

Peel the scorzonera with a vegetable peeler and trim both ends. Drop them into acidulated water as you work, to prevent discoloration. Drain the scorzonera and put them in a large, heavy-bottomed saucepan. Add sufficient water to cover the roots and bring them to the boil. Cook over high heat for 10 to 20 minutes, depending on the thickness of the scorzonera, until tender. Test the roots with the point of a sharp knife.

While the scorzonera is cooking, prepare the relish. Place all the remaining ingredients except the lamb's lettuce in a large bowl and combine them thoroughly.

Drain the scorzonera in a colander, arrange them on a hot serving dish and garnish with the lamb's lettuce. Spoon the relish over the roots and serve.

SUGGESTED ACCOMPANIMENT: *granary bread.*

EDITOR'S NOTE: *Salsify may be used instead of scorzonera.*

Boiled Yam with Hot Pepper Sauce

Serves 4
Working (and total) time: about 50 minutes

Calories **350**
Protein **8g**
Cholesterol **0mg**
Total fat **4g**
Saturated fat **0g**
Sodium **245mg**

1 tbsp	peanut oil	1 tbsp
2	large onions, chopped	2
750 g	tomatoes, skinned and seeded (page 14), chopped	1 ½ lb
1	hot yellow chili pepper, or one to two hot red chili peppers, seeded and very finely chopped (caution, page 25)	1
3 tbsp	tomato paste	3 tbsp
½ tsp	salt	½ tsp
1 tsp	vegetable extract	1 tsp
1 kg	firm yam, peeled	2 lb
1 tbsp	finely chopped parsley, for garnish	1 tbsp

In a heavy-bottomed saucepan, heat the oil over medium heat. Add the onions and cook them, stirring frequently, until they are golden — about 5 minutes. Add the tomatoes and chili pepper to the pan and stir them briskly for about 8 minutes, to cook them through. Stir in the tomato paste and 4 tablespoons of cold water, then add the salt and the vegetable extract. Mix the ingredients in the pan thoroughly. Reduce the heat, cover the pan, and simmer the sauce for 10 minutes. Set the sauce aside and keep it warm.

Rinse the yam under cold running water and cut it into thin slices about 1 cm (½ inch) thick. Place the slices in a large saucepan of water: the water should just cover the yam. Bring the water to the boil, reduce the heat to medium and cook the yam slices, with the pan partially covered, for 3 to 4 minutes, or until they feel soft when pierced with a sharp knife; be careful not to overcook them. Drain the slices in a colander.

Serve the yam slices with the hot pepper sauce, garnished with the chopped parsley.

SUGGESTED ACCOMPANIMENT: *chicory salad.*

EDITOR'S NOTE: *To avoid skin irritation, wear protective rubber gloves when peeling a yam.*

Chestnut-Stuffed Sweet Potatoes with Chili Sauce

Serves 4
Working time: about 1 hour and 10 minutes
Total time: about 2 hours

Calories **455**
Protein **6g**
Cholesterol **0mg**
Total fat **11g**
Saturated fat **2g**
Sodium **165mg**

2	sweet potatoes (about 500 g/1 lb each), scrubbed	2
400 g	fresh chestnuts, peeled (box, opposite)	14 oz
1 tbsp	virgin olive oil	1 tbsp
1	onion, finely chopped	1
1	garlic clove, crushed	1
¼ tsp	salt	¼ tsp
½	lime, juice only	½
1	bunch watercress, stemmed, washed and dried	1
½	orange, rind julienned, blanched for 1 minute in boiling water and drained, flesh segmented	½
Chili sauce		
1 tbsp	virgin olive oil	1 tbsp
½	onion, finely chopped	½
1	garlic clove, crushed	1
½	red chili pepper, fresh or dried, finely chopped (caution, page 25)	½
½ tsp	ground cumin	½ tsp
175 g	tomatoes, skinned and seeded (page 14), chopped	6 oz
2 tsp	demerara sugar	2 tsp
1 tsp	red wine vinegar	1 tsp

Preheat the oven to 200°C (400°F or Mark 6).

Prick the sweet potatoes with a fork and bake them on a rack in the oven for about 1½ hours, or until there is no resistance when the tip of a sharp knife is inserted. While the sweet potatoes are baking, prepare the chili sauce and chestnut stuffing.

For the chili sauce, heat the oil in a heavy-bottomed pan and fry the onion, garlic and chili for 4 to 5 minutes, until soft. Stir in the cumin, cover the pan, and cook over low heat for a further 4 minutes. Mix in the tomatoes, sugar and vinegar and simmer, covered, for 10 minutes. Let the sauce cool a little, then blend it in a food processor or blender until smooth.

To prepare the chestnut stuffing, simmer the peeled chestnuts in a pan of boiling water for 10 minutes, until they are soft. Drain them thoroughly and chop them. Heat the oil in a heavy non-reactive saucepan, add the onion and garlic, and cook them gently, over medium heat, until soft. Stir in the chopped chestnuts, together with the salt and lime juice. Keep the stuffing warm until the sweet potatoes are ready.

Cut the cooked sweet potatoes in half lengthwise and carefully scoop out the flesh into a bowl, leaving a 5 mm (¼ inch) thick shell. Mash the flesh, then spoon it back into the shells, making a well in the centre. Pile the chestnut stuffing into the well. Meanwhile, gently reheat the sauce, then transfer it to a bowl.

Arrange the stuffed sweet potatoes on a bed of watercress and garnish with the orange segments and rind. Serve the chili sauce with the potatoes.

Peeling Chestnuts

1 PREPARING THE CHESTNUTS. With a sharp
knife, cut a cross in the hull of each chestnut. Drop
the chestnuts into a saucepan of boiling water and
parboil them for about 10 minutes, to loosen their
hulls. Remove the pan from the heat.

2 PEELING OFF THE SKINS. With a slotted
spoon, lift the chestnuts out of the pan a few
at a time. Peel off the hulls and inner skins while
the chestnuts are still hot.

Sweet Potato Timbales with Two Paprika Sauces

Serves 6
Working time: about 1 hour
Total time: about 2 hours and 45 minutes (includes chilling)

Calories **140**
Protein **5g**
Cholesterol **10mg**
Total fat **5g**
Saturated fat **2g**
Sodium **185mg**

500 g	sweet potatoes, peeled and cut into chunks	1 lb
2 tbsp	double cream, chilled	2 tbsp
4	egg whites, chilled	4
1 tsp	finely cut chives, plus a few whole chives for garnish	1 tsp
1 tsp	virgin olive oil	1 tsp
3	sweet red peppers (about 500 g/1 lb) seeded, deribbed and thinly sliced	3
1	onion, thinly sliced	1
750 g	tomatoes, roughly chopped	1½ lb
1 tsp	paprika	1 tsp
½ tsp	salt	½ tsp
	freshly ground black pepper	
2 tbsp	fromage frais	2 tbsp

Put the sweet potatoes into a saucepan of cold water
and bring them to the boil. Cover the pan, reduce the
heat and simmer the sweet potatoes until they are
soft — 20 to 25 minutes. Drain the potatoes well, allow
them to cool for about 30 minutes, then chill them in
the refrigerator for 1 hour.

Line six 8 cl (3 fl oz) ramekins with non-stick parchment paper: cut a small disc to fit each base, and a
strip long enough to fit round the inside and wide ▶

enough to stand proud of the rim by 1 cm (½ inch). Preheat the oven to 180°C (350°F or Mark 4).

Put the sweet potatoes and cream into a food processor, purée the mixture until smooth, then transfer it to a large bowl. In another bowl, whisk the egg whites until they form soft peaks but are not yet stiff and dry. Using a metal spoon, fold the egg whites into the potato mixture as lightly as possible, then fold in the finely cut chives. Divide the mixture among the prepared ramekins, smoothing the tops with a wet teaspoon. Arrange the ramekins in a large baking dish, pour in enough hot water to come two thirds of the way up the sides of the ramekins, and cover them lightly with a sheet of non-stick parchment paper. Bake the timbales for 30 minutes, or until they are risen and puffy and just firm to the touch.

Meanwhile, prepare the paprika sauces. Heat the oil in a heavy frying pan over low heat, and sweat the peppers and onion in the oil for 5 minutes. Add the tomatoes and bring the mixture to the boil, then reduce the heat, cover, and simmer the vegetables for 15 minutes. Add the paprika and simmer, covered, for a further 5 minutes. Remove the pan from the heat.

When the mixture has cooled slightly, season it with the salt and with some black pepper, and purée it in a food processor or blender. Press the purée through a nylon sieve into a bowl, then divide the purée between two small saucepans. Add the *fromage frais* to one pan, stir well and warm through gently without boiling to make a creamy, pale sauce. Gently heat the contents of the second pan in the same way.

Unmould the timbales on to individual plates, garnish them with the whole chives and serve at once with a spoonful of each sauce.

SUGGESTED ACCOMPANIMENTS: *French beans; baby sweetcorn.*

Saffron and Potato Stew with Rouille

ROUILLE, A RED CHILI PEPPER AND GARLIC SAUCE FROM PROVENCE, IS USUALLY SERVED WITH FISH SOUPS. UNLIKE THE CLASSIC SAUCE, THIS VERSION CONTAINS NO OIL.

Serves 6
Working time: about 40 minutes
Total time: about 55 minutes

Calories **270**
Protein **7g**
Cholesterol **0mg**
Total fat **3g**
Saturated fat **trace**
Sodium **350mg**

750 g	potatoes, cut into 2 cm (¾ inch) chunks	1 ½ lb
1 tsp	virgin olive oil	1 tsp
2	beef tomatoes, skinned and seeded (page 14), cut into 1 cm (½ inch) chunks	2
2	leeks, washed thoroughly to remove all grit, white and green parts separated and sliced	2
1	onion, sliced	1
2 tsp	chopped fresh thyme, or ½ tsp dried thyme	2 tsp
3	bay leaves	3
1 tsp	caster sugar	1 tsp
2	strips thinly pared orange rind	2
1 tsp	saffron threads, soaked in 1 tbsp boiling water for 30 minutes	1 tsp
60 cl	unsalted vegetable stock (recipe, page 9)	1 pint
30 cl	medium white wine	½ pint
90 g	small pasta shapes	3 oz
250 g	courgettes, sliced	8 oz
3 tbsp	chopped parsley	3 tbsp
1	sweet yellow pepper, seeded, deribbed and sliced into fine strips	1
¾ tsp	salt	¾ tsp
	freshly ground black pepper	
45 g	thick Greek yogurt	1 ½ oz
Rouille		
60 g	white bread, crusts removed, broken into pieces	2 oz
8 cl	skimmed milk	3 fl oz
2	hot red chili peppers, seeded and roughly chopped (caution, page 25)	2
3	garlic cloves, roughly chopped	3
¼ tsp	salt	¼ tsp
1	small sweet red pepper, seeded, deribbed and roughly chopped	1

First make the *rouille*. Place the bread in a bowl with the milk and set it aside to steep until the bread has softened — about 5 minutes. Purée the chili peppers, garlic, salt and sweet red pepper with 2 tablespoons of water in a food processor or blender. Add the bread and milk, and blend again until smooth. Transfer the *rouille* to a serving bowl and set it aside.

Put the potatoes in a pan with enough cold water to cover them. Bring to the boil, then reduce the heat, cover the pan and simmer until the potatoes are almost tender — about 10 minutes. Drain them well.

While the potatoes are cooking, heat the oil in a large fireproof casserole over medium heat. Add the tomatoes, white parts of the leeks, onion, thyme and bay leaves, and cook, stirring, for 5 minutes. Stir in the sugar, orange rind, saffron and its soaking liquid, stock and wine, and bring the mixture to the boil. Add the pasta and cook, covered, for 5 to 7 minutes, until the pasta is almost *al dente*.

Stir in the potatoes, green parts of the leeks, courgettes, parsley, yellow pepper, salt and some black pepper and cook, stirring, for a further 3 to 5 minutes, until the potatoes are heated through but the yellow pepper and courgettes still retain their crispness.

Ladle the stew into individual serving bowls, and top each serving with a swirl of the yogurt and a spoonful of *rouille*. Serve the remaining *rouille* separately.

SUGGESTED ACCOMPANIMENT: *crusty wholemeal bread.*

Potato, Carrot and Celeriac Rösti

RÖSTI IS A NATIONAL SWISS DISH TRADITIONALLY MADE WITH POTATOES AS THE ONLY VEGETABLE. THIS VARIATION IS COOKED WITH SUBSTANTIALLY LESS BUTTER THAN THE CLASSIC VERSION.

Serves 4
Working time: about 40 minutes
Total time: about 1 hour and 10 minutes

Calories **200**
Protein **3g**
Cholesterol **25mg**
Total fat **9g**
Saturated fat **5g**
Sodium **165mg**

500 g	potatoes, scrubbed	1 lb
250 g	carrots, peeled	8 oz
300 g	celeriac, peeled	10 oz
¼ tsp	salt	¼ tsp
	freshly ground black pepper	
45 g	unsalted butter	1½ oz

Cook the potatoes, in their skins, in a saucepan of boiling water for 6 minutes, then drain them well. Carefully peel the potatoes while they are still hot. Allow to cool for 10 minutes, then chill them for 20 minutes.

Using a vegetable grater or mouli julienne machine, coarsely shred the potatoes, carrots and celeriac. Place the shredded vegetables in a large mixing bowl. Season them with the salt and with black pepper to taste, and mix them well together.

Heat half of the butter in a large non-stick frying pan until it begins to bubble. Reduce the heat to low and add the *rösti* mixture, pressing it down gently with a spatula to form a flat cake. Cook for about 10 minutes, until the *rösti* is golden-brown underneath, shaking the pan gently now and then to prevent sticking.

Place a large flat plate on top of the frying pan, remove it from the heat and carefully invert the *rösti* on to the plate. Return the frying pan to the heat, add the remaining butter and heat it until it is bubbling hot. Slide the *rösti* back into the pan and cook the second side for 5 to 6 minutes, until golden-brown. Turn the *rösti* on to a hot plate and serve immediately.

SUGGESTED ACCOMPANIMENT: *salad of red and white cabbage with chopped parsley, tossed in a vinaigrette dressing.*

Baked Potatoes with an Onion and Chive Filling

Serves 4
Working time: about 20 minutes
Total time: about 2 hours

Calories **270**
Protein **7g**
Cholesterol **3mg**
Total fat **3g**
Saturated fat **1g**
Sodium **245mg**

2	large potatoes (about 500 g/1 lb each), scrubbed and pricked	2
2	Spanish onions, unpeeled, halved lengthwise	2
250 g	thick Greek yogurt	8 oz
2 tbsp	finely cut chives	2 tbsp
½ tsp	salt	½ tsp
	freshly ground black pepper	

Preheat the oven to 200°C (400°F or Mark 6).

Place the potatoes and the onion halves on a rack in the middle of the oven and bake them until they are soft when pierced with a skewer; the onions will take about 45 minutes and the potatoes will need about 1½ hours. Do not turn off the oven at the end of this time.

When the onions are cooked, remove them from the oven. Allow them to cool a little, then peel them. Remove and reserve the centres of the onions and roughly chop the remainder.

Cut the cooked potatoes in half lengthwise. Using a spoon, scoop the flesh into a bowl, leaving a 1 cm (½ inch) thick potato shell. Mash the potato flesh, then mix in the yogurt, chives, salt and some black pepper.

Half fill the shells with the mashed potato mixture. Add a layer of chopped roast onion, and top the onion with the rest of the potato mixture. Garnish each potato half with a reserved onion centre. Return the stuffed potatoes to the oven for about 15 minutes, to heat them through.

SUGGESTED ACCOMPANIMENT: *radish and watercress salad.*

Scandinavian Salad

THIS IS AN ADAPTATION OF A SALAD THAT IN SCANDINAVIAN COUNTRIES TRADITIONALLY ACCOMPANIES CURED HERRINGS. THE CLASSIC MIXTURE INCLUDES HARD-BOILED EGGS AND A RICH, CREAMY DRESSING; HERE, THE PROPORTION OF EGGS IS REDUCED AND YOGURT REPLACES CREAM IN THE DRESSING.

Serves 6
Working time: about 45 minutes
Total time: about 2 hours and 15 minutes (includes chilling)

Calories **195**
Protein **7g**
Cholesterol **75mg**
Total fat **4g**
Saturated fat **1g**
Sodium **190mg**

750 g	small beetroots, washed and trimmed, 5 cm (2 inch) stem left on each	1 ½ lb
750 g	new potatoes, lightly scrubbed, halved if large	1 ½ lb
2	eggs, hard-boiled	2
1 tbsp	red wine vinegar	1 tbsp
1 tsp	molasses	1 tsp
2 tbsp	thick Greek yogurt	2 tbsp
1 tsp	caraway seeds, lightly toasted	1 tsp
	freshly ground black pepper	
	curly endive leaves, for garnish	
Mustard dressing		
2 tsp	mild Dijon mustard	2 tsp
1 tsp	dry mustard	1 tsp
1 tsp	yellow mustard seeds, toasted	1 tsp
½ tsp	freshly grated horseradish	½ tsp
1 tsp	white wine vinegar	1 tsp
2 tsp	virgin olive oil	2 tsp
15 cl	plain low-fat yogurt	¼ pint
2 tbsp	finely chopped fresh dill	2 tbsp

Preheat the oven to 200°C (400°F or Mark 6). Wrap the beetroots, in a single package, in aluminium foil. Bake the beetroots until they are tender — about 1 hour. Remove them from the oven and, when they are cool enough to handle, peel them, removing the stems, and cut them into 1 cm (½ inch) cubes. Place the beetroot cubes in a large bowl.

While the beetroots are cooking, steam the new potatoes until they are just tender — 15 to 20 minutes. Take care not to overcook them.

Cut one hard-boiled egg lengthwise into six wedges and set aside. Slice the second hard-boiled egg in half. Reserve the yolk for inclusion in the mustard dressing; dice the white finely and set it aside for garnish.

Put the red wine vinegar in a small bowl, add the molasses and stir until smoothly combined. Pour this dressing over the beetroot cubes and toss them in it thoroughly. Add the yogurt, the caraway seeds and some black pepper. Stir to combine all the ingredients, then set the bowl aside.

For the mustard dressing, sieve the reserved egg yolk into a small bowl and blend in the Dijon mustard. Add the dry mustard, mustard seeds and grated horse-radish, and stir thoroughly. Next, blend in the white wine vinegar, followed by the oil. Finally, mix in the yogurt and chopped dill.

Cut the potatoes into slightly larger cubes than the beetroots and place them in a large bowl. Pour on the mustard dressing and toss the cubes in it thoroughly.

Line a serving dish with the endive leaves. Pile the beetroot cubes in the centre of the dish, and arrange the potatoes and hard-boiled egg wedges in a circle around them. Sprinkle the chopped egg white over the beetroot. Chill the salad in the refrigerator for about 30 minutes before serving it.

SUGGESTED ACCOMPANIMENT: *a selection of breads.*

EDITOR'S NOTE: To toast caraway and mustard seeds, place them in small, dry frying pans and shake them over medium heat for about 3 minutes, until the seeds are hot and aromatic.

Jerusalem Artichoke and Walnut Soufflés

Serves 4
Working time: about 20 minutes
Total time: about 45 minutes

Calories **145**
Protein **8g**
Cholesterol **60mg**
Total fat **10g**
Saturated fat **2g**
Sodium **290mg**

250 g	Jerusalem artichokes, peeled and cut into small pieces	8 oz
2 tsp	cornflour	2 tsp
15 cl	skimmed milk	¼ pint
¼ tsp	ground mace	¼ tsp
½ tsp	salt	½ tsp
3 tbsp	chopped parsley	3 tbsp
	freshly ground black pepper	
60 g	shelled walnuts, finely chopped	2 oz
1	egg yolk	1
3	egg whites	3
1 tbsp	freshly grated Parmesan cheese	1 tbsp

Preheat the oven to 180°C (350°F or Mark 4). Lightly grease the sides of four 20 cl (7 fl oz) soufflé dishes and place them on a baking sheet.

Cook the Jerusalem artichokes in a saucepan of boiling water for 6 to 8 minutes, or until they are tender. Drain and mash them, and set them aside.

In a large, heavy-bottomed saucepan, blend the cornflour with a little of the milk. Stir in the remaining milk, followed by the mace, salt, parsley and some black pepper. Bring the contents of the pan to the boil, stirring continuously, then reduce the heat to medium and cook the sauce for about 2 minutes, until it has thickened. Remove the pan from the heat and stir in the mashed artichokes. Set aside 1 tablespoon of the walnuts, stir the remainder into the pan, together with the egg yolk, and mix the ingredients well.

Whisk the egg whites until stiff then, using a metal tablespoon, carefully fold a quarter of the whites at a time into the artichoke mixture. Divide the mixture equally among the prepared dishes. Sprinkle the top of the soufflés with the Parmesan and reserved walnuts, and bake them in the oven for 20 to 25 minutes, or until they are well risen and golden. Remove the soufflés from the oven and serve them immediately.

SUGGESTED ACCOMPANIMENTS: *crusty wholemeal bread; green salad with a garlic dressing.*

Curried Swede Soup

Serves 4
Working time: about 20 minutes
Total time: about 1 hour

Calories **185**
Protein **4g**
Cholesterol **0mg**
Total fat **7g**
Saturated fat **2g**
Sodium **425mg**

1 tbsp	safflower oil	1 tbsp
1	onion (about 125 g/4 oz), chopped	1
350 g	swedes, cut into 5 mm (¼ inch) dice	12 oz
175 g	parsnips, cut into 5 mm (¼ inch) dice	6 oz
1	small sweet red pepper, seeded, deribbed and cut into 5 mm (¼ inch) dice	1
1	small cooking apple (about 90g/3oz), cut into 5 mm (¼ inch) dice	1
30 g	brown basmati rice	1 oz
½ tsp	medium-hot curry powder	½ tsp
½ tsp	ground coriander	½ tsp
¼ tsp	ground cumin	¼ tsp
⅛ tsp	ground turmeric	⅛ tsp
⅛ tsp	ground ginger	⅛ tsp
1	garlic clove, crushed	1
½ tsp	salt	½ tsp
30 cl	tomato juice	½ pint
90 cl	unsalted vegetable stock (recipe, page 9)	1 ½ pints
15 g	sultanas	½ oz
15 g	desiccated coconut, toasted	½ oz

Heat the oil in a large, heavy-bottomed saucepan or fireproof casserole and sweat the onion, swedes and parsnips over medium heat for 5 minutes. Add the red pepper and cook for a further 2 to 3 minutes, stirring occasionally. Then add the apple, rice, spices and garlic and cook, stirring constantly, for 2 minutes. Finally, mix in the salt, tomato juice, stock and sultanas and bring the mixture to the boil. Reduce the heat to a simmer, cover the pan, and cook the soup for 30 minutes. Just before serving, stir in the coconut.

SUGGESTED ACCOMPANIMENT: *sourdough rye bread.* ·

EDITOR'S NOTE: *To toast desiccated coconut, spread the coconut out on a baking sheet and place it in a 180°C (350°F or Mark 4) oven for 10 minutes, stirring it once.*

Mixed Root Vegetables Cooked in Orange Sauce

Serves 4
Working time: about 30 minutes
Total time: about 1 hour

Calories **160**
Protein **4g**
Cholesterol **15mg**
Total fat **7g**
Saturated fat **4g**
Sodium **330mg**

30 g	unsalted butter	1 oz
1	onion, chopped	1
1	garlic clove, crushed	1
2 tsp	freshly grated ginger root	2 tsp
1 tsp	coriander seeds, crushed	1 tsp
175 g	parsnips, peeled if necessary, cut into 2.5 cm (1 inch) chunks	6 oz
175 g	carrots, peeled if necessary, cut into 2.5 cm (1 inch) chunks	6 oz
175 g	swedes, peeled if necessary, cut into 2.5 cm (1 inch) chunks	6 oz
175 g	kohlrabi, peeled if necessary, cut into 2.5 cm (1 inch) chunks	6 oz
175 g	celeriac, peeled if necessary, cut into 2.5 cm (1 inch) chunks	6 oz
175 g	turnips, trimmed and cut into 2.5 cm (1 inch) chunks	6 oz
30 cl	fresh orange juice, mixed with 15 cl (¼ pint) water	½ pint
1	lemon, coarsely grated rind only	1
1	orange, coarsely grated rind only	1
½ tsp	salt	½ tsp
	freshly ground black pepper	

Melt the butter in a large, heavy-bottomed saucepan or fireproof casserole over medium heat. Add the onion and garlic, and sauté them for 3 to 4 minutes, until the onion is transparent. Mix in the ginger and coriander, and cook the mixture for a further minute, stirring constantly. Add all the root vegetables, and the orange juice and water mixture. Bring the contents of the pan to the boil. Reduce the heat to low, cover the pan and simmer the vegetables for 20 minutes.

Stir in the grated lemon and orange rind, the salt and some freshly ground black pepper. Cover the saucepan or casserole again and simmer the vegetables for another 5 minutes. Finally, to reduce and thicken the orange sauce, remove the lid from the pan and boil the vegetables rapidly for 5 minutes. At the end of this time they should feel just tender when pierced with the tip of a sharp knife.

SUGGESTED ACCOMPANIMENT: *couscous or brown rice.*

EDITOR'S NOTE: *Since many valuable nutrients are contained in or just below the skin of root vegetables, select small, young specimens, which rarely need peeling, for this recipe.*

Stir-Fried Vegetables in a Sweet-and-Sour Sauce

Serves 4
Working (and total) time: about 30 minutes

Calories **240**			
Protein **9g**	1½ tbsp	safflower oil	1½ tbsp
Cholesterol **0mg**	350 g	baby sweetcorn, trimmed if necessary, halved lengthwise	12 oz
Total fat **13g**	1	large sweet red pepper, seeded, deribbed and cut into strips	1
Saturated fat **2g**			
Sodium **30mg**	350 g	young carrots, trimmed and thinly sliced diagonally	12 oz
	350 g	bean sprouts	12 oz
	350 g	mange-tout, strings removed	12 oz
	2 tsp	dark sesame oil	2 tsp
		freshly ground black pepper	

	Sweet-and-sour sauce	
3 tsp	arrowroot	3 tsp
30 cl	unsweetened pineapple juice	½ pint
2 tbsp	low-sodium soy sauce or shoyu	2 tbsp
1 tbsp	freshly grated ginger root	1 tbsp
1	garlic clove, crushed	1
15 cl	unsalted vegetable stock (recipe, page 9)	¼ pint
1 tsp	clear honey	1 tsp
5	spring onions, trimmed and finely sliced	5

To make the sweet-and-sour sauce, place the arrow-root in a medium-sized saucepan and gradually blend in the pineapple juice. Stir in the soy sauce or shoyu, grated ginger, garlic, vegetable stock, honey and sliced spring onions. Bring the contents of the pan to the boil, reduce the heat, and simmer the sauce for 5 minutes, stirring it frequently. Set the sauce aside while you cook the vegetables.

Heat the safflower oil in a wok or large, heavy frying pan over high heat. Add the sweetcorn, red pepper and carrots, and stir-fry them for 4 minutes. Add the bean sprouts and mange-tout, and stir-fry for a further 1 to 2 minutes, until the vegetables are cooked but still slightly crunchy.

Add the sweet-and-sour sauce to the wok. Reduce the heat and cook the mixture for 1 to 2 minutes more, still stirring, to warm the sauce through.

Season the stir-fry with the sesame oil and with some freshly ground black pepper. Serve immediately.

SUGGESTED ACCOMPANIMENT: *white or brown rice.*

Lohans' Feast

THIS IS ONE OF THE CLASSICS OF CHINESE BUDDHIST VEGETARIAN CUISINE, SOMETIMES KNOWN AS "BUDDHA'S DELIGHT" ON RESTAURANT MENUS. LOHANS ARE THE GUARDIAN ANGELS OF THE BUDDHA. A GRAND VERSION OF THIS DISH CONTAINS 18 DIFFERENT ITEMS — AMONG THEM RARE AND EXOTIC FUNGI — REPRESENTING THE 18 LOHANS. THIS COMPARATIVELY SIMPLE VERSION IS WHAT WOULD BE FOUND ON THE DINING TABLE OF MOST CONTEMPORARY CHINESE FAMILIES. COMMON TO ALL TRUE BUDDHIST VEGETARIAN DISHES, IT DOES NOT CONTAIN THE USUAL CHINESE FLAVOURINGS OF GARLIC, GINGER AND SPRING ONION, AS THESE ARE CONSIDERED BY BUDDHISTS AS RANK FLAVOURS AND ALSO BELIEVED TO AROUSE PASSION.

Serves 4
Working time: about 1 hour and 30 minutes
Total time: about 4 hours (includes soaking)

Calories **325**
Protein **11g**
Cholesterol **0mg**
Total fat **9g**
Saturated fat **1g**
Sodium **250mg**

15 g	dried hair algae, soaked for 20 minutes in cold water, or until pliable	½ oz
2½ tbsp	safflower oil	2½ tbsp
12	dried shiitake mushrooms, soaked for 20 minutes in warm water	12
20 g	dried lily buds (golden needles), soaked for 20 minutes in warm water	¾ oz
10 g	dried cloud-ear mushrooms, soaked for 20 minutes in warm water	⅓ oz
125 g	drained canned bamboo shoots, cut into 5 mm (¼ inch) thick slices	4 oz
75 g	dried bean curd sticks, soaked for 3 hours in cold water or until soft, drained and cut into 6 cm (2¼ inch) lengths	2½ oz
60 g	dried cellophane noodles, soaked for at least 5 minutes in cold water, drained 5 to 10 minutes before cooking	2 oz
90 g	shelled gingko nuts (about 36 nuts)	3 oz
1 tsp	dark sesame oil	1 tsp
½	carrot, sliced, slices cut into decorative shapes with aspic cutters, blanched in boiling water for 3 minutes and drained	½
Bean curd sauce		
45 cl	unsalted vegetable stock (recipe, page 9)	¾ pint
1 cube	red fermented bean curd, plus 1 tsp pickling liquid from the can or jar	1 cube
2 tbsp	low-sodium soy sauce or shoyu	2 tbsp
1½ tsp	sugar	1½ tsp

Drain the hair algae and rub into it 1 teaspoon of the safflower oil. Place the algae in a large bowl and cover them with fresh water. Stir the algae and rub them under the water to loosen any impurities lodged in the strands — the oil will help to loosen them and float them to the surface. Drain the algae carefully, pressing them against the side of the bowl. Repeat the oiling and rinsing twice more, then rinse the algae in fresh cold water at least three times, or until all traces of oil are removed. Squeeze the algae dry, separate the strands into bunches and knot the bunches into little balls. Set the balls aside.

Squeeze the shiitake mushrooms dry. Remove and discard the stalks and set the caps aside. Strain and reserve the soaking liquid.

Drain the lily buds, squeeze them dry and trim away and discard any hard bits at the stalk ends. Tie the buds into simple single knots — this is the traditional method and helps to preserve their crunchy texture. Set the knots aside.

Drain the cloud-ear mushrooms and rinse them in several changes of water to remove any grit. Remove any hard knobs with a sharp knife. Tear the fungus into bite-sized pieces, separating any large clusters as you do so. Leave the pieces to drain.

Next, prepare the bean curd sauce. Make the reserved mushroom-soaking liquid up to ½ litre (16 fl oz) with the stock and a little water if necessary. Blend the fermented bean curd with the teaspoon of its pickling liquid and a little of the stock solution until smooth. Pass the mixture through a fine sieve, pressing the bean curd with the back of a spoon and adding a little more stock if necessary to get it through the sieve. Add the soy sauce, sugar and remaining stock to the purée, and mix it thoroughly. Set the sauce aside.

Heat a wok or large, heavy frying pan over a high heat then add ½ teaspoon of the safflower oil and swirl it round in the wok to coat the sides. Add the lily buds and the cloud-ears, and let them sizzle in the oil for 30 seconds, continuously stirring them with a spatula. Remove them from the wok using a slotted spoon and set them aside. Add the remaining safflower oil to the wok and stir-fry the bamboo shoots and shiitake mushrooms for about 30 seconds; remove them from the wok and set them aside

Pour the bean curd sauce into a heavy-bottomed saucepan or fireproof casserole and bring it to the boil. Add the bean curd sticks and simmer them for 10 minutes. Add the previously browned lily buds, cloud ears, bamboo shoots and shiitake mushrooms to the casserole, together with the hair algae balls and gingko nuts. Simmer the ingredients for 10 minutes, then add the cellophane noodles and simmer for a further 10 minutes, until most of the liquid has been absorbed. (If you are using canned gingko nuts, add them with the cellophane noodles.)

Arrange the ingredients attractively on a heatproof serving platter. Sprinkle on the sesame oil and garnish the dish with the carrot shapes. Before serving, set the platter over a large pan of boiling water to steam for 10 to 15 minutes, to heat everything through.

SUGGESTED ACCOMPANIMENT: *boiled rice.*

EDITOR'S NOTE: *Lohans' Feast benefits from being cooked a day in advance, to allow the flavours to develop. All the unusual ingredients called for in this recipe can be obtained in Chinese grocery shops. Since most of the ingredients are dried, any unused surplus can be stored almost indefinitely and used on another occasion. Fermented bean curd, available in cans or jars, will keep for several months in its pickling liquid. Once a can is opened, the contents should be transferred to a sterile screw-top jar for storage.*

Okra and Sweet Pepper Stew

Serves 4
Working time: about 30 minutes
Total time: about 45 minutes

Calories **200**
Protein **9g**
Cholesterol **0mg**
Total fat **12g**
Saturated fat **3g**
Sodium **230mg**

2 tbsp	safflower oil	2 tbsp
2	Spanish onions, cut lengthwise into eight wedges	2
1 tbsp	palm oil	1 tbsp
2	beef tomatoes, skinned and seeded (page 14), chopped	2
1	sweet red pepper, seeded, deribbed and sliced into rings	1
1	sweet yellow pepper, seeded, deribbed and sliced into rings	1
6 ½ tbsp	tomato paste	6 ½ tbsp
30 cl	unsalted vegetable stock (recipe, page 9)	½ pint
750 g	okra, trimmed and sliced	1 ½ lb
500 g	button mushrooms, wiped and quartered	1 lb
2 tsp	ground coriander	2 tsp
½ tsp	salt	½ tsp

Heat the safflower oil in a large heavy-bottomed saucepan over medium heat. Add the onions and fry them gently for 5 minutes, stirring from time to time. Add the palm oil to the pan and, when it has melted, stir in the tomatoes and pepper rings. Reduce the heat to low, cover the pan and cook the vegetables gently for about 5 minutes.

Stir the tomato paste into the stock. When it has completely dissolved, pour this liquid into the saucepan. Add the okra, mushrooms and coriander and stir the mixture lightly.

Heat the contents of the pan slowly to simmering point. Cover the pan and continue to simmer for a further 15 minutes, or until the vegetables are tender, stirring from time to time. Stir in the salt and serve.

SUGGESTED ACCOMPANIMENT: *steamed yam.*

EDITOR'S NOTE: *Palm oil — misleadingly named since, at refrigerator temperature, it is the consistency of butter — is bright orange in colour and has a strong nutty flavour. It is available from African and Caribbean speciality food shops.*

Creamy Coconut Curry

Serves 4
Working time: about 45 minutes
Total time: about 1 hour

Calories **170**
Protein **5g**
Cholesterol **10mg**
Total fat **9g**
Saturated fat **2g**
Sodium **330mg**

15 g	ghee or unsalted butter	½ oz
1	onion, finely chopped	1
1 ½ tsp	ground turmeric	1 ½ tsp
2 tsp	ground coriander	2 tsp
1 tsp	ground fenugreek	1 tsp
2 tsp	black mustard seeds	2 tsp
350 g	carrots, coarsely chopped and blanched for 30 seconds in boiling water	12 oz
1	small cauliflower (about 750 g/1 ½ lb), broken into florets and blanched for 30 seconds in boiling water	1
½ tsp	salt	½ tsp
175 g	French beans, topped and tailed, cut in half and blanched for 30 seconds in boiling water	6 oz
60 g	raisins	2 oz
8	small hot green chili peppers, seeded and finely chopped (caution, page 25)	8
3	small bananas, peeled and diced	3
60 g	creamed coconut, grated	2 oz
½	lemon, juice only	½
1 tbsp	chopped fresh mint	1 tbsp
1 tbsp	chopped fresh coriander leaves	1 tbsp
	freshly ground black pepper	

Melt the ghee in a large, heavy-bottomed saucepan over medium heat. Add the onion and fry it, stirring frequently, until it is transparent — about 3 minutes. Stir in the turmeric, ground coriander, fenugreek and black mustard seeds, and fry the spices with the onion for about 2 minutes. Then mix in the blanched carrots and cauliflower, and the salt. Reduce the heat to low, cover the pan and cook the vegetables for 5 minutes. Add the French beans, re-cover the pan and cook for a further 3 minutes. Stir in 30 cl (½ pint) of water, then lightly stir in the raisins and half of the chopped chilies. Bring the mixture to the boil, cover the pan again and reduce the heat to low. Simmer for 10 minutes, or until the carrots are tender.

Gently mix in the bananas and creamed coconut, and simmer the curry, uncovered, for 3 minutes. Finally, add the lemon juice, mint, chopped coriander, remaining chilies and some freshly ground black pepper. If the curry seems dry, add a little extra water. Simmer the curry for 2 minutes more and serve.

SUGGESTED ACCOMPANIMENTS: *rice; coriander raita.*

EDITOR'S NOTE: *For a hotter curry, add a little chili powder with the ground coriander. To make coriander raita, whisk ½ teaspoon of chili powder into ¼ litre (8 fl oz) of chilled, plain low-fat yogurt. Stir in about 2 tablespoons of chopped coriander leaves, and sprinkle a few more on top as a garnish.*

Mexican Sweet Potato Stew

Serves 4
Working time: about 40 minutes
Total time: about 1 hour and 10 minutes

Calories **270**
Protein **7g**
Cholesterol **0mg**
Total fat **9g**
Saturated fat **1g**
Sodium **150mg**

600 g	sweet potatoes, cut into large chunks	1 ¼ lb
350 g	slice of pumpkin, seeded and chopped	12 oz
2 tbsp	safflower oil	2 tbsp
1	onion, finely chopped	1
2	garlic cloves, crushed	2
½ tsp	chili powder	½ tsp
250 g	okra, topped, tailed and chopped	8 oz
1	sweet green pepper, seeded, deribbed and chopped	1
4	fresh hot red chili peppers, seeded and finely chopped (caution, page 25)	4
175 g	fresh or frozen sweetcorn kernels	6 oz
400 g	canned tomatoes, with their juice	14 oz
5	cloves	5
30 cl	unsalted vegetable stock (recipe, page 9)	½ pint
2 tbsp	tomato paste	2 tbsp
⅛ tsp	salt	⅛ tsp
	freshly ground black pepper	

Put the sweet potatoes in a saucepan, cover them with water and bring to the boil. Cover the pan, reduce the heat and simmer the sweet potatoes until they are tender — about 10 minutes. Remove them from the pan with a slotted spoon and set them aside. Put the pumpkin into the same cooking water and bring it to the boil. Reduce the heat, cover the pan again and simmer the pumpkin until it, too, is tender — 5 to 7 minutes. Drain the pumpkin and set it aside while you cook the rest of the vegetables.

Heat the oil in a large, heavy-bottomed saucepan and sauté the onion and garlic over very gentle heat for about 7 minutes, or until the onion is tender. Add the chili powder, okra, sweet pepper, chili peppers, sweetcorn, tomatoes and their juice, cloves and stock. Bring the mixture to the boil, then reduce the heat and cook over medium-low heat for about 10 minutes, or until the liquid has reduced and thickened.

Add the tomato paste, sweet potatoes, pumpkin, salt and some black pepper to the pan and stir gently. Cover the pan and simmer the stew for a further 10 minutes. Serve it hot.

SUGGESTED ACCOMPANIMENTS: *tacos or tortillas; green salad.*

Hot and Sour Potato and Turnip Casserole

Serves 4
Working time: about 45 minutes
Total time: about 1 hour and 20 minutes

Calories **270**
Protein **7g**
Cholesterol **0mg**
Total fat **12g**
Saturated fat **3g**
Sodium **265mg**

1 tsp	coriander seeds	1 tsp
1 tsp	black peppercorns	1 tsp
5	cardamom pods	5
4	cloves	4
1 ½ tbsp	safflower oil	1 ½ tbsp
1	small onion, finely chopped	1
2	garlic cloves, crushed	2
1 tsp	freshly grated ginger root	1 tsp
1	fresh or dried red chili pepper, halved lengthwise and seeded (caution, page 25)	1
500 g	potatoes, diced	1 lb
250 g	turnips, diced	8 oz
250 g	French beans or wax beans, topped and tailed, cut into 2.5 cm (1 inch) lengths	8 oz
5 or 6	fresh curry leaves (optional)	5 or 6
½ tsp	salt	½ tsp
500 g	tomatoes, skinned, seeded (page 14), and chopped	1 lb
1 ½ tbsp	fresh lemon juice	1 ½ tbsp
2 tsp	sugar	2 tsp
150 g	thick Greek yogurt or 15 cl (¼ pint) soured cream	5 oz
2 tsp	ground turmeric	2 tsp
3 tbsp	chopped fresh coriander	3 tbsp

Toast the coriander seeds, peppercorns, cardamom pods and cloves in a dry frying pan over medium heat for 1 minute, to release their fragrance. Grind them finely, either in an electric coffee grinder or by hand in a mortar with a pestle.

Heat the oil over medium heat in a large fireproof casserole or heavy-bottomed saucepan. Fry the onion, garlic, ginger, ground spices and chili pepper for 5 minutes, stirring frequently. Add the potatoes, turnips, beans, curry leaves, if using, and salt. Stir the mixture well, cover the casserole and sweat the vegetables for 10 minutes, stirring occasionally.

Blend the tomatoes in a food processor or blender until smooth, and add them to the casserole. Continue simmering until the potatoes are almost done — about 15 minutes. Stir in 15 cl (¼ pint) of water and cook for 5 minutes, then stir in another 15 cl (¼ pint) and cook for 5 minutes more. Remove the casserole from the heat and mix in the lemon juice and 1 teaspoon of the sugar. Discard the curry leaves, if using, and also, if you wish, the chili pepper.

In a bowl, mix the yogurt with the remaining teaspoon of sugar and the turmeric. Stir half of the yogurt mixture into the casserole. Pour the rest of the yogurt mixture into the centre of the casserole, sprinkle over the chopped coriander and serve.

SUGGESTED ACCOMPANIMENT: *brown or white rice*

EDITOR'S NOTE: *Curry leaves are available from Indian grocers and some supermarkets.*

2 *Mung beans, chick-peas, wild rice, white and brown rice and red kidney beans are just a sample of the many pulses and grains used in this chapter.*

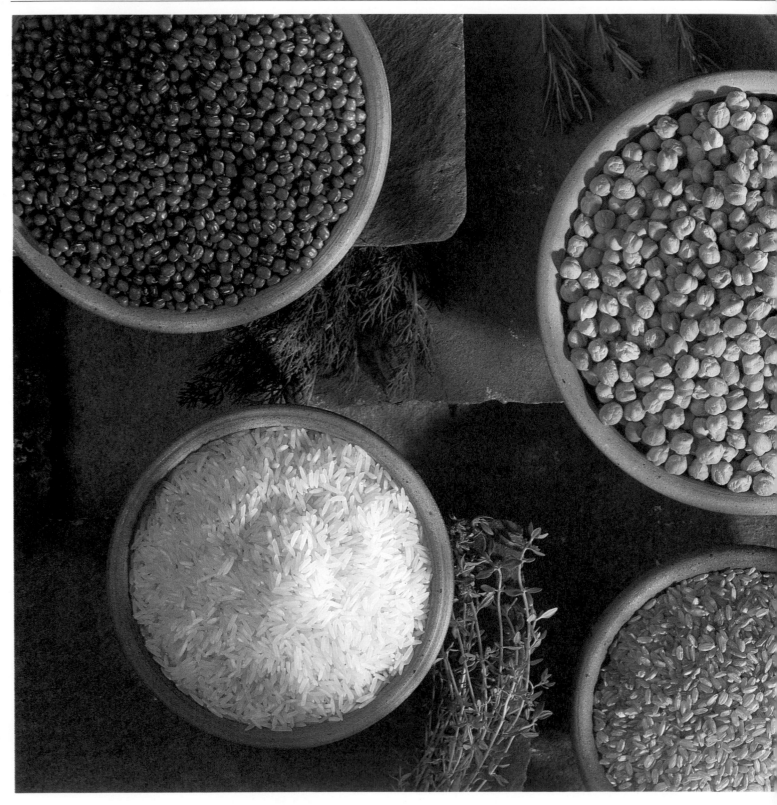

Stored Goodness

For ten thousand years or more, ever since Stone Age farmers first cultivated the banks of slow-flowing Asian rivers, grains and pulses have been central to human nutrition. Today, these two vast families of food (there are 2,500 varieties of rice alone) still provide most of the calories and more than two thirds of the protein consumed throughout the world. Their long association is no historical accident; eaten together, grains and pulses complement each other to create a perfect protein balance. In the wealthy Western countries of the world, where meat and fish are the principal sources of protein, health-conscious cooks are reawakening to this time-honoured way of eating. Low in saturated fats and high in dietary fibre and carbohydrates, grains and pulses are an ancient antidote to the modern ills of an affluent diet. As the recipes in this chapter suggest, they adapt easily to the sophisticated tastes of the 20th century.

Although most of the ingredients in this chapter are widely available from wholefood shops, many are not yet common to every Western larder. Millet, a tiny, delicately flavoured grain, is a staple of the African and Asian diet and is rich in protein, iron and B vitamins. Buckwheat is not strictly a wheat at all, being more closely related to rhubarb. The seeds or "groats", known as kasha in Russian cookery, add a robust, earthy tang to any dish. Wild rice is a costly but delectable grass seed native to the central northern United States. Even in small quantities, it enhances any dish with its distinctive though subtle flavour.

Several varieties of dried beans, peas and lentils are now to be found on the shelves of good grocery shops and supermarkets. Tofu, however, is still generally only available in health food or Oriental shops. This high-protein soya bean curd — nearly tasteless by itself — has a satisfying texture and a chameleon-like tendency to absorb flavours from other ingredients in which it is marinated or with which it is cooked.

There is one important caveat to bear in mind when preparing beans for any recipe. A number of varieties, particularly red beans, black beans and others in the kidney bean family, contain a potentially dangerous toxin. This is completely destroyed by 10 minutes of rapid boiling, after which the water should be changed and the beans simmered until they are tender. Reward yourself for this extra labour by cooking double the quantity of beans required. Cooked beans freeze well and are delicious in salads and soups.

Salad of Avocado, Flageolets, Almonds and Brown Rice

Serves 6
Working time: about 25 minutes
Total time: about 3 hours (includes soaking)

Calories **300**
Protein **10g**
Cholesterol **0mg**
Total fat **11g**
Saturated fat **2g**
Sodium **80mg**

125 g	dried flageolet beans, picked over	4 oz
250 g	brown rice	8 oz
¼ tsp	salt	¼ tsp
1	small ripe avocado	1
1	lemon, juice only, strained	1
60 g	blanched and skinned almonds, toasted	2 oz
6 tbsp	chopped parsley	6 tbsp
2 tbsp	chopped fresh wild fennel	2 tbsp
4 tbsp	plain low-fat yogurt	4 tbsp
1 tbsp	virgin olive oil	1 tbsp
1 tsp	Dijon mustard	1 tsp
1	garlic clove, crushed	1
1	large lettuce, leaves washed and dried, for garnish	1

Rinse the beans under cold running water, then put them into a large, heavy pan, and pour in enough cold water to cover them by about 7.5 cm (3 inches). Discard any beans that float to the surface. Cover the pan, leaving the lid ajar, and slowly bring the liquid to the boil. Boil the beans for 2 minutes, then turn off the heat, and soak the beans, covered, for at least 1 hour.

(Alternatively, soak the beans overnight in cold water.)

Rinse the beans, place them in a clean saucepan, and pour in enough water to cover them by about 7.5 cm (3 inches). Bring the liquid to the boil. Boil the beans for 10 minutes, then drain and rinse again. Wash out the pan, replace the beans and pour in enough water to cover them again by about 7.5 cm (3 inches). Bring the liquid to the boil, then reduce the heat to maintain a strong simmer and cook the beans, covered, until they are tender — about 1 hour. If the beans appear to be drying out at any point, pour in more hot water. Drain the beans in a colander, rinse them, and set them aside to cool for about 30 minutes.

Bring 2 litres (3½ pints) of water to the boil in a large saucepan. Stir in the rice and salt, reduce the heat and simmer, uncovered, until the rice is tender — about 40 minutes. Drain the rice in a strainer, rinse under cold water and leave to drain and cool thoroughly.

Halve, stone, peel and chop the avocado and coat the pieces in half of the lemon juice to prevent them from discolouring. In a large bowl, mix the avocado, almonds, parsley and fennel with the beans and the rice. In a small bowl, beat together the yogurt, olive oil, mustard, garlic and remaining lemon juice. Fold this dressing into the rice salad.

To serve, line a large bowl with the lettuce leaves and spoon the rice salad into the middle.

SUGGESTED ACCOMPANIMENT: *tomato salad.*

EDITOR'S NOTE: *To toast almonds, put them on a baking sheet in a preheated 180° C (350° F or Mark 4) oven for 10 minutes.*

Caribbean Spiced Rice

CARIBBEAN COOKING IS INFLUENCED BY MANY CULINARY
TRADITIONS: THE SIMPLE FOOD OF THE NATIVE INDIANS WAS
ADAPTED AND DEVELOPED BY THE SPANISH, AFRICAN AND
INDIAN PEOPLES WHO LIVED AND WORKED IN THE ISLANDS.

Serves 4
Working (and total) time: about 50 minutes

Calories **540**
Protein **9g**
Cholesterol **0mg**
Total fat **6g**
Saturated fat **2g**
Sodium **250mg**

350 g	basmati rice, rinsed under cold running water until the water runs clear	12 oz
1 tsp	ground allspice	1 tsp
½ tsp	salt	½ tsp
2	garlic cloves, sliced	2
	freshly ground black pepper	
90 cl	unsalted vegetable stock (recipe, page 9)	1 ½ pints
2	green bananas	2
1 tbsp	white wine vinegar	1 tbsp
1	small carrot, finely chopped	1
¼	sweet red pepper, finely chopped	¼
1	stick celery, finely chopped	1
125 g	okra, finely sliced	4 oz
2	small ripe mangoes	2
12	spring onions, finely sliced	12
6 tbsp	chopped parsley	6 tbsp
½	fresh lime, cut into slices, for garnish	½
Coriander sauce		
20 g	fresh coriander leaves	¾ oz
4	spring onions, roughly chopped	4
1	garlic clove, roughly chopped	1
½	onion, roughly chopped	½
1 cm	piece fresh ginger root, peeled and roughly chopped	½ inch
½	green chili pepper, seeded and roughly chopped (caution, page 25)	½
	freshly ground black pepper	
4 tsp	wine vinegar	4 tsp
½	fresh lime, juice only	½
2 tbsp	virgin olive oil	2 tbsp

First make the coriander sauce. Put all the ingredients in a blender with 2 tablespoons of water and blend until smooth. Turn the sauce into a small serving bowl, cover it and set it aside.

Put the rice in a saucepan with the allspice, salt, garlic and some black pepper, and pour in the unsalted vegetable stock. Bring the stock to a simmer, cover the pan and slowly simmer until the rice is cooked and the water absorbed — about 20 minutes.

Meanwhile, cut the bananas in half lengthwise without peeling them. With a sharp knife score the skin through to the flesh in a few places. Put the bananas in a saucepan, pour in enough cold water to cover them and add the vinegar. Bring the liquid to the boil and simmer for 20 minutes. When the bananas are cooked, drain and peel them. Cut each half length-wise into three or four thin slices. Set the bananas aside and keep them warm.

While the rice and bananas are cooking, steam the vegetables. Pour enough water into a saucepan to fill it 2.5 cm (1 inch) deep. Set a vegetable steamer in the saucepan, and bring the water to the boil. Put the carrot in the steamer and steam it for 3 minutes, then add the sweet red pepper, the celery and the okra. Steam the vegetables until they are cooked but still firm and crisp — a further 5 to 6 minutes. Set them aside and keep them warm.

Peel the mangoes. Cut off the two cheeks from each mango, slice them thinly and set them aside. Dice the remaining flesh and discard the stones.

When the rice is cooked, stir in the diced mangoes, spring onions, steamed vegetables and parsley, then turn the mixture into a serving dish. Serve the rice with the banana, mango slices and a slice of lime, accompanied by the coriander sauce.

Basmati and Wild Rice Moulds with Braised Artichokes

Serves 6
Working time: about 1 hour and 30 minutes
Total time: about 2 hours and 30 minutes (includes soaking)

Calories **405**
Protein **14g**
Cholesterol **25mg**
Total fat **12g**
Saturated fat **5g**
Sodium **245mg**

125 g	wild rice	4 oz
125 g	basmati rice, rinsed under cold running water until the water runs clear, then soaked in 60 cl (1 pint) water for 1 hour	4 oz
½ tsp	salt	½ tsp
6	globe artichokes	6
2	lemons, grated rind of one, juice of both	2
1 tbsp	virgin olive oil	1 tbsp
3 tbsp	chopped mint	3 tbsp
2	garlic cloves, finely chopped	2
125 g	fresh chestnuts, peeled (page 37), or 60g (2 oz) dried chestnuts, soaked in hot water for 8 hours or overnight	4 oz
60 g	unsalted butter	2 oz
	white pepper	

Pour 1.25 litres (2 pints) of water into a saucepan and bring it to the boil. Stir in the wild rice, reduce the heat and simmer the rice, uncovered, until it is tender but still has bite — about 45 minutes. Meanwhile, drain the basmati rice and place it in a large saucepan with the salt. Add 90 cl (1½ pints) of water, bring it to the boil and boil it rapidly, uncovered, for 5 minutes until the rice is cooked. Drain the basmati rice and set it aside.

While the wild rice is cooking, prepare the artichokes. Put 3 litres (5 pints) of water in a large bowl and add a third of the lemon juice. Break or cut the stem off one of the artichokes. Snap off and discard the outer leaves, starting at the base and continuing until you reach the pale yellow leaves at the core. Cut the top two thirds off the artichoke. Trim away any dark green leaf bases that remain on the artichoke bottom. Cut the artichoke bottom in half and remove the hairy choke and all the pinkish central leaves. Then cut each half into six wedges. Drop the wedges into the acidulated water until required. Repeat these steps to prepare the remaining artichokes.

Heat the oil in a large heavy frying pan over medium heat. Add the mint and garlic and cook for about 1 minute. Drain the artichokes, add them to the pan and stir-fry them for 1 minute. Add the remaining lemon juice and ¼ litre (8 fl oz) of water, cover and simmer for about 10 minutes. Remove the lid and cook for a further 5 to 10 minutes, until the artichokes are tender.

A few minutes before the end of cooking the artichokes, prepare the rice moulds. Drain the wild rice. Chop the chestnuts finely. Melt the butter in a pan, add the chestnuts and fry them for 2 to 3 minutes. Add the basmati and wild rice. Mix them well and heat through. Divide the rice mixture among six 20 cl (7 fl oz) moulds or cups and carefully turn each one out on to a hot individual serving plate.

Arrange the artichoke wedges alongside the rice. Stir the lemon rind and some white pepper into the juices left in the pan and spoon the mixture over the artichokes. Serve immediately.

Gateau of Crêpes with Wild Rice and Mushrooms

Serves 6
Working time: about 1 hour
Total time: about 2 hours

Calories **215**
Protein **8g**
Cholesterol **40mg**
Total fat **7g**
Saturated fat **2g**
Sodium **185mg**

125 g	plain flour	4 oz
1 tsp	freshly grated nutmeg	1 tsp
1	small egg	1
1	egg white	1
30 cl	skimmed milk	½ pint
60 g	wild rice	2 oz
30 g	dried ceps or other wild mushrooms	1 oz
1½ tbsp	dry Madeira	1½ tbsp
1½ tbsp	safflower oil	1½ tbsp
250 g	button mushrooms, wiped clean, thinly sliced	8 oz
½ tsp	salt	½ tsp
60 g	low-fat fromage frais	2 oz
	freshly ground black pepper	

First make the batter for the crêpes. Sift the flour into a bowl and mix in the nutmeg. Make a well in the centre and add the egg, egg white and a little of the milk. Beat the eggs and milk, gradually working in the dry ingredients; as the batter thickens, add the rest of the milk in several stages to make a smooth batter. Cover the bowl and let the batter stand for 1 hour.

Bring 30 cl (½ pint) of water to the boil in a saucepan. Stir in the wild rice, reduce the heat and simmer, uncovered, until the rice is tender but still has bite — approximately 45 minutes, then drain.

Meanwhile, put the ceps in a small bowl and add 1 tablespoon of the Madeira and 60 cl (1 pint) of tepid water to cover them. Set the mushrooms aside to soak for 20 to 30 minutes.

When the batter has rested, heat a 20 cm (8 inch) crêpe pan or non-stick frying pan over medium heat. Add ¼ teaspoon of the oil and spread it over the entire surface with a paper towel. Continue heating the pan until it is very hot and the oil is almost smoking. Put about 3 tablespoons of the batter into the hot pan and immediately swirl the pan to coat the bottom with a thin, even layer of batter. Pour any excess batter back into the bowl. Cook the crêpe until the bottom is browned — about 1 minute. Lift the edge with a spatula and turn the crêpe over. Cook the crêpe on the second side until it, too, is browned — 15 to 30 seconds. Slide the crêpe on to a plate. Repeat the process with the remaining batter to make six crêpes in all, brushing the pan lightly with more oil if the crêpes begin to stick, and stacking the cooked crêpes on the plate as you go. Cover the crêpes with a towel to prevent them from drying out, and set them aside.

Preheat the oven to 180°C (350°F or Mark 4).

Drain and rinse the ceps and strain their soaking liquid through muslin or a coffee filter paper; reserve the liquid. Heat the remaining oil in a heavy-bottomed saucepan. Add the button mushrooms and sauté them for about 3 to 5 minutes, until lightly cooked. Add the ceps, the reserved soaking liquid, the salt and the remaining ½ tablespoon of Madeira. Bring the liquid to the boil and boil it fast for 30 seconds. Reduce the heat, stir in the wild rice and cook over medium heat for about 2 minutes, to heat the rice through. Drain the rice and mushrooms, reserving the liquid. Return the mixture to the pan, season it with some black pepper, then cover it and keep it warm.

Pour the reserved liquid into a small saucepan and boil hard over high heat to reduce it to about 3 tablespoons. Take the pan off the heat and stir in the *fromage frais*. Reduce the heat to low, then gently warm the sauce; do not allow it to boil. Cover and keep warm while you make the gateau.

Place one crêpe on a large ovenproof plate. Spoon one fifth of the rice and mushroom mixture evenly over the crêpe, then cover the mixture with another crêpe, and continue alternating layers of rice and mushroom mixture with crêpes to make a gateau. Place the crêpe gateau in the oven for a few minutes to warm it through. Serve the gateau at once, cut into wedges, and accompanied by the sauce.

SUGGESTED ACCOMPANIMENT: *carrot ribbons and peas.*

Wild and Brown Rice Pilaff with a Mushroom Ragout

Serves 8
Working time: about 45 minutes
Total time: about 3 hours (includes soaking)

Calories **390**
Protein **14g**
Cholesterol **5mg**
Total fat **11g**
Saturated fat **2g**
Sodium **265mg**

250 g	dried flageolet beans, picked over	8 oz
2	bay leaves	2
125 g	wild rice	4 oz
15 cm	cinnamon stick	6 inch
1 tsp	salt	1 tsp
300 g	brown basmati rice, rinsed under cold running water until the water runs clear, then soaked in 1 ½ litres (2 ½ pints) of water for 15 minutes	10 oz
2	blades of mace	2
2 tsp	light brown sugar	2 tsp
400 g	baby sweetcorn, thickly sliced	14 oz
4 tbsp	hazelnut or walnut oil	4 tbsp
½ tsp	freshly grated nutmeg	½ tsp
	freshly ground black pepper	
Yogurt-mushroom ragout		
15 g	unsalted butter	½ oz
1	small onion, finely chopped	1
500 g	mixed fresh wild mushrooms, such as chanterelles, ceps, oyster or field mushrooms, wiped clean	1 lb
45 cl	unsalted vegetable stock (recipe, page 9)	¾ pint
2 tbsp	cornflour	2 tbsp
2 tbsp	thick Greek yogurt	2 tbsp
¼ tsp	salt	¼ tsp
	freshly ground black pepper	

Rinse the beans under cold running water, then put them into a large, heavy pan, and pour in enough cold water to cover them by about 7.5 cm (3 inches). Discard any beans that float to the surface. Cover the pan, leaving the lid ajar, and slowly bring the liquid to the boil. Boil the beans for 2 minutes, then turn off the heat and soak the beans, covered, for at least 1 hour. (Alternatively, soak the beans overnight in cold water.)

Rinse the beans, place them in a clean saucepan, and pour in enough water to cover them by about 7.5 cm (3 inches). Bring the liquid to the boil. Boil the beans for 10 minutes, then drain and rinse again. Wash out the pan, replace the beans and pour in enough water to cover them again by about 7.5 cm (3 inches). Add the bay leaves, bring the liquid to the boil, then reduce the heat to maintain a strong simmer, and cook the beans until they are tender — about 1 hour. If the beans appear to be drying out at any point, pour in more hot water. Drain the beans, rinse them and drain them again. Set the beans aside and keep them warm.

Preheat the oven to 170°C (325°F or Mark 3).

Place the wild rice with the cinnamon stick and ½ teaspoon of the salt in a small ovenproof dish. Bring 60 cl (1 pint) of water to the boil and pour it over the rice. Cover the dish with a lid and bake the rice for 1 hour. Drain off all but about 1 tablespoon of water. Leave the rice, covered, in a warm place for 15 minutes, to allow it to absorb the remaining liquid.

Drain the basmati rice and place it in a large saucepan with the mace and the remaining ½ teaspoon of salt. Add 3 litres (5 pints) of water and bring it to the boil. Reduce the heat to low, cover the pan and simmer the rice for 20 minutes, or until tender. When the rice is cooked, drain it, cover and keep warm.

While the basmati rice is cooking, prepare the mushroom ragout. Melt the butter in a large heavy-bottomed saucepan over medium heat, add the onion and cook it gently for 5 to 6 minutes, until it is softened but not browned. Add the mushrooms and cook for a further 2 to 3 minutes, until they are slightly softened. Pour in the stock and bring it to the boil, then cover the pan and reduce the heat. Simmer for 10 minutes, until the mushrooms are soft. Blend the cornflour with the yogurt and stir it into the mushrooms with the salt and some black pepper. Continue cooking for 3 to 4 minutes, until the sauce thickens slightly. Transfer the ragout to a serving bowl and keep it warm.

Meanwhile, bring about 4 cm (1 ½ inches) of water to the boil with the brown sugar in a large non-reactive saucepan. Add the sweetcorn and bring the water back to the boil, reduce the heat, and simmer, covered, until just tender — about 5 minutes. Drain the sweetcorn in a colander.

Place half the nut oil in a warmed serving bowl. Discard the bay leaves from the beans and the cinnamon stick and blades of mace from the rices. Transfer the beans, rices and sweetcorn to the oiled serving bowl. Pour over the remaining oil, add the nutmeg and some pepper, then toss all the ingredients together. Serve immediately, with the mushroom ragout.

EDITOR'S NOTE: *If wild mushrooms are unavailable, substitute button and chestnut mushrooms. The pilaff is also delicious served cold as a salad, with a little cider vinegar added.*

Pumpkin and Pecorino Risotto

Serves 4
Working (and total) time: about 1 hour and 15 minutes

Calories **305**
Protein **6g**
Cholesterol **5mg**
Total fat **6g**
Saturated fat **2g**
Sodium **280mg**

1 tbsp	virgin olive oil	1 tbsp
2	shallots, finely chopped	2
250 g	Italian round-grain rice	8 oz
500 g	pumpkin, peeled, seeded and finely grated	1 lb
¼ tsp	powdered saffron	¼ tsp
8 cl	dry white wine	3 fl oz
90 cl	unsalted vegetable stock (recipe, page 9)	1 ½ pints
1 tbsp	finely chopped fresh oregano, or 1 tsp dried oregano	1 tbsp
½ tsp	salt	½ tsp
	freshly ground black pepper	
30 g	pecorino cheese, finely grated	1 oz
2 tbsp	finely chopped flat-leaf parsley, for garnish (optional)	2 tbsp

Heat the oil in a 2 to 3 litre (3½ to 5 pint) fireproof casserole. Add the shallots and cook them over medium heat for about 5 minutes, stirring from time to time, until they are soft but not brown. Reduce the heat to low, add the rice, and stir to ensure that each grain is coated with a little oil. Add the grated pumpkin and stir well over medium heat for about 3 minutes, until it is evenly heated through. Stir the saffron into the white wine. Increase the heat and pour the wine into the casserole. Stir constantly until all the liquid has been absorbed — about 3 minutes. Meanwhile, heat the stock in a separate pan.

Reduce the heat under the rice and ladle in about 15 cl (¼ pint) of hot stock into the casserole. Stir well, then place the lid on the casserole to almost cover the top. Simmer gently until all the stock has been absorbed — about 5 minutes. Stir in another ladleful of stock and cover as before. This time, stir the contents of the casserole once or twice while the stock is being absorbed, replacing the lid after stirring. Mix in the oregano, then continue to add stock by the ladleful, stirring frequently, until the rice is soft but still a little resilient to the bite, and the pumpkin has almost melted into a sauce — about 30 minutes. Once this stage has been reached, stir in the remaining stock and replace the lid on the casserole. Turn off the heat and leave the risotto to stand for 5 minutes, during which time the remaining stock will be absorbed. Meanwhile, warm four serving bowls.

Season the risotto with the salt, some pepper and the pecorino cheese, stirring well until the cheese has melted. Serve immediately; if you like, sprinkle ½ tablespoon of chopped parsley over each portion.

Pea and Mushroom Risotto

Serves 6
Working time: about 45 minutes
Total time: about 1 hour and 15 minutes

Calories **410**
Protein **12g**
Cholesterol **20mg**
Total fat **10g**
Saturated fat **5g**
Sodium **430mg**

350 g	peas, shelled, or 125 g (4 oz) frozen peas, thawed	12 oz
30 g	unsalted butter	1 oz
125 g	shallots, chopped	4 oz
500 g	brown round-grain rice	1 lb
20 cl	dry white wine or dry vermouth	7 fl oz
45 cl	tomato juice	¾ pint
45 cl	unsalted vegetable stock (recipe, page 9)	¾ pint
250 g	tomatoes, skinned, seeded (page 14) and chopped	8 oz
½ tsp	salt	½ tsp
250 g	chestnut mushrooms, wiped clean and coarsely grated	8 oz
60 g	Parmesan cheese, grated	2 oz
	freshly ground black pepper	
	chopped parsley, for garnish	

If you are using fresh peas, boil them until barely tender — 3 to 4 minutes. Drain them, then refresh them under cold running water. Drain them again and set aside. (Frozen peas do not need precooking.)

In a large, heavy-bottomed saucepan, melt the butter and sauté the shallots over medium heat until they are transparent, stirring occasionally — 3 to 5 minutes. Stir the rice into the shallots and cook it for 2 to 3 minutes, stirring constantly to ensure that the grains are well coated with the butter.

Pour the wine into the rice and simmer, stirring frequently, until the wine has been absorbed by the rice. Pour in the tomato juice and 30 cl (½ pint) of the stock, bring the liquid to the boil, then reduce the heat to a simmer. Cover the saucepan and cook the rice, stirring occasionally, for about 20 minutes. Stir the tomatoes and the salt into the rice, cover and simmer for a further 10 minutes, adding more stock, a ladleful at a time, if the rice dries out.

Add the mushrooms, peas and any remaining stock to the pan, increase the heat to high and cook rapidly, stirring constantly, until the stock is absorbed but the rice is still very moist. Stir the Parmesan cheese into the risotto and season it generously with freshly ground pepper. Turn the risotto into a warmed serving dish and sprinkle it with chopped parsley.

SUGGESTED ACCOMPANIMENT: *salad of raw spinach leaves with a vinaigrette.*

EDITOR'S NOTE: *If preferred, 90 cl (1 ½ pints) of unsalted vegetable stock may be used instead of the combination of tomato juice and stock.*

60 g	mung beans, soaked for 1 to 2 hours in water	2 oz
60 g	adzuki beans, soaked for 1 to 2 hours in water	2 oz
12	dried shiitake mushrooms, soaked for 20 minutes in hot water	12
250 g	long-grain rice	8 oz
1 tsp	safflower oil	1 tsp
1 or 2	garlic cloves, finely chopped	1 or 2
½ tbsp	grated fresh ginger root	½ tbsp
175 g	bamboo shoots, finely diced	6 oz
2	carrots, diced	2
3	spring onions, white and green parts separated and diced	3
90 g	roasted unsalted peanuts	3 oz
¼ tsp	sugar	¼ tsp
¼ tsp	salt	¼ tsp
1 tsp	low-sodium soy sauce or shoyu	1 tsp

First prepare the rice stuffing. Simmer the chestnuts in water to cover for 20 to 25 minutes, until just tender. Bring the water to the boil and continue to boil until nearly all the liquid has evaporated, turning the chestnuts several times.

Drain the mung and adzuki beans, rinse them and drain them again. Simmer the two sorts of bean separately in fresh water to cover until tender — about 10 minutes for the mung beans, and up to 25 minutes for the adzuki beans — skimming several times during cooking. Drain and rinse the beans, reserving the liquid from the adzuki beans.

Drain the mushrooms, and strain and reserve their soaking liquid. Dice the mushrooms, discarding the stalks, and set them aside.

Rinse the rice several times in cold water. Mix the adzuki bean liquid with the mushroom-soaking liquid and make it up to ½ litre (16 fl oz) with water. Put this in a large saucepan with the rice and bring to a fast boil, then cook the rice, uncovered, for 10 to 15 minutes, until most of the liquid has evaporated. Cover the pan tightly, reduce the heat to the lowest setting possible, and cook very gently for a further 10 minutes. Turn off the heat and leave the rice to steam, covered, for about 10 minutes. Remove the lid, fluff up the rice with a pair of chopsticks and leave to cool. (The rice will be tinted pale pink from the adzuki bean liquid.)

Heat a wok or large, heavy frying pan until very hot. Add the oil and drop in the garlic and ginger to sizzle and become aromatic, then add the mushrooms, bamboo shoots, carrots, chestnuts and white parts of the spring onions at 10 to 12 second intervals, tossing and stirring all the time with a wok scoop or spatula. Transfer the contents of the pan to a large bowl, add the rice, the green parts of the spring onions, the peanuts, sugar, salt and soy sauce, and mix well together to complete the stuffing.

Make up four lotus-leaf parcels, each filled with a quarter of the rice stuffing (Steps 1 to 3, opposite). Steam the parcels in a bamboo or metal steamer over boiling water for 20 to 25 minutes.

Eight Treasures in Lotus Leaves

IN CHINESE TRADITION, CERTAIN NUMBERS SUCH AS THREE, FIVE AND EIGHT ARE CONSIDERED TO BRING LUCK; HENCE DISHES CONTAINING THREE MAIN INGREDIENTS ARE USUALLY KNOWN AS "THREE DELICACIES", WHILE THOSE WITH EIGHT OR MORE ARE KNOWN AS "EIGHT TREASURES".

Serves 4
Working time: about 1 hour and 30 minutes
Total time: about 12 hours (includes soaking)

Calories **553**
Protein **19g**
Cholesterol **0mg**
Total fat **14g**
Saturated fat **3g**
Sodium **250mg**

4	dried lotus leaves, soaked for 30 minutes in hot water, rinsed in cold water and dried carefully on a tea towel	4
500 g	fresh lotus roots, or 90 g (3 oz) dried lotus roots, soaked for 8 hours or overnight in tepid water	1 lb
45 cl	unsalted vegetable stock (recipe, page 9), or water	¾ pint
2 tbsp	rice wine or medium-dry sherry	2 tbsp
½ tsp	sugar	½ tsp
⅛ tsp	salt	⅛ tsp
1.25 cm	piece fresh ginger root, sliced	½ inch
1	garlic clove	1
3	spring onions, each cut into three pieces	3
45 g	canned skinned whole lotus nuts, drained	1½ oz
1 tsp	low-sodium soy sauce or shoyu	1 tsp
4 or 5	fresh coriander sprigs, leaves only, for garnish	4 or 5
Rice stuffing		
24	fresh chestnuts, peeled (page 37), or dried chestnuts, soaked for at least 8 hours or overnight in hot water and drained	24

Meanwhile, scrub the fresh lotus roots well and cut them diagonally into 5 mm (¼ inch) slices. (If you are using reconstituted dried lotus roots, rinse them thoroughly before slicing.)

Bring the stock or water to the boil, add the rice wine, sugar, salt, ginger, garlic and spring onions, and return to the boil. Add the whole lotus nuts and sliced roots, and simmer for 35 minutes. Remove the nuts, ginger, garlic and spring onions with a slotted spoon; reserve the nuts and keep them warm, and discard the ginger, garlic and onions. (If you are using dried roots, simmer them for another 15 minutes.) Add the soy sauce to the cooking liquid, bring to the boil, and reduce it until the sauce becomes syrupy — 10 to 12 minutes. Return the nuts to the sauce to heat through.

Place a steamed lotus parcel on each of four individual plates and cut a square window in the parcel with scissors *(Step 4, opposite)*. Serve the rice-stuffed parcels with the braised lotus roots and nuts, garnished with coriander leaves.

EDITOR'S NOTE: *All the unusual ingredients called for in this recipe can be obtained in Chinese grocery shops. Since most of the ingredients are dried, any unused surplus can be stored almost indefinitely and used on another occasion.*

Shaping a Lotus Leaf Parcel

1 *PREPARING A LEAF. Lay a lotus leaf flat on the work surface. Using a pair of kitchen scissors, snip off the centre core where the stalk meets the leaf. Cut the leaf in half to make two semicircles.*

2 *BEGINNING THE PARCEL. Lay the leaf halves on the work surface vein side down and with their cut edges overlapping by about 5 cm (2 inches). Place the stuffing in the centre of the circle and shape the stuffing into a roughly square mound with a knife blade. Fold over two opposite edges of the leaf circle by about 5 cm (2 inches), as below, left, then fold these edges firmly over the stuffing (below, right), to make a long package.*

3 *COMPLETING THE PARCEL. Fold in the sides of one of the flaps that remain, so that the flap tapers. Make a fold 2 cm (¾ inch) from the end of the flap, then fold again so that the flap covers the stuffed part of the leaf. Repeat with the other flap, then secure the parcel with a wooden cocktail stick. Complete the remaining three parcels in the same way.*

4 *OPENING THE COOKED PARCEL. When the parcels have been steamed (recipe, opposite), snip a square window in the top of the parcel, using kitchen scissors. Replace the lid on the parcel to serve.*

Rice Cakes with Onion Relish

Serves 4
Working time: about 35 minutes
Total time: about 1 hour and 45 minutes (includes soaking)

Calories **255**
Protein **8g**
Cholesterol **15mg**
Total fat **6g**
Saturated fat **3g**
Sodium **300mg**

175 g	basmati rice, rinsed under cold running water until the water runs clear, then soaked for 1 hour in 1 litre (1 ¾ pints) water	6 oz
½ tsp	safflower oil	½ tsp
1	onion, finely chopped	1
125 g	carrots, grated	4 oz
2	hot green chili peppers, finely chopped (caution, page 25)	2
2	garlic cloves, crushed	2
½ tsp	cardamom seeds, crushed	½ tsp
1 tbsp	chopped fresh coriander	1 tbsp
½ tsp	ground cumin	½ tsp
¼ tsp	ground turmeric	¼ tsp
60 g	Cheddar cheese, grated	2 oz
¼ tsp	salt	¼ tsp
Onion relish		
1	onion, cut into paper-thin rings	1
½	sweet red pepper, finely chopped	½
1	lime, finely grated rind and juice	1
¼ tsp	salt	¼ tsp
½ tsp	paprika	½ tsp
½ tsp	brown sugar	½ tsp

First make the onion relish. Place the onion in a bowl with the sweet red pepper, and add the lime rind, lime juice, salt, paprika and sugar. Toss the ingredients together until well combined, then transfer them to a serving bowl and set them aside for the flavours to develop while you prepare the rice cakes.

Drain the rice and put it in a large saucepan, add 1.5 litres (2½ pints) of water and bring to the boil. Boil the rice rapidly, uncovered, until thoroughly tender — about 10 minutes. The rice needs to be well cooked so that the rice cakes will hold together when they are grilled. Drain the rice and set it aside.

Heat the oil in a heavy frying pan over medium heat and fry the chopped onion for 3 to 4 minutes, until softened and beginning to brown. Stir in the carrots, chili peppers, garlic, cardamom, coriander, cumin and turmeric, and cook, stirring continuously, until the carrots have softened — about 2 minutes. Remove the pan from the heat, stir in the rice, cheese and salt, and mash the mixture with a potato masher, until the rice is broken up and sticky.

Preheat the grill to medium. Lightly flour your hands and shape the mixture into 20 small balls. Thread five balls on to each of four skewers. Place the skewers on a foil-covered rack and grill the cakes for about 15 minutes, turning once, until they are a pale golden colour. Serve hot, accompanied by the onion relish.

SUGGESTED ACCOMPANIMENTS: *Indian bread; tomato salad.*

EDITOR'S NOTE: *If you use wooden skewers, soak them in water for about 10 minutes before threading them with the rice balls to prevent them from burning under the grill.*

Buckwheat and Lentil Pilaff

Serves 8
Working time: about 1 hour
Total time: about 1 hour and 15 minutes

Calories **355**
Protein **19g**
Cholesterol **0mg**
Total fat **7g**
Saturated fat **1g**
Sodium **175mg**

1.5 kg	fresh peas, shelled, or 500 g (1 lb) frozen peas, thawed	3 lb
350 g	green lentils, picked over and rinsed	12 oz
250 g	buckwheat groats (kasha)	8 oz
1 tsp	salt	1 tsp
3 tbsp	virgin olive oil	3 tbsp
2	small aubergines, cut into 1 cm (½ inch) cubes	2
2	sweet red peppers, seeded, deribbed and sliced	2
2	sweet green peppers, seeded, deribbed and sliced	2
8	garlic cloves, finely chopped	8
2	large onions, sliced	2
500 g	tomatoes, skinned, seeded (page 14) and roughly chopped	1 lb
4 tbsp	finely cut chives	4 tbsp
2 tbsp	chopped mint, or 1 tsp dried mint	2 tbsp
4 tbsp	chopped parsley	4 tbsp
4 tbsp	capers, rinsed (optional)	4 tbsp
	freshly ground black pepper	

If you are using fresh peas, parboil them until they are barely tender — 3 to 4 minutes. Drain them, then refresh them under cold running water. Drain the peas again and set them aside. (If using frozen peas, there is no need to parboil them.)

Put the lentils in a large, heavy-bottomed saucepan with 2.5 litres (4½ pints) of water. Bring the water to the boil, then reduce the heat and simmer the lentils until they are tender — about 20 minutes. When the lentils are cooked, drain them in a strainer.

While the lentils are cooking, pour 60 cl (1 pint) of water into a saucepan, and bring to the boil. Add the buckwheat and ½ teaspoon of the salt and cook the buckwheat, stirring frequently, until the grains have trebled in size but still have bite — about 5 minutes. Drain the grains in a strainer, rinse them well, and drain them again. Transfer them to a large bowl.

Heat the olive oil over medium heat in a large, heavy frying pan. Add the aubergines, peppers, garlic and onions to the pan, and sauté them for 10 to 15 minutes, stirring constantly, until they become soft. Add the lentils, the buckwheat, tomatoes and peas to the aubergine mixture. Gently heat all the ingredients, stirring continuously.

Remove the pan from the heat. Add the chopped chives, mint and parsley and, if you are using them, the capers. Season with the remaining ½ teaspoon of salt and some black pepper. Serve immediately.

Semolina Gnocchi with Julienned Vegetables

Serves 6
Working time: about 1 hour
Total time: about 3 hours (includes chilling)

Calories **270**
Protein **13g**
Cholesterol **5mg**
Total fat **8g**
Saturated fat **3g**
Sodium **295mg**

250 g	celeriac, finely julienned, placed in acidulated water	8 oz
350 g	carrots, finely julienned	12 oz
18	spring onions, trimmed, quartered lengthwise and cut into 5 cm (2 inch) pieces	18
3	garlic cloves, crushed	3
30 cl	unsalted vegetable stock (recipe, page 9)	½ pint
½	lemon, grated rind and juice	½
1 ½ tsp	cornflour	1 ½ tsp
30 g	pine-nuts	1 oz
½ tsp	caster sugar	½ tsp
½ tsp	salt	½ tsp
	freshly ground black pepper	
Semolina gnocchi		
60 cl	skimmed milk	1 pint
200 g	semolina	7 oz
15 g	unsalted butter	½ oz
½ tsp	salt	½ tsp
½ tsp	freshly grated nutmeg	½ tsp
4 tbsp	freshly grated Parmesan cheese	4 tbsp

First make the gnocchi. Pour the skimmed milk into a heavy-bottomed saucepan and bring it to the boil. Add the semolina gradually, stirring constantly, then cook for 4 to 5 minutes over medium heat until the mixture is very thick. Beat in half the butter, the salt, the nutmeg and 3 tablespoons of the cheese. Turn out the mixture into an 18 by 18 by 4 cm (7 by 7 by 1 ½ inch) baking tray lined with plastic film and spread it flat using a dampened palette knife. Allow the mixture to cool for 20 minutes, then cover the tin loosely with film and place the mixture in the refrigerator until well chilled — at least 2 hours, or overnight.

Preheat the oven to 180°C (350°F or Mark 4). Using a sharp, thin-bladed knife, cut the chilled mixture into thirty-six 2.5 cm (1 inch) squares. Transfer the gnocchi to a lightly greased baking sheet. Gently melt the remaining butter in a small saucepan and brush it over the gnocchi. Sprinkle them with the remaining Parmesan cheese. Bake the gnocchi until they are golden and crisp on top — 20 to 25 minutes.

About 15 minutes before the gnocchi are cooked, put the celeriac, carrots, spring onions and garlic into a non-reactive saucepan and pour in the vegetable stock. Bring the stock to the boil. Reduce the heat and simmer for 3 to 4 minutes, until the vegetables are softened. Stir in the lemon rind and juice. Blend the cornflour with 1 tablespoon of water and stir it into the stock. Add the pine-nuts, sugar, salt and some black pepper. Bring the mixture back to the boil and cook over high heat, stirring continuously, until the stock has formed a thick sauce — about 2 minutes. Spoon the vegetables on to warmed individual plates and top them with the baked gnocchi.

SUGGESTED ACCOMPANIMENT: *steamed broccoli.*

Chili Beans with Cornbread Topping

Serves 4
Working time: about 30 minutes
Total time: about 3 hours (includes soaking)

Calories **340**
Protein **15g**
Cholesterol **60mg**
Total fat **10g**
Saturated fat **1g**
Sodium **405mg**

100 g	dried red kidney beans, picked over	3 ½ oz
1 tbsp	safflower oil	1 tbsp
1	onion, chopped	1
½ tsp	chili powder	½ tsp
2	garlic cloves, chopped	2
750 g	ripe tomatoes, skinned, seeded (page 14) and chopped, or 400 g (14 oz) canned tomatoes, chopped	1 ½ lb
1	sweet green pepper, seeded, deribbed and coarsely chopped	1
1	sweet red pepper, seeded, deribbed and coarsely chopped	1
2	sticks celery, trimmed and sliced	2
1 tbsp	tomato paste	1 tbsp
60 g	stoned green olives, rinsed and quartered or halved	2 oz
Cornbread topping		
125 g	cornmeal	4 oz
30 g	strong plain flour	1 oz
¼ tsp	salt	¼ tsp
¼ tsp	freshly ground black pepper	¼ tsp
2 tsp	baking powder	2 tsp
1	egg, beaten	1
12.5 cl	skimmed milk	4 fl oz
2 tbsp	chopped parsley	2 tbsp
30 g	Edam cheese, finely grated	1 oz

Rinse the kidney beans under cold running water, then put them into a large saucepan with enough cold water to cover them by about 7.5 cm (3 inches). Discard any beans that float to the surface. Cover the saucepan, leaving the lid ajar, and slowly bring the liquid to the boil. Boil the beans for 2 minutes, then turn off the heat and soak the beans, covered, for at least an hour. (Alternatively, soak the beans overnight in cold water).

Rinse the beans and place them in a clean saucepan with enough cold water to cover them by about 7.5 cm (3 inches). Bring to the boil. Boil the kidney beans for 10 minutes, then rinse them and discard the water. Wash out the pan, replace the beans and cover them again by about 7.5 cm (3 inches) of fresh water, then simmer them until tender — about 1 hour. Check the water level from time to time and add more hot water if necessary. When the beans are cooked, drain and rinse them.

Preheat the oven to 200°C (400°F or Mark 6).

Heat the oil in a heavy-bottomed saucepan, and fry the onion over medium heat until soft — about 5 minutes. Add the chili powder and garlic, and fry for a further minute. Stir in the tomatoes, peppers, celery and tomato paste, cover and cook over medium-low heat for 10 minutes. Add the olives and cooked beans and cook for a further 5 minutes, stirring occasionally. Divide the bean mixture among four shallow 35 cl (12 fl oz) ovenproof dishes and set them aside.

To make the topping, mix the cornmeal, flour, salt, pepper and baking powder in a large bowl, and make a well in the centre. In a separate bowl, beat together the egg, milk and parsley, using a wooden spoon. Pour the egg and milk into the cornflour, and beat until the mixture is smooth and thick. Spoon the topping over the chili beans, using a fork to spread it to the edges of the dishes. Sprinkle on the grated cheese.

Place the dishes in the oven and bake until the topping is firm — 15 to 20 minutes. Serve hot.

SUGGESTED ACCOMPANIMENT: *mixed leaf salad*.

Polenta Pizza

Serves 4
Working time: about 40 minutes
Total time: about 1 hour

Calories **470**
Protein **19g**
Cholesterol **25mg**
Total fat **12g**
Saturated fat **5g**
Sodium **390mg**

½ tsp	salt	½ tsp
350 g	cornmeal	12 oz
1 tbsp	virgin olive oil	1 tbsp
1	red onion, finely sliced	1
1	large garlic clove, chopped	1
2	carrots, chopped	2
4	sticks celery, finely sliced	4
500 g	tomatoes, skinned, seeded (page 14) and chopped	1 lb
6 tbsp	tomato paste, dissolved in 17.5 cl (6 fl oz) hot water	6 tbsp
1 tbsp	chopped fresh basil, or 1 tsp dried basil	1 tbsp
½ tbsp	chopped fresh oregano, or ½ tsp dried oregano	½ tbsp
	cayenne pepper	
	freshly ground black pepper	
125 g	low-fat mozzarella cheese, very thinly sliced	4 oz
1 tbsp	freshly grated Parmesan cheese	1 tbsp
½ tbsp	finely chopped parsley, for garnish	½ tbsp

Preheat the oven to 180°C (350°F or Mark 4). Thoroughly grease a 30 by 22 by 2.5 cm (12 by 9 by 1 inch) baking tin or dish.

Put 1.6 litres (2 ¾ pints) of water into a large saucepan with the salt, and bring it to the boil. Sprinkle in the cornmeal, stirring continuously with a wooden spoon. Reduce the heat to medium and cook the polenta, stirring constantly, until all the liquid has been absorbed and the polenta is quite stiff — 10 to 15 minutes. Spoon the polenta into the prepared baking tin and spread it out to a uniform thickness. Cover the dish with aluminium foil, and bake the polenta in the oven for 20 minutes.

While the polenta is baking, make the sauce. Heat the oil in a heavy-bottomed saucepan, add the onion and sauté it over medium heat until it is soft and transparent — about 10 minutes. Add the garlic, carrots, celery and tomatoes. Stir well for a few minutes, then mix the tomato paste solution into the sauce. Finally, add the basil, the oregano, some cayenne and some black pepper. Simmer the sauce gently, covered, for 10 to 15 minutes.

When the polenta is ready, spread the sauce over it. Cover the sauce with the sliced mozzarella, then sprinkle over the Parmesan cheese. Return the polenta to the oven for about 10 minutes, until the cheese has melted. Serve the polenta immediately, garnished with the chopped parsley.

SUGGESTED ACCOMPANIMENT: *steamed purple sprouting broccoli, tossed in a little lemon juice with some freshly ground black pepper.*

Polenta Ring with Pine-Nuts and Mozzarella

Serves 6
Working time: about 45 minutes
Total time: about 1 hour and 45 minutes (includes cooling)

Calories **300**
Protein **13g**
Cholesterol **20mg**
Total fat **14g**
Saturated fat **4g**
Sodium **265mg**

500 g	tomatoes, skinned (page 14, Step 1)	1 lb
2 tbsp	virgin olive oil	2 tbsp
1 tsp	paprika	1 tsp
2	garlic cloves, one crushed, the other chopped	2
½ tsp	salt	½ tsp
150 g	cornmeal	5 oz
125 g	low-fat mozzarella cheese, thinly sliced	4 oz
1	onion, thinly sliced	1
1	sweet red pepper, seeded, deribbed and cut into 2.5 cm (1 inch) strips	1
1	sweet green pepper, seeded, deribbed and cut into 2.5 cm (1 inch) strips	1
1 tsp	ground cumin	1 tsp
60g	pine-nuts	2 oz

Thinly slice three of the tomatoes crosswise, and the remainder lengthwise; keep them separate. Grease a 20 cm (8 inch) ring mould with ½ tablespoon of the oil.

Pour ¾ litre (1¼ pints) of water into a large saucepan, and bring it to the boil. Add the paprika, crushed garlic and salt, then stir in the cornmeal. Reduce the heat to medium and continue to cook, stirring, for 10 to 15 minutes, or until the cornmeal has formed a thick porridge. Remove the pan from the heat and immediately pour half the polenta into the prepared ring mould. Press it down firmly, using the back of a spoon. Quickly place the crosswise-sliced tomatoes and the mozzarella on top, and cover them with the remaining polenta. Set the polenta aside, until it is completely cool — at least 1 hour.

Meanwhile, preheat the oven to 180°C (350°F or Mark 4). When the polenta has cooled, carefully loosen all round the edges of the mould, using a small palette knife. Turn out the polenta ring on to a large, flat heat-proof plate and bake it in the oven for about 15 minutes, or until the mozzarella has melted.

While the polenta is baking, heat the remaining oil in a heavy frying pan over low heat. Put the onion and the chopped garlic in the pan and cook them gently to soften them — about 3 minutes. Add the peppers, cover the pan and cook over very low heat for 10 minutes, then add the remaining tomato slices, the cumin and half of the pine-nuts. Cover the pan again and cook for a further 2 minutes over very low heat.

Spoon some of the vegetables into the centre of the polenta ring and the remainder round the edge. Sprinkle the remaining pine-nuts over the vegetables. Serve the polenta hot.

Provençal Casserole

Serves 6
Working time: about 30 minutes
Total time: about 3 hours (includes soaking)

Calories **180**
Protein **11g**
Cholesterol **0mg**
Total fat **3g**
Saturated fat **1g**
Sodium **90mg**

250 g	dried flageolet beans, picked over	8 oz
1 tbsp	virgin olive oil	1 tbsp
1	large onion, sliced	1
1	garlic clove, crushed	1
1	sweet red pepper, seeded, deribbed and sliced	1
500 g	courgettes, thickly sliced	1 lb
1	aubergine, cut into large dice	1
500 g	tomatoes, skinned, seeded (page 14) and roughly chopped, or 300 g (10 oz) canned tomatoes, drained and roughly chopped	1 lb
125 g	button mushrooms, wiped clean, stems trimmed	4 oz
15 cl	unsalted vegetable stock (recipe, page 9)	¼ pint
2 tsp	chopped fresh oregano, or ½ tsp dried oregano	2 tsp
¼ tsp	freshly ground black pepper	¼ tsp
¼ tsp	salt	¼ tsp

Rinse the beans under cold running water, then put them into a large saucepan, and pour in enough cold water to cover them by about 7.5 cm (3 inches). Dis-card any beans that float to the surface. Bring the water to the boil and cook the beans for 2 minutes. Turn off the heat, partially cover the pan, and soak the beans for at least 1 hour. (Alternatively, soak the beans overnight in cold water)

Rinse the beans, place them in a clean pan, and pour in enough water to cover them by about 7.5 cm (3 inches). Bring the liquid to the boil. Boil the beans for 10 minutes, then drain and rinse them again. Wash out the pan, replace the beans, cover them again by 7.5 cm (3 inches) of water and bring it to the boil. Reduce the heat to maintain a strong simmer, and cook the beans, covered, until they are tender — about 1 hour. If the beans appear to be drying out at any point, pour in more hot water. When they are cooked, drain and rinse the beans in a colander.

Heat the oil in a large, fireproof casserole or heavy-bottomed saucepan and cook the onion and garlic over low heat for a few minutes, until softened but not browned. Add the sweet red pepper, courgettes, aubergine and tomatoes, and cook over medium-low heat for 1 to 2 minutes, stirring frequently. Reduce the heat to low and add the mushrooms, beans, stock, oregano, black pepper and salt. Mix well, cover, and simmer over low heat, stirring occasionally, for 25 minutes, or until the vegetables are tender. Serve hot.

SUGGESTED ACCOMPANIMENT: *garlic rolls.*

Tandoori Patties

Serves 4
Working time: about 45 minutes
Total time: about 2 hours and 45 minutes (includes soaking)

Calories **305**
Protein **14g**
Cholesterol **0mg**
Total fat **6g**
Saturated fat **1g**
Sodium **290mg**

250 g	dried pinto beans, picked over	8 oz
1 tbsp	safflower oil	1 tbsp
1	onion, chopped	1
2	garlic cloves, chopped	2
3 tsp	tandoori spice	3 tsp
1 tsp	ground cumin	1 tsp
30 g	fresh wholemeal breadcrumbs	1 oz
2 tbsp	chopped fresh coriander	2 tbsp
2 tbsp	tomato paste	2 tbsp
125 g	parsnips or carrots, finely grated	4 oz
½ tsp	salt	½ tsp
	freshly ground black pepper	
3 tbsp	wholemeal flour	3 tbsp
1 tsp	paprika	1 tsp
Coriander-yogurt sauce		
15 cl	plain low-fat yogurt	¼ pint
½ tsp	ground coriander	½ tsp
1 tsp	tomato paste	1 tsp
1	garlic clove, crushed	1
2 tsp	chopped fresh coriander	2 tsp

Rinse the beans under cold running water, put them into a large, heavy pan, and pour in enough cold water to cover them by about 7.5 cm (3 inches). Discard any beans that float to the surface. Cover the pan, leaving the lid ajar, and slowly bring the liquid to the boil. Boil the beans for 2 minutes, then turn off the heat and soak the beans, covered, for at least 1 hour. (Alternatively, soak the beans overnight in cold water.)

Rinse the beans, place them in a clean saucepan, and pour in enough water to cover them by about 7.5 cm (3 inches). Bring the liquid to the boil. Boil the beans for 10 minutes, then drain and rinse them again. Wash out the pan, replace the beans and again pour in enough water to cover them by about 7.5 cm (3 inches). Bring the liquid to the boil, reduce the heat to maintain a strong simmer, cover the pan, and cook the beans until they are tender — about 1 hour. Check the water level in the pan from time to time and pour in more hot water if the beans appear to be drying out. Drain the cooked beans in a colander, rinse them under cold running water and set them aside.

Heat ½ tablespoon of the oil in a heavy frying pan and fry the onion over medium heat for about 3 minutes, until soft. Add the chopped garlic, 2 teaspoons of the tandoori spice and the ground cumin, and fry for a further minute.

Put the onion mixture and the beans into a food processor or blender with the breadcrumbs, fresh coriander, tomato paste, parsnips or carrots, salt and some pepper. Blend until smooth, scraping down the sides of the processor bowl as necessary.

Preheat the grill to medium high. Mix the flour with the remaining tandoori spice and the paprika. Dampen your hands and shape the blended mixture into eight balls, then flatten the balls into patties. Roll the patties in the spiced flour to coat them. Brush the patties with the remaining oil and grill them for 3 to 4 minutes on each side, until they are crisp.

Meanwhile, mix all the sauce ingredients together. Serve the patties hot, with the coriander-yogurt sauce.

SUGGESTED ACCOMPANIMENTS: *endive and cucumber salad; hot potato salad.*

EDITOR'S NOTE: *Tandoori spice, a curry powder containing coriander, chili, ginger, turmeric, fenugreek, garlic and other spices, is used in Indian cuisine to flavour food baked in a ''tandoor'', a clay oven.*

Gingered Black Beans with Saffron Rice

Serves 6
Working time: about 35 minutes
Total time: about 2 hours and 45 minutes (includes soaking)

Calories **390**
Protein **12g**
Cholesterol **0mg**
Total fat **14g**
Saturated fat **2g**
Sodium **150mg**

175 g	dried black kidney beans, picked over	6 oz
2 tbsp	virgin olive oil	2 tbsp
7.5 cm	piece fresh ginger root, peeled, 5 cm (2 inches) thinly sliced, the remainder grated	3 inch
1 tbsp	chopped fresh oregano, or 1 tsp dried oregano	1 tbsp
1 tsp	chopped fresh sage, or ¼ tsp dried sage	1 tsp
1 tsp	saffron threads	1 tsp
½ tsp	salt	½ tsp
250 g	long-grain white rice	8 oz
90 g	shelled walnuts, roughly chopped	3 oz
3	garlic cloves, crushed	3
60 g	dried cloud-ear mushrooms, soaked for 20 minutes in hot water and drained	2 oz
125 g	button mushrooms, wiped and sliced	4 oz
2	limes, grated rind and juice	2
	freshly ground black pepper	
¼ tsp	paprika, for garnish	¼ tsp

Rinse the beans under cold running water, then put them into a large, heavy pan and pour in enough cold water to cover them by about 7.5 cm (3 inches). Discard any beans that float to the surface. Cover the pan, leaving the lid ajar, and slowly bring the liquid to the boil. Boil the beans for 2 minutes, then turn off the heat and soak the beans, covered, for at least 1 hour.

(Alternatively, soak the beans overnight in cold water.)

Rinse the beans, place them in a clean saucepan, and pour in enough water to cover them again by about 7.5 cm (3 inches). Bring the liquid to the boil. Boil the beans for 10 minutes, then drain and rinse again.

In a large, clean saucepan, heat 1 tablespoon of the oil over medium heat; add the sliced ginger root, the oregano and sage, and sauté them for 1 minute. Add the beans and enough cold water to cover them by 7.5 cm (3 inches). Bring to the boil, reduce the heat to maintain a strong simmer, and cook the beans until tender — about 1 hour. Drain them, return them to the pan with all the flavourings and keep them warm.

Bring 60 cl (1 pint) of water to the boil in a saucepan. Add the saffron, salt and rice, and stir once. Cover the pan and simmer for about 15 minutes, or until the rice is just cooked and the water is absorbed. Remove the pan from the heat and stir in the walnuts. Cover the pan again and leave it to stand for a few minutes while the walnuts warm through.

Meanwhile, heat the remaining oil in a wok or large, heavy frying pan over medium heat, then add the garlic, cloud-ear and button mushrooms and the grated ginger. Increase the heat to high and stir-fry them for 5 to 6 minutes, until soft. Add them to the beans, with the lime rind and juice and some pepper.

Pile up the bean mixture in the centre of a large platter and arrange the rice round it. Sprinkle the rice with the paprika and serve at once.

SUGGESTED ACCOMPANIMENT: *watercress, curly endive and orange salad.*

Borlotti Beans Tuscan-Style

THIS ADAPTATION OF A TRADITIONAL TUSCAN RECIPE
REPLACES THE USUAL SAUSAGES WITH CEPS AND USES LESS
OIL AND MORE TOMATOES.

Serves 4
Working time: about 45 minutes
Total time: about 3 hours (includes soaking)

Calories **330**
Protein **22g**
Cholesterol **0mg**
Total fat **6g**
Saturated fat **trace**
Sodium **245mg**

350 g	dried borlotti beans, picked over	12 oz
2	bay leaves	2
1 tbsp	virgin olive oil	1 tbsp
2	garlic cloves, crushed	2
3	fresh rosemary sprigs	3
6	leaves fresh sage, finely shredded	6
250 g	fresh ceps, or 20 g (¾ oz) dried ceps, soaked for 20 minutes in hot water, drained and well rinsed	8 oz
1 kg	fresh tomatoes, skinned, seeded (page 14) and chopped	2 ½ lb
1 tbsp	red wine vinegar	1 tbsp
1 tbsp	molasses sugar	1 tbsp
½ tsp	salt	½ tsp
	freshly ground black pepper	
12	basil leaves, torn into pieces	12

Rinse the beans under cold running water, then put them into a large, heavy pan and pour in enough cold water to cover them by about 7.5 cm (3 inches). Discard any beans that float to the surface. Cover the pan, leaving the lid ajar, and slowly bring the liquid to the boil. Boil the beans for 2 minutes, then turn off the heat and soak the beans, covered, for at least 1 hour. (Alternatively, soak the beans overnight in cold water.)

Rinse the beans, place them in a clean saucepan, and pour in enough water to cover them again by

about 7.5 cm (3 inches). Bring the liquid to the boil. Boil the beans for 10 minutes, then drain and rinse them. Wash out the pan, replace the beans and again add enough water to cover them by about 7.5 cm (3 inches). Add the bay leaves, bring the liquid to the boil, then reduce the heat to maintain a strong simmer and cook the beans until they are tender — about 1 hour. Check the water level in the pan from time to time, and pour in more hot water if necessary. Drain the beans in a colander and discard the bay leaves. Rinse the beans, drain again and set aside.

Heat the oil in a large, fireproof casserole; fry the garlic in the oil for 2 minutes. Add the rosemary, reduce the heat to the lowest possible setting, cover, and leave for 10 minutes to allow the rosemary to infuse the oil. Discard the rosemary and add the beans to the casserole with the sage, stirring well to coat the beans evenly. Increase the heat to medium low, add the mushrooms, and cook, stirring constantly, for about 2 minutes, until thoroughly heated through. Cover the casserole closely and set it aside.

In a large, shallow saucepan, combine the tomatoes with the vinegar, sugar, salt and some pepper. Cook briefly over high heat to allow excess moisture to evaporate as the tomatoes break down into a sauce. Pour the sauce over the beans and mushrooms, and add the torn basil leaves. Set the casserole over medium-high heat, and simmer briefly until the beans are just heated through; do not overcook.

SUGGESTED ACCOMPANIMENT: *crusty bread.*

EDITOR'S NOTE: *If you use dried ceps, the soaking liquid can be added to the water in which the beans are cooked to enhance their flavour. Strain the liquid through a double layer of muslin or a coffee filter paper before adding it.*

Butter Beans Baked with a Herbed Crust

Serves 6
Working time: about 30 minutes
Total time: about 3 hours (includes soaking)

Calories **310**
Protein **19g**
Cholesterol **0mg**
Total fat **5g**
Saturated fat **1g**
Sodium **280mg**

500 g	dried butter beans, picked over	1 lb
2	onions, one finely chopped	2
1	large carrot, trimmed	1
1	small leek, trimmed, washed thoroughly to remove all grit	1
2	fresh thyme sprigs, one chopped	2
2	fresh rosemary sprigs, one chopped	2
2	bay leaves	2

1 ½ tbsp	virgin olive oil	1 ½ tbsp
1.5 kg	fresh tomatoes, skinned, seeded (page 14) and roughly chopped	3 lb
2	garlic cloves, one crushed, one chopped	2
1 tsp	salt	1 tsp
	freshly ground black pepper	
125 g	fresh wholemeal breadcrumbs	4 oz
30 g	parsley, chopped	1 oz
1	lemon, grated rind only	1

Rinse the beans under cold running water, then put them into a large saucepan with enough cold water to cover them by about 7.5 cm (3 inches). Discard any beans that float to the surface. Cover the saucepan, leaving the lid ajar, and slowly bring the liquid to the boil. Boil the beans for 2 minutes, then turn off the heat and soak the beans, covered, for at least 1 hour. (Alternatively, soak the beans overnight in cold water.)

Rinse the beans, place them in a clean saucepan, and pour in enough water to cover them by 7.5 cm (3 inches). Bring the liquid to the boil. Boil the beans for 10 minutes, then drain and rinse again.

Put the beans in a clean saucepan with the whole onion, the carrot, the leek, the whole sprigs of thyme and rosemary and one bay leaf. Add cold water to cover them by about 7.5 cm (3 inches) and bring to the boil. Reduce the heat, cover the pan and simmer until the beans are tender — about 1 hour. Check the water level from time to time, and add more hot water if necessary. Drain the beans in a colander. Discard the vegetables and herbs and set the beans aside.

Heat 1 teaspoon of the oil in a heavy-bottomed saucepan over medium heat, add the chopped onion, half the chopped thyme and rosemary and the remaining bay leaf, and sauté for 3 minutes. Add the tomatoes and the crushed garlic, bring to the boil, then lower the heat. Season with the salt and some pepper and simmer, uncovered, for 30 to 40 minutes, or until the mixture has reduced and thickened to a sauce.

Meanwhile, preheat the oven to 180°C (350°F or Mark 4). In a bowl, combine the chopped garlic, remaining rosemary and thyme, the breadcrumbs and parsley, to form a green-flecked, crumbly mixture. Add the lemon rind and remaining oil, and mix well.

When the tomato mixture is ready, add the beans to the saucepan, stir gently, then transfer the mixture to a large gratin dish. Spread the herbed crumbs on top of the beans and bake them in the oven, uncovered, for about 40 minutes, until the crust is crisp.

SUGGESTED ACCOMPANIMENT: *asparagus or broccoli, or a crisp green salad.*

Butter Bean Succotash

SUCCOTASH IS AN AMERICAN INDIAN DISH TRADITIONALLY
MADE WITH GREEN CORN AND LIMA BEANS.

Serves 4
Working time: about 30 minutes
Total time: about 2 hours and 45 minutes (includes soaking)

Calories **325**
Protein **15g**
Cholesterol **10mg**
Total fat **6g**
Saturated fat **2g**
Sodium **300mg**

200 g	dried butter beans, picked over	7 oz
½ tbsp	safflower oil	½ tbsp
1	onion, sliced	1
2	garlic cloves, crushed	2
3	sticks celery, trimmed and sliced	3
1	large potato, chopped	1
1	sweet green pepper, seeded, deribbed and chopped	1
1	savory sprig	1
350 g	fresh or frozen sweetcorn kernels	12 oz
½ tsp	salt	½ tsp
1 tsp	sugar	1 tsp
	freshly ground black pepper	
3 tbsp	soured cream	3 tbsp
1 tsp	fresh lemon juice	1 tsp
2 tbsp	chopped parsley	2 tbsp

Rinse the beans under cold running water, then put them into a large saucepan with enough cold water to cover them by about 7.5 cm (3 inches). Discard any beans that float to the surface. Cover the pan, leaving the lid ajar, and slowly bring the liquid to the boil. Boil the beans for 2 minutes, then turn off the heat and soak the beans, covered, for at least 1 hour. (Alternatively, soak the beans overnight in cold water.)

Rinse the beans, place them in a clean pan and pour in enough cold water to cover them by about 7.5 cm (3 inches). Bring the liquid to the boil. Boil the beans for 10 minutes, then drain and rinse again.

Put the beans into a clean saucepan, and pour in enough water to cover them again by about 7.5 cm (3 inches). Bring the liquid to the boil, reduce the heat to maintain a strong simmer, and cook the beans until they are tender — about 1 hour. Check the liquid in the pan from time to time, and pour in more hot water if necessary. Drain the beans in a strainer over a bowl, and reserve the cooking liquid. Rinse the beans under cold water. Drain them again, and set aside.

Heat the oil in a heavy-bottomed saucepan and fry the onion for about 3 minutes, until soft. Add the garlic, celery, potato, green pepper, savory and the reserved bean-cooking liquid, made up to 60 cl (1 pint) with water, if necessary. Cover the saucepan, bring the liquid to the boil and simmer for 10 minutes.

Add the cooked beans to the saucepan, with the sweetcorn, salt, sugar and some black pepper. Cook the mixture for a further 10 minutes. Remove the pan from the heat and stir in the soured cream and lemon juice. Ladle the succotash into individual bowls and sprinkle over the chopped parsley.

SUGGESTED ACCOMPANIMENT: *crusty bread*.

Cabbage Stuffed with Black-Eyed Peas and Mushrooms

Serves 4
Working time: about 1 hour
Total time: about 3 hours and 15 minutes

Calories **155**			
Protein **8g**	60 g	dried black-eyed peas, picked over	2 oz
Cholesterol **20mg**	1 tbsp	virgin olive oil	1 tbsp
Total fat **7g**	15 g	unsalted butter	½ oz
Saturated fat **2g**	1	firm green cabbage (about 1 kg/2½ lb), hollowed out (box, right), 250 g (8 oz) inner leaves reserved and chopped	1
Sodium **220mg**	3	garlic cloves, chopped	3
	1	onion, chopped	1
	125 g	mushrooms, wiped clean and chopped	4 oz
	15 g	flaked millet	½ oz
	15 cl	unsalted vegetable stock (recipe, page 9)	¼ pint
	½ tsp	salt	½ tsp
		freshly ground black pepper	
	1 tbsp	finely chopped fresh coriander	1 tbsp
	1 tbsp	finely chopped summer savory	1 tbsp

Rinse the black-eyed peas under cold running water, then put them into a large saucepan and pour in enough cold water to cover them by about 7.5 cm (3 inches). Discard any peas that float to the surface. Bring the water to the boil and cook the peas for 2 minutes. Turn off the heat, cover the pan, and soak the peas for at least 1 hour. (Alternatively, soak the peas overnight in cold water.)

Discard the soaking water and rinse the peas. Place them in a clean saucepan and pour in enough water to cover them again by about 7.5 cm (3 inches). Bring the liquid to the boil, then reduce the heat to medium low, cover the pan tightly and simmer the peas, occasionally skimming any foam from the surface of the

liquid, until they are tender — about 1 hour. Check the water level in the pan from time to time, and pour in more hot water if necessary. Transfer the peas to a colander to drain, rinse them and drain them again, then set them aside.

Preheat the oven to 200°C (400°F or Mark 6).

In a large frying pan, heat the oil and butter together until the butter has melted. Add the reserved chopped cabbage, garlic, onion and mushrooms, and cook, stirring frequently, over medium heat for 5 to 7 minutes, until the vegetables are softened but not browned. Remove the pan from the heat.

Stir the cooked black-eyed peas into the vegetables. Add the millet and pour in the stock. Stir lightly, return the pan to the heat and bring the mixture to a simmer. Simmer for 5 minutes. Remove the pan from the heat, season the stuffing with the salt and some black pepper, then mix in the coriander and summer savory.

Fill the hollowed-out cabbage to the top with the stuffing. Put the cabbage "lid" over the stuffing, and place the cabbage in the middle of a 50 cm (20 inch) square of non-stick parchment paper. Fold the paper up to enclose the cabbage completely.

Place the wrapped cabbage on a baking sheet and bake it for 30 to 40 minutes, or until the cabbage is tender. Leave it to rest for a few minutes before unwrapping it. Remove the lid and serve the stuffed cabbage cut into wedges.

SUGGESTED ACCOMPANIMENT: *tomato coulis.*

Hollowing a Whole Cabbage for Stuffing

SCOOPING OUT THE CENTRE. Trim the protruding stem of the cabbage just enough to allow the cabbage to be stood on end. Cut a lid about 10 cm (4 inches) in diameter and 1 cm (½ inch) thick off the top of the cabbage and set it aside. With a sturdy tablespoon, dig into the exposed centre and scoop out leaves until the cabbage walls are about 1 cm (½ inch) thick. Reserve the inner leaves for the stuffing.

Chick-Pea and Okra Casserole with Couscous

Serves 4
Working time: about 30 minutes
Total time: about 3 hours and 30 minutes (includes soaking)

Calories **450**
Protein **15g**
Cholesterol **0mg**
Total fat **10g**
Saturated fat **1g**
Sodium **320mg**

125 g	dried chick-peas, picked over	4 oz
2 tbsp	virgin olive oil	2 tbsp
1	large onion, chopped	1
1 tbsp	paprika	1 tbsp
1 tsp	ground turmeric	1 tsp
3	fresh thyme sprigs	3
2	fresh bay leaves	2
90 cl	unsalted vegetable stock (recipe, page 9) or water	1½ pints
½ tsp	salt	½ tsp
250 g	carrots, thickly sliced	8 oz
60 g	dried apricots	2 oz
125 g	baby sweetcorn	4 oz
125 g	dried pears	4 oz
30 g	currants	1 oz
250 g	small okra, trimmed	8 oz
250 g	wholemeal couscous	8 oz

Rinse the chick-peas under cold running water, then put them in a large, heavy pan and pour in enough cold water to cover them by about 7.5 cm (3 inches). Discard any that float to the surface. Cover the pan, leaving the lid ajar, and slowly bring the liquid to the boil. Boil the chick-peas for 2 minutes, then turn off the heat and soak them for at least 1 hour. (Alternatively, soak the peas overnight in cold water.)

Drain and rinse the chick-peas, return them to the pan and pour in enough water to cover them again by about 7.5 cm (3 inches). Bring the liquid to the boil, reduce the heat to maintain a strong simmer, and cook the peas until they are just tender — about 1 hour. If the chick-peas appear to be drying out at any point, pour in more hot water. Drain the peas and rinse them under cold running water.

In a large saucepan, heat half the oil and sauté the onion over medium heat until transparent — about 3 minutes. Add the paprika and turmeric and cook, stirring, for 1 to 2 minutes. Add the thyme, bay leaves, chick-peas and stock and bring to the boil. Reduce the heat, cover and simmer for 45 minutes. Add the salt, carrots, apricots, sweetcorn, pears and currants. Cover and simmer for a further 15 minutes.

Heat the remaining tablespoon of oil in a heavy frying pan and sauté the okra for 5 minutes. Using a slotted spoon, add the okra to the vegetable mixture and simmer for a further 15 minutes.

Meanwhile, place the couscous in a bowl and pour ½ litre (16 fl oz) of boiling water over it. Stir it with a fork, then leave it to absorb the water — about 10 minutes.

Arrange the couscous on a large serving dish and pile the fruit and vegetable stew in the centre, discarding the bay leaves and thyme sprigs.

Chick-Pea and Burghul Kofta

KOFTA IS AN INDIAN DISH, USUALLY MADE OF HERBED MINCED MEAT SHAPED INTO SMALL BALLS OR OVALS. IN THIS RECIPE, THE MEAT IS REPLACED WITH CHICK-PEAS.

Serves 4
Working time: about 45 minutes
Total time: about 4 hours (includes soaking and chilling)

Calories **430**
Protein **21g**
Cholesterol **0mg**
Total fat **12g**
Saturated fat **2g**
Sodium **60mg**

250 g	dried chick-peas, picked over	8 oz
125 g	burghul, soaked in warm water for 30 minutes, drained and squeezed dry in paper towels	4 oz
2 tbsp	tahini	2 tbsp
6 tbsp	plain low-fat yogurt	6 tbsp
1	small onion, grated	1
1	garlic clove, crushed	1
4 tbsp	chopped parsley	4 tbsp
4 tbsp	chopped mint	4 tbsp
1	lemon, juice only	1
	lettuce leaves, washed and dried, and lemon wedges, for garnish	
Chili-tomato relish		
1 tbsp	virgin olive oil	1 tbsp
500 g	tomatoes, chopped	1 lb
1	small onion, very finely chopped	1
1	cucumber, very finely chopped	1
2 or 3	fresh hot red or green chili peppers, seeded and finely chopped (caution, page 25)	2 or 3

Rinse the chick-peas under cold running water, then transfer them to a large pan and pour in enough water to cover them by about 7.5 cm (3 inches). Discard any chick-peas that float to the surface. Cover the pan, leaving the lid ajar, and bring the liquid to the boil. Boil the peas for 2 minutes, then turn off the heat, cover the pan and soak the peas for at least 1 hour. (Alternatively, soak the peas overnight in cold water.)

Drain and rinse the chick-peas, return them to the pan and pour in enough water to cover them by about 7.5 cm (3 inches). Bring the liquid to the boil, then reduce the heat to maintain a strong simmer and cook the peas, covered, until they are soft — about 1½ hours — adding more hot water as required.

Drain the chick-peas, then purée them in a food processor. Stir in the burghul, tahini, yogurt, onion, garlic, parsley, mint and lemon juice. Using your hands, form the mixture into 16 boat shapes; chill them for 1 hour.

Meanwhile, begin to make the relish. Heat the oil in a heavy-bottomed pan over low heat. Add the tomatoes and cook them gently, covered, for 15 minutes. Sieve the tomatoes and chill the purée for 1 hour.

Preheat the grill to high and cover a grill rack with foil. Grill the kofta until golden-brown — 3 to 4 minutes on each side. Meanwhile, stir the onion, cucumber and chilies into the tomato purée. Serve the kofta hot, garnished with the lettuce leaves and lemon wedges.

Chick-Pea Salad in Artichoke Cups

Serves 4
Working time: about 1 hour
Total time: about 3 hours (includes soaking)

Calories **230**
Protein **13g**
Cholesterol **5mg**
Total fat **10g**
Saturated fat **2g**
Sodium **135mg**

150 g	dried chick-peas, picked over	5 oz
1	small onion	1
1	garlic clove	1
1	chili pepper, seeded and halved (caution, page 25)	1
2	bay leaves	2
6	fresh sage leaves	6
4	large globe artichokes	4
1	large lemon, halved	1
	salad leaves, for garnish	
Yogurt dressing		
1½ tbsp	virgin olive oil	1½ tbsp
1	garlic clove	1
125 g	thick Greek yogurt	4 oz
15 g	dry-packed sun-dried tomatoes, soaked in boiling water for 10 minutes, drained and finely diced	½ oz
1 tbsp	finely chopped parsley	1 tbsp
2	fresh sage leaves, finely sliced	2
¼ tsp	cayenne pepper	¼ tsp
¼ tsp	salt	¼ tsp

Rinse the chick-peas under cold running water, then put them in a large, heavy pan and pour in enough cold water to cover them by about 7.5 cm (3 inches). Discard any chick-peas that float to the surface. Cover the pan, leaving the lid ajar, and slowly bring the liquid to the boil over medium-low heat. Boil the chick-peas for 2 minutes, then turn off the heat, and soak them, covered, for at least 1 hour. (Alternatively, soak the chick-peas overnight in cold water.)

Drain and rinse the chick-peas, return them to the pan and pour in enough water to cover them again by about 7.5 cm (3 inches). Bring the liquid to the boil, then reduce the heat to medium low and add the onion, garlic, chili, bay leaves and sage. Cover the pan and simmer the chick-peas gently until tender — about 1 hour — adding more hot water as necessary. Leave them to cool in their cooking liquid.

Trim the artichokes *(Step 1, below)*, using one lemon half to rub the cut surfaces. Place the artichokes in a large, non-reactive saucepan wide enough to hold them in a single layer.

Grate the rind and squeeze the juice from the un-used lemon half. Set the rind and 1 tablespoon of juice aside for the dressing. Add the remaining juice to the artichokes. Pour cold water into the pan to come level with the tops of the artichokes, bring it to the boil, cover the pan and cook for 30 to 40 minutes, until the centre and base of each artichoke can be pierced easily with the tip of a sharp knife.

While the artichokes are cooking, make the yogurt dressing. Place the oil and garlic clove in a small, heavy-bottomed saucepan, and heat gently until the garlic sizzles. Remove the pan from the heat and allow the oil to infuse for 5 to 10 minutes. Discard the garlic and blend the oil into the yogurt. Add the sun-dried tomatoes to the yogurt with the parsley, sage, cayenne pepper and salt. Stir in the reserved lemon rind and enough of the remaining juice to sharpen the dressing to your liking.

Drain the chick-peas and discard the flavouring ingredients, then stir the chick-peas into the dressing.

Using a slotted spoon, lift the artichokes from the pan; set them upside down to drain. When the artichokes are cool enough to handle, remove the choke from the centre of each *(Step 2, below)*. Remove a few more leaves from the centre of each artichoke to form a cup large enough to hold a quarter of the dressed chick-peas.

Place the artichoke cups on individual plates and pile the chick-peas into them. Serve with a garnish of salad leaves.

EDITOR'S NOTE: *If you cook and dechoke the artichokes in advance, return them to their cooking liquid until required; this will prevent them from discolouring and drying out. Drain them upside down before filling them with the chick-peas.*

Preparing Artichokes for Stuffing

1 *TRIMMING THE LEAVES. Cut off the stem and small outer leaves from the base of each artichoke with a stainless steel knife. Rub the cut surfaces with freshly cut lemon to keep them from turning brown. Cut off the top third of each artichoke, then snip off the sharp tips of the outer leaves with kitchen scissors. Cook the artichokes according to the instructions in the recipe.*

2 *REMOVING THE CHOKE. Lift the artichokes from the pan and set them upside down to drain and cool. With a teaspoon, scoop out the tiny inner leaves and the hairy choke from the centre of each artichoke to reveal the smooth, edible green heart.*

Indonesian Vegetable Stew

Serves 6
Working time: about 45 minutes
Total time: about 1 hour and 20 minutes

Calories **290**
Protein **10g**
Cholesterol **0mg**
Total fat **10g**
Saturated fat **1g**
Sodium **30mg**

200 g	small aubergines, cut into 1 cm (½ inch) cubes	7 oz
1 tsp	salt	1 tsp
3 tbsp	safflower oil	3 tbsp
1 tbsp	black mustard seeds	1 tbsp
1 tbsp	ground fenugreek	1 tbsp
2	dried hot red chili peppers, seeded and broken into small pieces (caution, page 25)	2
2	fresh hot green chili peppers, seeded and thinly sliced (caution, page 25)	2
6	garlic cloves, chopped	6
1 tsp	freshly ground green cardamom pods	1 tsp
1 tsp	concentrated tamarind paste	1 tsp
125 g	dried mung beans, picked over, rinsed	4 oz
1.25 litres	unsalted vegetable stock (recipe, page 9)	2 pints
500 g	potatoes, thickly sliced	1 lb
125 g	dried ceps, soaked in hot water for 20 minutes, drained and roughly chopped	4 oz
250 g	okra, trimmed and sliced	8 oz
500 g	French beans, trimmed and halved	1 lb
2	spears fresh lemon grass, finely chopped (optional)	2
1	lemon, grated rind and juice	1
2 tbsp	grated creamed coconut	2 tbsp

In a bowl, toss the cubed aubergines with the salt. Place the aubergines in a colander, weight them down with a plate and let them drain for 30 minutes. Rinse the aubergines under cold running water to remove the salt, and drain them well.

Meanwhile, in a large, heavy-bottomed saucepan, heat the oil over medium-high heat. Add the mustard seeds, fenugreek, dried and fresh chili peppers, garlic, cardamom and tamarind paste. Sauté these ingredients for about 2 minutes, stirring them occasionally, then add the mung beans and stock. Bring the contents of the pan to the boil, reduce the heat and simmer, uncovered, for 15 minutes.

Add the potatoes, aubergines, ceps and okra to the pan, and simmer, covered, for a further 10 minutes. Stir in the French beans, and the lemon grass, if you are using it. Simmer the stew for 10 minutes more. Finally, mix the lemon rind, lemon juice and coconut into the stew, and simmer for a further minute. Before serving, allow the stew to rest, uncovered, off the heat for about 5 minutes, to allow the coconut and lemon flavours to develop.

SUGGESTED ACCOMPANIMENTS: *a mixture of wild and brown rice; onion and chili chutney; fruit pickle.*

Lentils with Spinach and Carrots

Serves 4
Working time: about 20 minutes
Total time: about 50 minutes

Calories **330**			
Protein **18g**	250 g	lentils, picked over and rinsed	8 oz
Cholesterol **0mg**	1	bay leaf	1
Total fat **10g**	2 tbsp	safflower oil	2 tbsp
Saturated fat **1g**	1	garlic clove, crushed	1
Sodium **80mg**	1 tbsp	freshly grated ginger root	1 tbsp
	250 g	carrots, peeled and cut into bâtonnets	8 oz
	12	spring onions, cut into 2.5 cm (1 inch) lengths	12
	350 g	spinach, stems discarded, leaves washed, dried and roughly chopped	12 oz
	2 tbsp	low-sodium soy sauce or shoyu	2 tbsp
	6 tbsp	dry sherry	6 tbsp
	1 tbsp	sesame seeds, toasted	1 tbsp

Put the lentils in a large, heavy-bottomed saucepan with ¾ litre (1¼ pints) of water. Bring the water to the boil, then reduce the heat to medium, add the bay leaf, cover the pan tightly and simmer the lentils until they are tender — about 40 minutes. Drain the lentils and remove the bay leaf. Rinse the lentils under cold running water and drain them again.

Heat the oil in a wok or large, heavy frying pan over high heat. Add the garlic and ginger, and stir them until the garlic sizzles. Add the carrots and spring onions and stir-fry them for 1 minute, then transfer them to a plate using a slotted spoon.

Place the spinach in the pan and stir it over high heat until it begins to wilt — 2 to 3 minutes. Return the carrots and spring onions to the pan, add the cooked lentils and stir them for 2 minutes to heat them through. Add the soy sauce and the sherry and bring them to the boil. Stir the ingredients once more, then transfer them to a heated serving dish. Scatter the toasted sesame seeds over the lentils and vegetables, and serve immediately.

SUGGESTED ACCOMPANIMENT: *long-grain brown rice.*

EDITORS NOTE: *To toast sesame seeds, heat them in a small, heavy frying pan over medium-low heat until they are golden — 1 to 2 minutes.*

Lentil and Potato Cakes with Mustard Pickle

Serves 4
Working time: about 40 minutes
Total time: about 1 hour and 40 minutes

Calories **295**
Protein **15g**
Cholesterol **10mg**
Total fat **4g**
Saturated fat **1g**
Sodium **245mg**

250 g	floury potatoes, peeled and cut into 2.5 cm (1 inch) cubes	8 oz
½ tsp	safflower oil	½ tsp
12	spring onions, trimmed, white parts chopped, green parts sliced into rings	12
2.5 cm	piece fresh ginger root, peeled and finely chopped	1 inch
¼ tsp	ground cinnamon	¼ tsp
¼ tsp	grated nutmeg	¼ tsp
½ tsp	salt	½ tsp
	freshly ground black pepper	
175 g	split red lentils, picked over, rinsed	6 oz
45 cl	unsalted vegetable stock (recipe, page 9)	¾ pint
½ tsp	garam masala	½ tsp
175 g	thick Greek yogurt	6 oz
Mustard pickle		
¼ tsp	safflower oil	¼ tsp
1	small onion, finely chopped	1
1 tbsp	mustard seeds, lightly crushed	1 tbsp
2 tbsp	white wine vinegar	2 tbsp
4 tbsp	dry white wine	4 tbsp
1 tbsp	soft brown sugar	1 tbsp
1 tbsp	grainy mustard	1 tbsp
1	red-skinned mango, peeled and stoned, flesh roughly diced	1

First make the mustard pickle. Heat the oil in a small, heavy-bottomed saucepan, add the onion and mustard seeds, and cook over medium heat, stirring, for about 3 minutes, until the onions have softened. Stir in the vinegar, wine, sugar, mustard and mango. Bring to the boil, then reduce the heat, cover, and cook gently for about 15 minutes, until the mango is tender and the mixture thick and pulpy. Transfer the contents of the pan to a bowl, and set it aside.

Cook the potatoes in boiling water for about 20 minutes, until tender. Drain them well, then mash them with a potato masher. Set the mashed potatoes aside.

Heat the oil in a large frying pan and add the white parts of the spring onions, the ginger, cinnamon, nutmeg, salt and some pepper. Cook over medium heat, stirring continuously, for 3 minutes. Add the lentils and stock. Bring to the boil, then cover, reduce the heat, and simmer gently for about 25 minutes, stirring frequently, until the lentils are completely soft. Remove the lid and increase the heat, stirring continuously until the mixture is dry — about 2 minutes. Beat in the mashed potatoes and garam masala, then set the mixture aside to cool.

Preheat the grill to medium, and lightly grease a baking sheet. Using your hands, shape the mixture into 12 flat cakes about 7.5 cm (3 inches) in diameter, and place them on the baking sheet. Grill the cakes for 5 minutes on each side, until golden, then transfer them to individual serving plates. Top the cakes with the Greek yogurt and mustard pickle, and garnish with the green spring onion rings.

SUGGESTED ACCOMPANIMENT: *stir-fried cucumber wedges.*

EDITOR'S NOTE: *Garam masala is a mixture of ground spices used in Indian cookery. It usually contains coriander, cumin, cloves, ginger and cinnamon. In this recipe, a pinch each of some or all of these spices can be substituted if garam masala is not available.*

Lentils with Cumin and Onion

Serves 4
Working time: about 15 minutes
Total time: about 1 hour

Calories **215**
Protein **9g**
Cholesterol **0mg**
Total fat **7g**
Saturated fat **1g**
Sodium **225mg**

350 g	lentils, picked over and rinsed	12 oz
1 tsp	ground cumin	1 tsp
½ tsp	salt	½ tsp
60 g	brown rice	2 oz
1 tbsp	virgin olive oil	1 tbsp
500 g	onions, thinly sliced	1 lb
90 g	radishes, thinly sliced	3 oz
2 tbsp	chopped parsley	2 tbsp

In a heavy-bottomed saucepan, bring 1.5 litres (2½ pints) of water to the boil. Add the lentils, cumin and salt, and boil, uncovered, for 20 minutes. Add the rice and cook for a further 30 to 40 minutes, until the liquid has been absorbed but the rice is still moist.

Meanwhile, heat the oil in a frying pan, and fry the onions over low heat, partially covered, until they are soft and golden-brown, stirring them frequently while they are cooking — about 15 minutes.

Stir half of the fried onions into the lentils. Transfer the mixture to the centre of a shallow serving dish. Distribute the remaining fried onions round the lentil mixture, then arrange the radishes round the onions at the edge of the dish. Sprinkle the chopped parsley over the lentils. Serve hot.

SUGGESTED ACCOMPANIMENT: *salad of lettuce and cucumber.*

Lentil Soufflés Baked in Sweet Pepper Cases

Serves 6
Working time: about 40 minutes
Total time: about 2 hours

Calories **165**
Protein **10g**
Cholesterol **75mg**
Total fat **5g**
Saturated fat **1g**
Sodium **130mg**

1 tbsp	virgin olive oil	1 tbsp
1	large onion, finely chopped	1
1	large carrot, finely chopped	1
1	garlic clove, crushed	1
175 g	split red lentils, picked over, rinsed	6 oz
45 cl	unsalted vegetable stock (recipe, page 9)	¾ pint
¼ tsp	salt	¼ tsp
2 tbsp	tomato paste	2 tbsp
3	large sweet green peppers	3
	freshly ground black pepper	
2	eggs, separated	2

Heat the oil in a large, heavy-bottomed saucepan over medium heat. Add the onion and carrot and cook gently for 5 minutes. Stir in the garlic, lentils, stock, salt and tomato paste. Bring the mixture to the boil, then reduce the heat, cover the pan tightly and simmer for 45 minutes, until the lentils are soft and the stock has been absorbed.

Meanwhile, carefully remove the stalk from each pepper. Cut the peppers in half horizontally and remove their seeds and any thick white ribs. Cook the pepper cups in gently simmering water to cover for 4 to 5 minutes until softened, then drain them well on paper towels. Place the cups in a lightly oiled, shallow ovenproof dish.

Preheat the oven to 190°C (375°F or Mark 5).

Remove the cooked lentils from the heat and allow them to cool for 10 minutes. Season with some pepper, then beat in the egg yolks. Whisk the egg whites until stiff but not dry; fold 1 tablespoon into the lentil mixture to lighten it, then fold in the remainder. Spoon the soufflé mixture into the pepper cups and cook for 30 to 35 minutes, until the soufflés are well risen and lightly browned. Serve immediately.

SUGGESTED ACCOMPANIMENTS: *tomato salad; crusty bread.*

Tofu with Sweet Pepper and Peanuts, Sichuan-Style

SICHUAN CUISINE, ONE OF THE FIVE STYLES OF CHINESE COOKING, IS CHARACTERIZED BY ITS USE OF PEPPERS AND IMAGINATIVE SEASONINGS.

Serves 6
Working (and total) time: about 35 minutes

Calories **220**
Protein **15g**
Cholesterol **0mg**
Total fat **15g**
Saturated fat **1g**
Sodium **50mg**

2 tbsp	safflower oil	2 tbsp
1 kg	firm tofu, well drained (box, opposite), cut into 2 cm (¾ inch) cubes	2 lb
2	garlic cloves, thinly sliced	2
4 cm	piece fresh ginger root, peeled and finely shredded	1½ inch
3	fresh or dried red chili peppers, seeded and thinly sliced (caution, page 25)	3
8	spring onions, green and white parts separated and thinly sliced	8
2	small sweet green peppers, seeded, deribbed and cut into 1.5 cm (¾ inch) squares	2
⅛ tsp	salt	⅛ tsp
1 tbsp	rice wine or sherry	1 tbsp
45 g	shelled peanuts, skinned and toasted	1½ oz
Seasoning sauce		
2 tbsp	low-sodium soy sauce or shoyu	2 tbsp
2 tsp	rice or wine vinegar	2 tsp
1½ tsp	sugar	1½ tsp
10 cl	unsalted vegetable stock (recipe, page 9) or water	3½ fl oz
1½ tsp	cornflour	1½ tsp
½ tsp	Tabasco or chili sauce	½ tsp

In a non-stick frying pan, heat 2 teaspoons of the oil and fry half of the tofu cubes over medium-high heat for 3 to 5 minutes, until they are golden-brown all over; turn the cubes continuously with a spatula to prevent the tofu from sticking to the pan. Transfer the cubes to paper towels to drain. Pour another 2 teaspoons of the oil into the pan, fry the remaining tofu cubes in the same way, and transfer them to paper towels.

In a small bowl, mix together all the ingredients for the sauce. Set the sauce aside.

Heat the remaining oil in a wok or large, heavy frying pan, swirling it round to coat the sides. Drop in the garlic and allow it to sizzle for a few seconds. Add the ginger and fry, stirring continuously, until it is golden-brown — about 2 minutes. Add the chilis and the white parts of the spring onions, and stir-fry for 10 seconds, turning and tossing the ingredients with a spatula. Add the sweet peppers, stir-fry for 10 seconds, then add the tofu cubes and stir-fry for a further 20 seconds. Add the salt and wine.

Stir the sauce well and pour it into the wok. Continue to stir over the heat until the sauce thickens; add the peanuts. Remove the wok from the heat and mix in most of the green parts of the spring onions. Transfer the tofu stir-fry to a serving dish and sprinkle over the remaining spring onions.

SUGGESTED ACCOMPANIMENT: *plain boiled rice or Chinese egg noodles.*

EDITOR'S NOTE: *To toast peanuts, place them on a baking sheet and put them under a hot grill for 2 to 3 minutes, stirring them from time to time.*

Storing and Draining Tofu

Tofu (the Japanese name for soya bean curd) is usually sold in a pressed form, either fresh or vacuum packed. Fresh tofu may be stored in the refrigerator, submerged in cold water, for up to a week; change the water daily. Unopened vacuum-packed tofu will keep for many months. Once opened, however, it should be treated in the same way as fresh tofu.

Because it is stored under water, tofu is moist, and for many recipes it needs to be drained thoroughly before use. To drain tofu, wrap it in a double layer of muslin or a clean tea towel, and place it between two flat, heavy boards; raise one end of the boards a few centimetres, and position the lower end over a sink or tray to catch the fluid that drains away. Leave the tofu to drain for 30 minutes to 1 hour.

Tofu and Vegetable Dumplings

Serves 4
Working time: about 45 minutes
Total time: about 1 hour

Calories **220**	500 g	firm tofu, well drained (page 85)	1 lb
Protein **16g**	4½ tbsp	cornflour	4½ tbsp
Cholesterol **0mg**	1	egg white	1
Total fat **8g**	½ tsp	salt	½ tsp
Saturated fat **trace**			
Sodium **235mg**	60 g	shelled peas, blanched for 1 minute, drained and refreshed under cold running water, or frozen peas, thawed	2 oz
	60 g	carrots, peeled and very finely diced, blanched for 1 minute, drained and refreshed under cold running water	2 oz
	6	fresh water chestnuts, peeled and finely diced, or canned water chestnuts, drained and finely diced	6
	2½ tsp	sesame seeds, toasted	2½ tsp
	45 cl	unsalted vegetable stock (recipe, page 9)	¾ pint
	250 g	baby sweetcorn	8 oz
	250 g	centre leaves of small bok choy	8 oz
	125 g	mange-tout, strings removed	4 oz

Put the tofu in a food processor with the cornflour and blend for about 1 minute. In a bowl, whisk the egg white with the salt until it is stiff but not dry. Add the egg white to the tofu, and process the ingredients briefly to form a smooth paste. Transfer the paste to a bowl, cover it, and chill it for 30 minutes.

Mix the peas, carrots, water chestnuts and 2 teaspoons of the toasted sesame seeds into the tofu paste, then divide the mixture into 16 equal portions and mould each portion into a ball. Bring a large saucepan of water to the boil. Line a steamer with muslin and set it over the pan; carefully place the tofu dumplings in the steamer in a single layer. Steam the dumplings over high heat for 12 minutes, then set them aside and keep them warm.

Meanwhile, bring the vegetable stock to the boil in a saucepan. Add the sweetcorn to the stock, and cook them for 3 minutes; add the bok choy leaves and continue to cook for 2 minutes, then add the mange-tout and cook for a further 2 minutes.

Reduce the heat to low and gently lower the dumplings into the stock. Heat them through for about 1 minute. Transfer the dumplings and vegetables to individual plates, sprinkle the remaining sesame seeds over the dumplings, and serve immediately.

EDITOR'S NOTE: *To toast sesame seeds, heat them in a small, heavy frying pan over medium-low heat until they are golden — 1 to 2 minutes.*

Tofu and Vegetable Stir-Fry with Noodles

Serves 4
Working (and total) time: about 30 minutes

Calories **480**
Protein **18g**
Cholesterol **0mg**
Total fat **15g**
Saturated fat **2g**
Sodium **340mg**

2 tbsp	low-sodium soy sauce or shoyu	2 tbsp
2 tbsp	clear honey	2 tbsp
½ tsp	Chinese five-spice powder	½ tsp
225 g	firm tofu, cut into thin slices	7½ oz
4 tsp	light sesame oil	4 tsp
1	garlic clove, crushed	1
8	spring onions, sliced	8
125 g	mange-tout, strings removed	4 oz
1	large sweet yellow pepper, seeded, deribbed and sliced	1
1	large sweet red pepper, seeded, deribbed and sliced	1
125 g	baby sweetcorn	4 oz
350 g	fresh Chinese egg noodles, or 250 g (8 oz) dried vermicelli or thin spaghetti	12 oz

In a medium-sized bowl, mix together the soy sauce, honey and five-spice powder. Add the tofu to the bowl, spoon the marinade over it, and leave it to absorb the flavours while you cook the vegetables.

Heat 3 teaspoons of the sesame oil in a wok or a large, heavy frying pan, and stir in the garlic and spring onions. Add the mange-tout, peppers and sweetcorn, and fry over medium heat, stirring frequently, for 4 to 5 minutes, until the vegetables are cooked but still crisp. Using a slotted spoon, transfer the vegetables to a heated dish. Cover with foil and keep warm.

Meanwhile, bring 4 litres (7 pints) of lightly salted water to the boil. When the water boils, add the noodles. Cook the noodles until they are *al dente*: start testing them after 3 minutes. Drain the cooked noodles in a colander, rinse them under cold running water, and set them aside.

Drain the tofu, reserving the marinade. Add the remaining teaspoon of oil to the wok and cook the tofu slices for about 20 seconds on each side.

Pour boiling water over the noodles in the colander to reheat them. Place the noodles on a heated serving dish, cover them with the vegetables, and arrange the tofu on top of the vegetables.

Pour the reserved marinade into the wok with 2 tablespoons of water. Heat the liquid through, and pour it over the tofu. Serve immediately.

Tofu, Courgette and Mushroom Kebabs

Serves 4
Working (and total) time: about 45 minutes

Calories **240**
Protein **15g**
Cholesterol **0mg**
Total fat **15g**
Saturated fat **2g**
Sodium **100mg**

4	courgettes (about 175 g/6 oz each), topped and tailed	4
24	small shallots (about 250 g/8 oz)	24
1	sweet red pepper (about 250 g/8 oz), seeded, deribbed and cut into 2.5 cm (1 inch) squares	1
500 g	firm tofu, well drained (page 85), cut into 24 cubes	1 lb
24	small mushrooms (about 500 g/1 lb), wiped clean	24
2 tbsp	virgin olive oil	2 tbsp
	white pepper	
Olive and caper sauce		
4	black olives, stoned and finely chopped	4
1 tbsp	finely chopped capers	1 tbsp
2 tsp	grainy mustard	2 tsp
1 tbsp	finely chopped parsley	1 tbsp
5 tbsp	low-fat plain yogurt	5 tbsp
2 tbsp	fresh lemon or lime juice	2 tbsp

In a small bowl, mix together all the ingredients for the olive and caper sauce, then set the sauce aside to allow the flavours to develop.

Using a canelle knife or the point of a small, sharp knife, remove thin strips of peel lengthwise from each courgette to create a striped effect. Slice the courgettes into 2.5 cm (1 inch) thick rounds. Blanch the courgettes, shallots and pepper squares in boiling water for 2 minutes, refresh them under cold running water, and drain them well. Preheat the grill to high.

Allowing three skewers per serving, thread two each of the courgette rounds, shallots, tofu cubes, mushrooms and pepper squares in turn on to each of 12 skewers. Brush the kebabs with the olive oil and season them with some white pepper.

Place the kebabs under the grill until they are lightly browned — 4 to 6 minutes on each side. Arrange the kebabs on a serving platter and serve the olive and caper sauce separately.

SUGGESTED ACCOMPANIMENT: *long-grain rice flavoured with 1 to 2 tablespoons of tomato paste.*

Barley and Mushroom Broth with Smoked Tofu

Serves 4
Working time: about 30 minutes
Total time: about 1 hour

Calories **140**
Protein **6g**
Cholesterol **0mg**
Total fat **5g**
Saturated fat **trace**
Sodium **85mg**

60 g	pot barley, rinsed under cold running water and drained	2 oz
1.5 litres	unsalted vegetable stock (recipe, page 9)	2½ pints
1 tbsp	safflower oil	1 tbsp
125 g	onion, finely chopped	4 oz
125 g	carrot, diced	4 oz
2	sticks celery, diced	2
125 g	button mushrooms, wiped clean and sliced	4 oz
2 tbsp	mushroom ketchup	2 tbsp
2 tbsp	tomato paste	2 tbsp
125 g	smoked tofu, cut into 1 cm (½ inch) cubes	4 oz
	freshly ground black pepper	
2 tbsp	chopped parsley	2 tbsp
2 tbsp	freshly cut chives	2 tbsp

Place the barley in a large saucepan with the vege-table stock, and bring the liquid to the boil. Reduce the heat to a simmer, cover the pan and cook the barley for 30 minutes.

Meanwhile, heat the oil in a heavy frying pan, add the onion, carrot and celery, and sweat them over medium heat for about 10 minutes. Add the mush-rooms and cook for a further 2 minutes.

Add the sweated vegetables, the mushroom ketch-up and the tomato paste to the barley and stock, and simmer, covered, for 20 minutes. Add the tofu to the saucepan and simmer, covered, for a further 10 minutes. Season the broth with some black pepper and stir in the parsley and chives. Serve hot.

SUGGESTED ACCOMPANIMENT: *rye bread.*

3 Bread, pasta and the ingredients of numerous pastry dishes await metamorphosis into satisfying vegetarian meals.

A Sustaining Trio

Pasta, pastry and bread are the nutritious corner-stones of many vegetarian dishes. They derive nearly all of their goodness from wheat flour, which is rich in carbohydrates and includes six of the eight essential amino acids. Plain flour is also a good source of B vitamins, calcium and iron, while its wholemeal form contains even higher concentrations of these valuable nutrients. Combined with vegetables and pulses and small quantities of dairy products or eggs, the time-honoured staples made with flour create perfectly balanced meatless meals.

Pasta is not only one of the simplest of foods; provided that one bears in mind a few basic techniques, it is also very easy to cook. Boil it in plenty of water — at least 5 litres (8 pints) for 500 g (1 lb) of fresh or dried pasta. Cooking times given in any recipe are no more than guidelines; you only really know when pasta is done by testing it. When it is tender but still slightly resistant to the bite — that is, *al dente* — drain it immediately or it will continue to cook.

Shortcrust pastry is indispensable to any cook's repertoire. For a light, crumbly pie crust, keep the ingredients cool. Make sure that the fat is chilled; if your fingertips are warm, use a pastry blender to combine the fat and flour. Mix the dry and liquid ingredients just enough to form a compact ball; do not overwork the dough, or the pastry will be tough.

Yeast pastry prefers a heavy-handed approach, requiring a period of vigorous kneading after the ingredients have been combined. Dry or fresh yeast work equally well to create this bread-like crust. Take care, however, that the liquid is at the correct temperature when activating the yeast: too cold a temperature will retard its development; too hot will kill it. Ideally, the liquid should be 43°C (110°F), a temperature that feels hot to the touch.

Phyllo pastry — paper-thin and crisp — makes an ideal wrapping for low fat vegetarian dishes. It can be made at home — and still is in some Greek and Turkish households — but it is now also available ready-made from many supermarkets as well as from Middle Eastern speciality shops. After peeling a sheet of phyllo from its stack, work swiftly so that the pastry does not dry out and tear, and keep the remaining sheets covered by a damp cloth.

Bread, the most ancient and revered of the flour-paste foods, is a universal accompaniment to virtually all meals. At the conclusion of this chapter, the staff of life also lends its able support to a variety of ingredients — from Brie to okra — in a number of inventive main course dishes.

Ricotta and Courgette Tortellini with Mint-Yogurt Sauce

Serves 6
Working and total time: about 1 hour and 40 minutes

175 g	courgettes	6 oz
¼ tsp	salt	¼ tsp
175 g	strong plain flour	6 oz
1	egg	1
1	egg white	1
1 tbsp	safflower oil	1 tbsp
150 g	low-fat ricotta cheese	5 oz
	freshly ground black pepper	
	chopped mint leaves, for garnish	
Mint-yogurt sauce		
200 g	low-fat fromage frais	7 oz
100 g	thick Greek yogurt	3½ oz
12.5 cl	plain low-fat yogurt	4 fl oz
4	mint sprigs, leaves only, chopped	4
	white pepper	

Calories **215**
Protein **11g**
Cholesterol **45mg**
Total fat **7g**
Saturated fat **4g**
Sodium **145mg**

Grate the courgettes into a bowl, sprinkle them with the salt and set them aside for 30 minutes.

Meanwhile, make the pasta dough. Put the flour into a bowl and make a well in the centre. Add the egg, egg white and oil, and stir them with a fork or wooden spoon, gradually mixing in the flour. Transfer the dough to a lightly floured surface and knead it for a few minutes. The dough should come cleanly away from the surface; if it is too wet, add flour by the tablespoon until the dough is no longer sticky. If the dough is too dry and crumbly to work with, add water by the teaspoon until it is pliable. Continue kneading the dough until it is smooth and elastic — about 10 minutes. (Alternatively, place the dough ingredients in a food processor and process for about 30 seconds.) Wrap the dough in greaseproof paper or plastic film

and let it rest for 15 minutes before rolling it out.

To prepare the filling, break up the ricotta with a fork in a large bowl and season it with some black pepper. Squeeze the courgettes dry, a quarter at a time, in a double layer of muslin or a clean tea towel, and add them to the ricotta. Mix well together and set aside.

Divide the dough into three equal portions. Cover two with plastic film or an inverted bowl to keep them from drying out. Using a rolling pin, roll out the third on a floured surface into a sheet about 1 mm (1/16 inch) thick. With a 6 cm (2½ inch) round cutter, cut out 24 circles from the pasta and form them into tortellini, as demonstrated below, using 1 teaspoon of filling for each circle. Repeat the procedure with the remaining pieces of dough and filling to make about 72 tortellini. Set them aside.

To make the sauce, place all the ingredients in a food processor or blender, and blend them until smooth. Transfer the sauce to a small saucepan and warm over very gentle heat while you cook the pasta. Do not allow the sauce to boil.

Add the tortellini to 3 litres (5 pints) of boiling water with 1½ teaspoons of salt. Start testing the tortellini 1 minute after the water returns to the boil, and cook them until they are *al dente*. Drain the pasta and serve it immediately, with the mint-yogurt sauce and a little chopped mint sprinkled over the top.

SUGGESTED ACCOMPANIMENT: *a salad of sliced sweet red and yellow peppers.*

EDITOR'S NOTE: *Instead of kneading and rolling out the pasta by hand, you can use a pasta machine.*

Shaping Tortellini

1 FILLING THE TORTELLINI. With a 6 cm (2½ inch) pastry cutter, cut circles from the dough. Stack them or store them under a bowl to keep them from drying out. Place some filling on a circle, then moisten one half of the circle with water.

2 ENCLOSING THE FILLING. Fold the circle in half so that the moist and dry edges meet. Press the edges together firmly to seal them.

3 JOINING THE ENDS. Curl the ends round the filling and pinch these together, moistening the inner surfaces, if necessary, to make them stick. Repeat the steps with the remaining circles.

Vegetable Lasagne

Serves 6
Working time: about 1 hour and 30 minutes
Total time: about 2 hours and 15 minutes

Calories **295**
Protein **13g**
Cholesterol **55mg**
Total fat **12g**
Saturated fat **5g**
Sodium **280mg**

1 tbsp	virgin olive oil	1 tbsp
1	onion, finely chopped	1
1	leek, trimmed, washed thoroughly to remove all grit, thinly sliced	1
2	garlic cloves, crushed	2
175 g	broccoli florets	6 oz
125 g	French beans, topped and tailed, cut into 2.5 cm (1 inch) lengths	4 oz
6	sticks celery, thinly sliced	6
1	small sweet yellow pepper, seeded, deribbed and thinly sliced	1
1 tsp	mixed dried herbs	1 tsp
1 tbsp	chopped parsley	1 tbsp
400 g	canned tomatoes, sieved	14 oz
¼ tsp	salt	¼ tsp
	freshly ground black pepper	
30 g	Parmesan cheese, grated	1 oz
Spinach pasta dough		
175 g	strong plain flour	6 oz
250 g	fresh spinach, washed, stemmed, blanched for 1 minute in boiling water, squeezed dry and finely chopped, or 150 g (5 oz) frozen chopped spinach, thawed	8 oz
1	egg	1
1	egg white	1
1 tbsp	safflower oil	1 tbsp
Nutmeg sauce		
30 g	unsalted butter	1 oz
30 g	plain flour	1 oz
30 cl	skimmed milk	½ pint
½ tsp	freshly grated nutmeg	½ tsp
⅛ tsp	salt	⅛ tsp
	freshly ground black pepper	

To prepare the vegetable filling, heat the oil in a large, heavy-bottomed saucepan over medium heat. Add the onion and leek and cook for 6 to 8 minutes, until softened. Stir in the garlic, all of the remaining vegetables and herbs, the sieved tomatoes, the salt and some black pepper. Bring the mixture to the boil, then reduce the heat and partially cover the saucepan with a lid. Cook gently for 45 minutes, until the vegetables are tender and the liquid has thickened.

Meanwhile, make the pasta. Put the flour into a mixing bowl and make a well in the centre. Add the spinach, egg, egg white and oil and stir them, using a fork or wooden spoon, gradually incorporating the flour. Transfer the dough to a lightly floured surface and knead it for a few minutes. The dough should come cleanly away from the surface; if it is too wet, add flour by the tablespoon until the dough is no longer sticky. If the dough is too dry and crumbly, add water by the teaspoon until it is pliable. Continue kneading the dough until it is smooth and elastic — about 10 minutes. (Alternatively, place the ingredients in a food processor and process them for about 30 seconds.) Wrap the dough in greaseproof paper or plastic film and let it rest for 15 minutes.

Roll out the dough on a floured surface into a rectangle about 60 by 45 cm (24 by 18 inches); it should be about 1 mm ($\frac{1}{16}$ inch) thick. Cut the rectangle lengthwise into three 15 cm (6 inch) strips, then cut each of these strips crosswise into six 10 cm (4 inch) wide pieces, to make a total of 18 sheets of lasagne.

Preheat the oven to 200°C (400°F or Mark 6).

Cook the lasagne for 1 minute, three or four sheets at a time, in 3 litres (5 pints) of gently boiling water. Lift the sheets out of the water with a slotted spoon and spread them on a clean tea towel to drain.

Grease a 25 by 20 by 5 cm (10 by 8 by 2 inch) oven-proof dish and line the bottom with six sheets of lasagne. Pour in half of the vegetable filling and cover it with another six sheets of lasagne. Pour in the rest of the vegetables and arrange the remaining lasagne sheets over the top.

To make the sauce, melt the butter in a saucepan over medium heat. Add the flour, then gradually stir in the milk. Bring the sauce to the boil, stirring continuously until it thickens. Stir in the nutmeg, salt and some black pepper. Reduce the heat to low and simmer the sauce for 5 minutes, stirring frequently. Pour the sauce over the top of the lasagne and spread it to cover the entire surface. Sprinkle the Parmesan evenly over the sauce. Cook the lasagne in the oven for 40 minutes, until golden-brown and bubbling hot.

SUGGESTED ACCOMPANIMENT: *mixed salad.*

EDITOR'S NOTE: *Instead of kneading and rolling out the pasta by hand, you can use a pasta machine. Dried lasagne sheets may be used in place of the fresh pasta.*

Penne Rigati with Celery and Soft Cheese

Serves 8
Working (and total) time: about 30 minutes

Calories **320**
Protein **14g**
Cholesterol **15mg**
Total fat **6g**
Saturated fat **3g**
Sodium **275mg**

500 g	penne rigati, or other short, tubular pasta	1 lb
250 g	celery, trimmed and finely chopped	8 oz
175 g	low-fat soft cheese	6 oz
500 g	thick Greek yogurt	1 lb
½ tsp	freshly grated nutmeg	½ tsp
½ tsp	salt	½ tsp
	freshly ground black pepper	
1 tbsp	virgin olive oil	1 tbsp
60 g	shallots, finely chopped	2 oz
5 tbsp	finely chopped parsley	5 tbsp
3 tbsp	fresh lime juice	3 tbsp

Add the penne rigati to 5 litres (8 pints) of boiling water with 1½ teaspoons of salt. Start testing the pasta after 10 minutes and continue to cook until it is *al dente.*

Meanwhile, pour enough water into a saucepan to fill it about 2.5 cm (1 inch) deep. Set a vegetable steamer in the pan and bring the water to the boil. Put the celery in the steamer, cover the pan, and steam the celery until it is tender but still firm — 3 to 4 minutes.

Mash the soft cheese and yogurt together in a bowl with a fork until smooth, then season with the nutmeg, salt and some black pepper. Set the mixture aside.

Heat the oil in a heavy frying pan, add the steamed celery, the shallots and 4 tablespoons of the chopped parsley, and sauté them over medium heat for about 5 minutes, until soft. Drain the pasta and stir it into the celery mixture. Remove the pan from the heat and gently stir the cheese mixture into the pasta and celery. Return the pan to a low heat, cover with a lid and gently warm the pasta mixture through for about 3 minutes. Stir in the lime juice and serve immediately, garnished with the remaining chopped parsley.

SUGGESTED ACCOMPANIMENT: *grilled tomatoes or a fresh tomato salad.*

Goat Cheese and Parsley Ravioli

Serves 4
Working (and total) time: about 1 hour and 15 minutes

Calories **430**
Protein **23g**
Cholesterol **75mg**
Total fat **14g**
Saturated fat **2g**
Sodium **490mg**

175 g	strong plain flour	6 oz
1	egg	1
1	egg white	1
1 tbsp	safflower oil	1 tbsp
175 g	soft goat cheese	6 oz
90 g	fine fresh white breadcrumbs	3 oz
100 g	parsley, finely chopped	3½ oz
45 g	spring onions, finely chopped	1½ oz
Tomato sauce		
1 tsp	virgin olive oil	1 tsp
1	small onion, chopped	1
750 g	fresh tomatoes, skinned (page 14) and roughly chopped	1½ lb
½ tsp	salt	½ tsp
	freshly ground black pepper	

To prepare the dough, put the flour into a mixing bowl and make a well in the centre. Add the egg, egg white and oil and stir them, using a fork or wooden spoon, gradually mixing in the flour. Transfer the dough to a lightly floured surface and knead it for a few minutes. The dough should come cleanly away from the surface. If it is too wet, add flour by the tablespoon until it is no longer sticky. If the dough is too dry and crumbly, add water by the teaspoon until it is pliable. Continue kneading the dough until it is smooth and elastic — about 10 minutes. (Alternatively, place the dough ingredients in a food processor and process them for about 30 seconds.) Wrap the dough in greaseproof paper or plastic film and let it rest for 15 minutes.

Meanwhile, make the tomato sauce. Heat the olive oil in a heavy frying pan over medium heat, then sauté the onion in the oil for about 3 minutes, until softened. Add the tomatoes, salt and some pepper. Bring the contents of the pan to the boil and cook over high heat, until the tomatoes soften — about 5 minutes. Reduce the heat and simmer, uncovered, for a further 15 minutes. Remove the pan from the heat. When the mixture has cooled a little, purée it in a blender. Sieve the purée into a clean saucepan and set it aside.

To make the ravioli filling, combine the goat cheese, breadcrumbs, 90 g (3 oz) of the chopped parsley and the spring onions in a bowl. Divide the dough into two portions. Cover one with plastic film or an inverted bowl to keep it moist. Using a rolling pin, roll out the other portion very thinly on a well-floured surface into a rectangle measuring about 75 by 15 cm (30 by 6 inches); it should be about 1 mm ($\frac{1}{16}$ inch) thick. Then, following the steps shown opposite, form it into 18 ravioli, each about 6 by 5 cm (2½ by 2 inches). Repeat the process with the second portion of dough.

Gently reheat the tomato sauce over low heat. Add the ravioli to 3 litres (5 pints) of boiling water with 1½ teaspoons of salt. Start testing the ravioli after 1 minute and cook them until they are *al dente*, then drain them. Serve immediately with the sauce, and sprinkled with the remaining chopped parsley.

EDITOR'S NOTE: *Instead of kneading and rolling out the pasta by hand, you can use a pasta machine.*

Making Ravioli

1 ADDING THE FILLING. Spread the rolled dough sheet on a lightly floured surface. Place 18 small spoonfuls of the filling on one half of the sheet, taking care to space them evenly, about 4 cm (1 ½ inches) apart.

2 COVERING THE FILLING. Brush the other half of the sheet lightly with water. Fold it carefully over the mounds of filling, matching the dough edges as closely as possible.

3 CUTTING THE RAVIOLI. Starting from the folded edge, use your fingers or the side of your hand to force out the air between the mounds of filling and to seal the dough. Cut out the ravioli with a fluted pastry wheel.

Spaghetti with Omelette Strips and Stir-Fried Vegetables

Serves 6
Working (and total) time: about 40 minutes

Calories **290**
Protein **13g**
Cholesterol **75mg**
Total fat **9g**
Saturated fat **2g**
Sodium **100mg**

2	eggs	2
¼ tsp	salt	¼ tsp
¼ tsp	cayenne pepper	¼ tsp
2 tsp	chopped fresh coriander	2 tsp
350 g	dried wholemeal spaghetti	12 oz
2 tbsp	safflower oil	2 tbsp
300 g	bok choy (Chinese chard), washed and dried, stalks removed and julienned, leaves cut into strips	10 oz
2.5 cm	piece fresh ginger root, julienned	1 inch
12	spring onions, white parts only, thinly sliced	12
2	large sweet red peppers, seeded, deribbed and julienned	2
2 ½ tbsp	low-sodium soy sauce or shoyu	2 ½ tbsp

First make two thin, flat omelettes. Break the eggs into a bowl, add the salt, cayenne pepper and coriander, and whisk well. Pour half of the egg mixture into a hot, lightly oiled non-stick frying pan and cook over medium heat until the underside begins to set — about 1 minute. Carefully lift the edge of the omelette with a spatula and allow any uncooked egg to run underneath; repeat until there is no liquid left on the surface of the omelette. Flip the omelette over and cook for a further 30 seconds. Slide the omelette on to a plate and make another omelette in the same way. Set them aside to cool, then slice them into strips.

Cook the pasta in 5 litres (8 pints) of boiling water with 2 teaspoons of salt; start testing it after 10 minutes and cook it until it is al dente. When it is almost ready, heat the oil in a wok or large, heavy frying pan. At 20 second intervals and stirring after each addition, add the bok choy stalks, the ginger, the spring onions together with the red peppers, and finally the bok choy leaves. Drain the pasta thoroughly and add it to the wok together with the omelette strips. Add the soy sauce, stir well and serve.

SUGGESTED ACCOMPANIMENT: a salad of carrot strips and cucumber dressed with a lemon and mint vinaigrette.

Saffron Fettuccine with a Hazelnut and Tarragon Sauce

Serves 4
Working time: about 1 hour
Total time: about 1 hour and 15 minutes

Calories **385**
Protein **23g**
Cholesterol **55mg**
Total fat **11g**
Saturated fat **2g**
Sodium **150mg**

175 g	strong plain flour	6 oz
60 g	semolina	2 oz
¼ tsp	saffron threads, ground with ¼ teaspoon of salt	¼ tsp
1	egg	1
1 tsp	safflower oil	1 tsp
Hazelnut and tarragon sauce		
1 tsp	virgin olive oil	1 tsp
1	garlic clove, crushed	1
60 g	blanched hazelnuts, toasted and coarsely ground	2 oz
250 g	tomatoes, skinned, seeded (page 14) and chopped	8 oz
15 cl	unsalted vegetable stock (recipe, page 9)	¼ pint
300 g	low-fat fromage frais	10 oz
2 tbsp	chopped fresh tarragon	2 tbsp
¼ tsp	salt	¼ tsp
	freshly ground black pepper	

Mix the flour, semolina and saffron together in a mixing bowl, then make a well in the centre. Add the egg, oil and 6 tablespoons of water to the well and stir them with a fork or wooden spoon, gradually mixing in the flour. Transfer the dough to a lightly floured surface and knead it for a few minutes. The dough should come cleanly away from the surface; if it is too wet, add flour by the tablespoon until the dough is no longer sticky. If the dough is too dry and crumbly to work with, add water by the teaspoon until it is pliable. Continue kneading the dough until it is smooth and elastic — about 10 minutes. (Alternatively, place the dough ingredients in a food processor and process for about 30 seconds.) Wrap the dough in greaseproof paper or plastic film and let it rest for 15 minutes.

Meanwhile, heat the oil in a heavy frying pan over medium heat and sauté the garlic until just golden — about 3 minutes. Stir in the toasted hazelnuts and tomatoes, and add the stock. Simmer the sauce for 2 to 3 minutes, then set the pan aside.

Divide the pasta dough into four portions. Cover three of the portions with plastic film or an inverted bowl to keep them moist. Using a rolling pin, roll out the fourth portion on a surface liberally sprinkled with semolina, into a sheet about 1 mm (¹⁄₁₆ inch) thick. Cut the sheet into 5 mm (¼ inch) wide strips. Roll out the remaining three portions of dough and cut them into strips. Add the fettuccine to 3 litres (5 pints) of boiling water with 1½ teaspoons of salt. Start testing the pasta after 1 minute and cook it until it is *al dente*. Drain the pasta, return it to the pan and keep it warm.

Stir the *fromage frais* and tarragon into the hazelnut sauce, season it with the salt and some black pepper, then return the pan to a low heat and warm the sauce through gently. Divide the fettuccine among four serving plates and top the pasta with the sauce.

EDITOR'S NOTE: *Instead of kneading and cutting the pasta by hand, you can use a pasta machine. To toast hazelnuts, place them on a baking sheet in a preheated 180° C (350° F or Mark 4) oven for 10 minutes.*

Summer Beans with Fresh Fettuccine and Basil

Serves 4
Working (and total) time: about 1 hour and 15 minutes

Calories **350**
Protein **14g**
Cholesterol **75mg**
Total fat **14g**
Saturated fat **4g**
Sodium **265mg**

30 cl	unsalted vegetable stock (recipe, page 9)	½ pint
1 kg	fresh broad beans, shelled, coarse outer skins removed	2 lb
125 g	French beans, trimmed and cut into 2.5 cm (1 inch) lengths	4 oz
125 g	small mange-tout, strings removed	4 oz
10 cl	single cream	3½ fl oz
2 tbsp	sesame seeds, toasted and ground	2 tbsp
1	garlic clove, crushed	1
4 tbsp	chopped fresh basil, plus basil sprigs for garnish	4 tbsp
½ tsp	salt	½ tsp
	freshly ground black pepper	
Pasta dough		
175 g	strong plain flour	6 oz
1	egg	1
1	egg white	1
1 tbsp	safflower oil	1 tbsp

First make the pasta dough. Put the flour into a mixing bowl and make a well in the centre. Add the egg, egg white and oil and stir them with a fork or wooden spoon, gradually incorporating the flour. Transfer the dough to a lightly floured surface and knead it for a few minutes. The dough should come cleanly away from the surface; if it is too wet, add flour by the tablespoon until the dough is no longer sticky. If the dough is too dry and crumbly to work with, add water by the teaspoon until it is pliable. Continue kneading the dough until it is smooth and elastic — about 10 minutes. (Alternatively, place the dough ingredients in a food processor and process them for about 30 seconds.) Wrap the dough in greaseproof paper or plastic film and let it rest for 15 minutes before rolling it out.

To make the sauce, bring the vegetable stock to the boil in a heavy-bottomed saucepan and add the broad beans. Reduce the heat and simmer the beans for 5 minutes. Add the French beans and simmer for 3 to 4 minutes, until just tender. Add the mange-tout and simmer for a further minute. Reserving the stock, drain the vegetables and keep them warm. Return the stock to the pan and reduce it to 15 cl (¼ pint) by fast boiling, then set it aside while you prepare the fettuccine.

Divide the pasta dough into four portions. Cover three of the portions with plastic film or an inverted bowl to keep them from drying out. Using a rolling pin, roll out the fourth portion very thinly on a floured surface into a sheet about 1 mm (1/16 inch) thick. Cut the sheet into 5 mm (¼ inch) strips. Roll out the remaining three portions of dough and cut them into strips. Add the fettuccine to 3 litres (5 pints) of boiling water with 1½ teaspoons of salt. Start testing the pasta after 1 minute and cook it until it is *al dente*. Drain the pasta, return it to the pan and keep it warm.

Stir the cream, ground sesame seeds, garlic, basil, salt and a generous amount of freshly ground black pepper into the reduced stock. Add the beans, mange-tout and freshly cooked pasta, and toss carefully over low heat until warmed through. Serve garnished with sprigs of fresh basil.

SUGGESTED ACCOMPANIMENT: *radicchio salad tossed in a garlic dressing.*

EDITOR'S NOTE: *Instead of kneading and cutting the pasta by hand, you can use a pasta machine. To toast sesame seeds, warm them in a small, heavy frying pan over medium-low heat until they are golden — 1 to 2 minutes. Grind the sesame seeds in a coffee grinder.*

Nut and Avocado Dumplings with a Citrus Sauce

Serves 4
Working time: about 1 hour and 15 minutes
Total time: about 1 hour and 40 minutes

Calories **330**
Protein **9g**
Cholesterol **55mg**
Total fat **14g**
Saturated fat **3g**
Sodium **320mg**

175 g	strong plain flour	6 oz
¾ tsp	salt	¾ tsp
1	egg, beaten	1
1 tsp	safflower oil	1 tsp
4	spring onions, trimmed and finely chopped	4
140 g	celeriac, peeled and finely diced	4½ oz
30 g	shelled Brazil nuts, finely chopped	1 oz
2	garlic cloves, crushed	2
1 cm	piece fresh ginger root, peeled and grated	½ inch
1	avocado	1
	freshly ground black pepper	
12	chives	12
Citrus sauce		
½	orange, rind pared into thin strips with a potato peeler, juice strained	½
½	lime, rind pared into thin strips with a potato peeler, juice strained	½
2 tbsp	redcurrant jelly	2 tbsp
½ tsp	grainy mustard	½ tsp
½ tsp	cornflour	½ tsp

Sift the flour and ¼ teaspoon of the salt into a bowl and make a well in the centre. Add the beaten egg and 2 tablespoons of water and, using a round-bladed knife, mix the ingredients to a firm dough, adding water by the teaspoon if the mixture is too dry. Knead the dough for 8 to 10 minutes, until it is smooth and elastic. Cover the dough and chill it for 20 minutes.

Meanwhile, make the filling. Heat the oil in a heavy-bottomed saucepan. Add the spring onions and celeriac, and cook them over medium heat until softened — about 5 minutes. Transfer them to a bowl and mix in the Brazil nuts, garlic and ginger. Halve the avocado; remove the stone and skin, and dice the flesh. Add the avocado to the bowl, together with the remaining ½ teaspoon of salt and some black pepper.

Divide the dough into 12 balls. Roll out each ball on a floured surface to form a circle about 10 cm (4 inches) in diameter. Place one twelfth of the filling in the centre of each circle. Brush the rims with water and gather them up over the filling to form bundles. Tie a chive round the neck of each bundle.

Bring a large saucepan of water to the boil. Place six dumplings in a steamer, cover and steam the dumplings for about 10 minutes, until they are puffed up. Transfer them to a heated dish and keep them warm while you steam the remaining dumplings.

Meanwhile, place the strips of orange and lime rind in a small saucepan of boiling water, and boil them for 1 minute. Drain the peel, set it aside and discard the water. Pour the orange and lime juices into the pan together with the redcurrant jelly and mustard, and cook gently until the jelly has dissolved. Blend the cornflour with 3 tablespoons of water and stir it into the sauce. Bring the sauce to the boil, stirring until it has thickened. Pour the sauce into a warmed bowl, and add the reserved citrus strips.

Spoon a little sauce on to warmed serving plates and place three dumplings on each plate. Serve immediately with the remaining sauce in the bowl.

SUGGESTED ACCOMPANIMENT: *basmati or wild rice.*

Herbed Spring Rolls with Peanut Sauce

Serves 4
Working time: about 45 minutes
Total time: about 1 hour and 15 minutes

Calories **425**
Protein **15g**
Cholesterol **55mg**
Total fat **13g**
Saturated fat **4g**
Sodium **125mg**

125 g	plain flour	4 oz
	freshly ground black pepper	
1	egg, beaten	1
30 cl	semi-skimmed milk	½ pint
1 tsp	finely chopped parsley	1 tsp
125 g	fine Chinese noodles	4 oz
1 tsp	dark sesame oil	1 tsp
1 or 2	garlic cloves, crushed	1 or 2
4	spring onions, chopped	4
1	leek, washed thoroughly to remove all grit, sliced	1
125 g	carrots, julienned	4 oz
60 g	mange-tout, strings removed, shredded	2 oz
1 tbsp	low-sodium soy sauce or shoyu	1 tbsp
1 tbsp	Chinese rice wine or sherry	1 tbsp
1 tsp	cornflour, dissolved in 1 tbsp water	1 tsp
30 g	sunflower seeds	1 oz
1 tbsp	sesame seeds	1 tbsp
1 tsp	safflower oil	1 tsp
	Chinese cabbage or iceberg lettuce, washed, dried and shredded	
Peanut sauce		
1 tsp	sesame or safflower oil	1 tsp
1	garlic clove, crushed	1
4	spring onions, chopped	4
1 tsp	clear honey	1 tsp
1 tsp	tomato paste	1 tsp
½ tsp	Tabasco sauce	½ tsp
2 tbsp	smooth peanut butter	2 tbsp
1 tbsp	fresh lemon juice	1 tbsp

First make the batter for the pancakes. Sift the flour and some pepper into a bowl, then make a well in the centre and add the egg, milk and parsley. Whisk the mixture with an electric mixer or hand whisk to incorporate the flour. Cover the batter and allow it to stand for 30 minutes.

Meanwhile, make the filling. Cook the noodles as directed on the packet, then drain them thoroughly. Heat the sesame oil in a heavy-bottomed non-stick saucepan or frying pan over medium heat and cook the garlic for 2 minutes, until soft. Add the spring onions, leek, carrots and mange-tout, and cook for 4 to 5 minutes, stirring frequently, until the vegetables are tender but still slightly crisp. Stir the soy sauce and rice wine into the cornflour solution and add this mixture to the vegetables, then add the sunflower seeds, sesame seeds and noodles. Mix the filling ingredients thoroughly and remove the pan from the heat.

To make the pancakes, heat a 15 cm (6 inch) crêpe pan or non-stick frying pan over medium-high heat. Add ¼ teaspoon of the safflower oil and spread it over the surface of the pan with a paper towel. (Do not discard the paper towel.) Pour about one eighth of the batter into the hot pan and immediately swirl it round to coat the bottom of the pan with a thin, even layer of the batter. Pour any excess batter back into the bowl. Cook the pancake until the bottom is browned — about 1 minute. Lift the edge with a spatula and turn the pancake over. Cook the pancake on the second side until it, too, is browned — 15 to 30 seconds — then slide it on to a plate. Repeat the process with the remaining batter to make eight pancakes in all; re-oil the pan between cooking pancakes by wiping it over with the oiled paper towel, adding a little extra oil as required. Stack the cooked pancakes on top of one another on the plate.

Preheat the oven to 190°C (375°F or Mark 5). Lay a pancake flat on the work surface and place an eighth of the filling on one half, to come within 2.5 cm (1 inch) of the edges. Fold the side edges of the pancake over, then, starting from the end containing the filling, roll up the pancake tightly. Repeat with the remaining pancakes and filling. Place the pancakes in a lightly greased dish or on a lightly greased baking sheet, with the joins underneath. Brush them lightly with the remaining oil and bake them in the oven for 15 minutes; cover the pancakes loosely with foil after half the cooking time, to prevent them from drying out.

While the pancakes are in the oven, make the sauce. Heat the oil in a saucepan over medium heat and cook the garlic and spring onions for 1 minute. Add the remaining ingredients, together with 15 cl (¼ pint) of water, and whisk the sauce well while bringing it to the boil. Pour the sauce into a bowl.

Serve the pancakes on a bed of Chinese cabbage or iceberg lettuce, accompanied by the sauce.

Individual Raised Pies with Carrot and Broccoli Filling

Serves 6
Working time: about 1 hour
Total time: about 2 hours

Calories **450**	500 g	carrots, chopped	1 lb
Protein **17g**	1	egg, beaten	1
Cholesterol **110mg**	60 g	pine-nuts, ground	2 oz
Total fat **25g**	150 g	low-fat fromage frais	5 oz
Saturated fat **6g**	¼ tsp	salt	¼ tsp
Sodium **375mg**		freshly ground black pepper	
	125 g	broccoli florets	4 oz
	½	bunch watercress, stems removed, very finely chopped	½
	2 tbsp	skimmed milk, for glazing	2 tbsp
	Hot-water crust pastry		
	350 g	wholemeal flour	12 oz
	1	egg yolk	1
	60 g	polyunsaturated margarine	2 oz
	60 g	hard white vegetable fat, diced	2 oz

First prepare the vegetable fillings. Steam the carrots over a saucepan of boiling water for 10 to 20 minutes, until they are tender. Mash the carrots roughly and transfer them to a bowl. Mix in the beaten egg, pine-nuts, *fromage frais*, salt and some black pepper.

Steam the broccoli for about 10 minutes, or until tender, then chop it finely and transfer it to a bowl. Stir in the watercress.

Preheat the oven to 200°C (400°F or Mark 6). Lightly grease six 15 cl (¼ pint) ramekins.

To make the pastry, place the flour in a large bowl and make a well in the centre. Put the egg yolk into the well. Gently heat the margarine, vegetable fat and 17.5 cl (6 fl oz) of water in a small saucepan, until the fat melts. Increase the heat, and bring the liquid to a rolling boil. Immediately pour the boiling liquid into the well in the flour, stirring with a round-bladed knife at the same time to mix the ingredients to a soft dough. Knead the dough on a lightly floured surface until smooth, then cut off one third of it. Wrap this in plastic film to prevent it from drying out, and set it aside.

Divide the large piece of dough into six equal portions. Roll out each one on a lightly floured surface into a circle large enough to line a ramekin — the circles should be about 15 cm (6 inches) in diameter. Carefully lift each circle of dough into a ramekin, pressing it neatly into the base and easing it up the sides; leave a little dough standing proud of the rim at the top.

Distribute half of the carrot mixture among the pastry cases and press it down gently. Divide the broccoli and watercress mixture among the pies, smoothing it into an even layer on top of the carrot mixture. Then spoon in the remaining carrot mixture and smooth the top of each pie filling.

Cut the reserved dough into six equal portions, and roll out each one into a 10 cm (4 inch) circle, to make a lid. Brush the raised edges of the pies with cold water and place a lid over each filling. Press the edges firmly together, to seal them. Flute the pastry edges, and cut a small hole in the top of each pie to allow steam to escape. Glaze the pies with the skimmed milk.

Place the ramekins on a baking sheet and bake the pies for 40 minutes, until the pastry is crisp. Remove the pies from the oven and allow them to stand for 3 to 4 minutes, then unmould them before serving.

SUGGESTED ACCOMPANIMENTS: *salad of mixed lettuce leaves; watercress sauce.*

EDITOR'S NOTE: *To make a watercress sauce, stir finely chopped watercress leaves into plain yogurt, adding a little lemon juice and some crushed garlic.*

Asparagus and Morel Tart

Serves 6
Working time: about 1 hour
Total time: about 2 hours

Calories **220**
Protein **14g**
Cholesterol **35mg**
Total fat **14g**
Saturated fat **4g**
Sodium **285mg**

125 g	firm white button mushrooms, finely chopped	4 oz
1 tsp	fresh lemon juice	1 tsp
1 tsp	Dijon mustard	1 tsp
15 g	unsalted butter	½ oz
7	dried morels, soaked for 20 minutes in tepid water, thoroughly rinsed and drained	7
500 g	asparagus, trimmed and peeled	1 lb
250 g	quark or low-fat fromage frais	8 oz
1	egg yolk	1
1 tbsp	cornflour	1 tbsp
1 tsp	dry mustard	1 tsp
½ tsp	salt	½ tsp
⅛ tsp	white pepper	⅛ tsp
Coriander dough		
75 g	wholemeal flour	2 ½ oz
75 g	plain flour	2 ½ oz
¼ tsp	ground coriander	¼ tsp
75 g	polyunsaturated margarine, chilled	2 ½ oz
1	egg white, lightly beaten	1

First make the dough. Stir together the flours and coriander in a mixing bowl, and rub in the margarine with your fingertips until the mixture resembles fine breadcrumbs. Using a round-bladed knife, blend in the egg white to form a dough. Knead the dough briefly on a lightly floured surface, until it is smooth. Roll out the dough and use it to line a 25 cm (10 inch) tart tin. Prick the insides of the pastry case with a fork, and chill it in the refrigerator for 30 minutes. Meanwhile, preheat the oven to 200°C (400°F or Mark 6).

Place the button mushrooms in a small, heavy-bottomed saucepan with the lemon juice, Dijon mustard and half of the butter. Cover the pan and sweat the mushrooms gently for about 10 minutes, stirring them from time to time. Remove the lid and continue cooking, stirring frequently, until almost all the moisture has evaporated. Cover the pan again, and set the mushrooms aside.

Bake the pastry case for 15 minutes, then remove it from the oven and set it aside. Reduce the oven temperature to 180°C (350°F or Mark 4).

Cut six of the morels in half lengthwise. Cut one slice, crosswise, from the widest part of the seventh morel and reserve the trimmings. Place the morel halves and the slice in a steamer basket. Trim the stalks of six large asparagus spears to a uniform length of 5 cm (2 inches), and reserve the offcuts. Place the six asparagus spears in the steamer basket with the morels.

Fill a saucepan that will fit under the steamer basket with water to a depth of 5 cm (2 inches). Bring the water to the boil and add the remaining asparagus spears and offcuts, and the morel trimmings to the pan. Fit the steamer basket over the top. Reduce the heat and cook for about 10 minutes, until the asparagus stalks in the pan beneath the steamer basket are tender. Heat the remaining butter in another pan, and add the asparagus and morels from the steamer basket. Shake them very gently, to coat them in melted butter.

Drain the asparagus and morel pieces from the pan beneath the steamer basket and place them in a food processor or blender. Blend them until smooth. Sieve the purée and return it to the food processor, then blend in the quark, egg yolk, cornflour, dry mustard, salt and pepper. Stir in the button mushrooms, then pour the filling into the baked pastry case. Return the tart to the oven for 15 minutes.

Carefully cut the butter-coated asparagus in half lengthwise. Arrange the pieces decoratively on top of the tart, tips radiating outwards. Lay the morel halves between the asparagus tips and place the morel slice in the centre of the tart. Cover the tart loosely with foil or non-stick parchment paper and return it to the oven for a further 20 minutes, or until the filling has set. Serve the tart warm rather than hot.

SUGGESTED ACCOMPANIMENT: *green salad.*

Savoury Pumpkin Pie

Serves 6
Working time: about 30 minutes
Total time: about 1 hour and 15 minutes

Calories **175**
Protein **13g**
Cholesterol **75mg**
Total fat **3g**
Saturated fat **1g**
Sodium **80mg**

500 g	pumpkin or squash, peeled and cut into 1 cm (½ inch) chunks	1 lb
200 g	quark	7 oz
2	eggs, beaten	2
1	onion, sliced into rings	1
1 tsp	safflower oil, plus a little extra for glazing	1 tsp
1	garlic clove, crushed	1
½ tsp	ground ginger	½ tsp
½ tsp	chili powder	½ tsp
⅛ tsp	salt	⅛ tsp
	white pepper	
Yeast dough		
175 g	wholemeal flour	6 oz
1 tsp	easy-blend dried yeast	1 tsp
12.5 cl	skimmed milk	4 fl oz

To make the dough, mix together the flour and yeast in a large bowl. Heat the milk in a saucepan until it is hot to the touch — about 43°C (110°F) — then pour it into the dry ingredients. Knead the mixture well for 10 minutes, adding a little extra water if necessary, to make a smooth, soft dough. Leave the dough to rest for 10 minutes. Roll out the dough and use it to line a lightly greased 20 cm (8 inch) flan tin.

Preheat the oven to 200°C (400°F or Mark 6).

Steam the pumpkin chunks over a saucepan of boiling water for 10 to 15 minutes, until they are soft. Transfer them to a bowl and mash them. When the purée has cooled slightly, beat in the quark and eggs.

Meanwhile, set a quarter of the onion rings aside and chop the remainder. Heat the oil in a small, heavy-bottomed saucepan over medium heat. Add the chopped onion and garlic, and sauté them for about 3 minutes, until softened but not browned. Stir in the ginger and chili powder.

Transfer the pumpkin mixture to a food processor, and add the contents of the saucepan, the salt and some pepper. Blend the mixture until it is smooth. Pour the filling into the pastry case and level the surface. Press the reserved onion rings lightly into the filling and brush them with the extra safflower oil.

Bake the pie in the oven for 30 to 40 minutes, until it is golden-brown and firm in the centre.

SUGGESTED ACCOMPANIMENT: *steamed fresh vegetables.*

Mustard Cauliflower Flan

Serves 4
Working time: about 40 minutes
Total time: about 1 hour and 30 minutes

Calories **330**
Protein **11g**
Cholesterol **55mg**
Total fat **15g**
Saturated fat **4g**
Sodium **285mg**

1	cauliflower trimmed and divided into small florets (about 350 g/12 oz),	1
1 tsp	virgin olive oil	1 tsp
1	onion, finely chopped	1
1	large cooking apple, peeled, cored and roughly chopped	1
1 ½ tbsp	Dijon mustard	1 ½ tbsp
2 tbsp	plain flour	2 tbsp
1	egg, lightly beaten	1
30 cl	skimmed milk	½ pint
¼ tsp	salt	¼ tsp
	white pepper	
	paprika	
Herb pastry		
125 g	wholemeal flour	4 oz
60 g	polyunsaturated margarine, chilled	2 oz
2 tbsp	finely chopped fresh coriander	2 tbsp
2 tbsp	finely chopped flat-leaf parsley	2 tbsp

First make the pastry. Put the flour in a mixing bowl and rub in the margarine with your fingertips until the mixture resembles fine breadcrumbs. Stir in the coriander and parsley. Using a round-bladed knife, blend 3 to 4 tablespoons of water into the dry ingredients to form a dough. Gather the dough into a ball and knead it briefly on a lightly floured surface, until it is smooth. Roll out the dough and use it to line a flan tin 20 cm (8 inches) in diameter, and about 4 cm (1½ inches) deep. Prick the inside of the pastry case with a fork, and chill it in the refrigerator for 30 minutes. Preheat the oven to 200°C (400°F or Mark 6).

Bake the pastry case for 10 to 15 minutes, until the pastry is crisp. Remove it from the oven and reduce the temperature to 180°C (350°F or Mark 4).

Meanwhile, parboil the cauliflower florets in a saucepan of boiling water until just tender — about 5 minutes. Drain, rinse under cold running water and drain again thoroughly. Set the florets aside. Heat the oil in a heavy frying pan over medium heat. Add the onion and fry gently until soft and transparent — about 3 minutes. Add the apple and cook for another 4 minutes, until the apple is just tender.

Spread the onion and apple mixture inside the flan case and arrange the cauliflower florets on top. In a bowl, blend the mustard and flour to form a smooth paste. Using an electric hand-held whisk, beat in the egg, then the milk, a little at a time. Add the salt and some pepper, and pour the mixture into the flan case.

Bake the flan in the oven for 30 to 45 minutes, until the filling is set. Serve the flan either hot or cold, sprinkled with a little paprika.

SUGGESTED ACCOMPANIMENTS: *salad of mixed lettuce leaves; sliced tomatoes.*

Granary Pizza with Sweetcorn and Pineapple

Serves 4
Working time: about 40 minutes
Total time: about 1 hour and 45 minutes

Calories **395**
Protein **17g**
Cholesterol **15mg**
Total fat **8g**
Saturated fat **4g**
Sodium **390mg**

2 tbsp	grainy mustard	2 tbsp
350 g	sweetcorn kernels, cut from two large ears, or 350 g (12 oz) frozen sweetcorn, thawed	12 oz
½ tsp	safflower oil	½ tsp
1	large onion, sliced into rings	1
2 tsp	chopped fresh basil, plus shredded basil leaves, for garnish	2 tsp
⅛ tsp	paprika	⅛ tsp
½	small ripe pineapple, skinned, cored and cut into small dice	½
1	sweet orange or red pepper, seeded, deribbed and cut into 1 cm (½ inch) dice	1
4	black olives, stoned and quartered	4
90 g	Gouda cheese, grated	3 oz
Pizza dough		
125 g	granary flour	4 oz
125 g	plain flour	4 oz
½ tsp	salt	½ tsp
30 g	fresh yeast, or 1 tsp dried yeast	1 oz

First make the dough for the pizza base. Mix both types of flour in a bowl with the salt. In a small bowl, crumble the fresh yeast over 15 cl (¼ pint) of warm water. Leave the mixture in a warm place for about 10 minutes, until its surface has become frothy. If using dried yeast, activate it according to the manufacturer's instructions. Make a well in the centre of the dry ingredients and pour in the yeast liquid. Using a wooden spoon, mix the ingredients to a soft dough. Turn the dough out on to a floured surface and knead it for 5 minutes. Return the dough to the bowl, cover it with plastic film and leave it in a warm place for about 10 minutes, until it has doubled in size.

Knock back the dough to its original size, then roll it out on a floured surface into a circle about 30 cm (12 inches) in diameter. Place the circle on a lightly greased baking sheet or pizza pan. Brush the dough with the mustard, leaving a 1 cm (½ inch) border of dough round the edge. Cover the dough and leave it in a warm place for about 10 minutes while it rises again.

While the dough is rising, preheat the oven to 200°C (400°F or Mark 6) and prepare the filling. Cook the sweetcorn kernels in a pan of simmering water for 3 minutes, then drain them. Heat the oil in a heavy frying pan over medium heat. Add the onion rings and fry them gently for 5 to 6 minutes, until soft. Stir in the chopped basil.

Arrange the onion and basil over the pizza base and sprinkle them with the paprika. Mix the sweetcorn with the pineapple and scatter the mixture over the onion. Add the sweet pepper and olives, and finally sprinkle over the grated cheese.

Bake the pizza in the oven for 20 to 25 minutes, until the dough is crusty round the edges and the cheese has melted. Serve the pizza hot, garnished with the shredded basil leaves.

Pastry-Wrapped Pears with a Walnut, Stilton and Leek Stuffing

Serves 4
Working time: about 1 hour
Total time: about 2 hours

Calories **605**
Protein **14g**
Cholesterol **65mg**
Total fat **17g**
Saturated fat **7g**
Sodium **430mg**

150 g	leeks, trimmed, leaves separated and washed thoroughly to remove all grit	5 oz
4	firm dessert pears (about 175 g/6 oz each)	4
2 tbsp	fresh lemon juice	2 tbsp
30 g	Stilton cheese, rind removed	1 oz
30 g	shelled walnuts, chopped	1 oz
4 tbsp	finely chopped parsley	4 tbsp
1	egg yolk	1
1 tbsp	skimmed milk	1 tbsp
60 g	dry breadcrumbs	2 oz
	oakleaf lettuce leaves, for garnish	
8	walnut halves, for garnish	8
Shortcrust pastry		
250 g	plain flour	8 oz
90 g	polyunsaturated margarine, chilled	3 oz
1	egg white, lightly beaten	1

First make the pastry. Sift the flour into a mixing bowl and rub in the margarine with your fingertips until the mixture resembles fine breadcrumbs. Using a round-bladed knife, mix in the egg white and 2 to 3 teaspoons of iced water to form a dough. Knead the dough briefly on a lightly floured surface until smooth, then wrap it in plastic film and chill it in the refrigerator for at least 15 minutes.

Meanwhile, blanch the leek leaves in a saucepan of boiling water for 20 seconds. Remove the pan from the heat, refresh the leaves under cold running water and allow them to drain. Chop the leeks finely and squeeze out any remaining water in a piece of muslin.

Peel the pears and brush them with some of the lemon juice to prevent discoloration. Cut the pears in half and trim away the stalks and the centre rib. Using a teaspoon, remove the cores and discard them. Scoop out and reserve more flesh from each pear half until only 1 cm (½ inch) thick shells remain. Chop the reserved pear flesh, sprinkle it with a little lemon juice and leave it to drain. Brush the insides of the pear shells with the remaining lemon juice and leave them to drain also, while you prepare the stuffing.

Crumble the cheese into a bowl and mix in the walnuts, leeks, pear flesh and parsley. Chill the stuffing mixture in the refrigerator until required.

Make a paper template slightly larger all round than the flat side of a pear half, then make a second template large enough to cover the convex side of a pear half, with 1 cm (½ inch) to tuck under all round. Roll out the dough into a large rectangle measuring about 65 by 40 cm (26 by 16 inches). With the point of a sharp knife, cut out eight shapes from each tem-

plate. Re-roll the pastry trimmings and fashion eight stalks and eight leaves. Arrange all the shapes on a flat tray and chill them for 10 to 15 minutes. Meanwhile, preheat the oven to 220°C (425°F or Mark 7).

Remove the eight small pastry pear shapes from the refrigerator and prick them well with a fork. Place them on a baking sheet and bake them for 10 minutes, until crisp and lightly coloured. Leave them to cool.

In a small bowl, mix the egg yolk and the milk together to make a glaze. Fill the pear shells with the stuffing mixture, dip the flat sides into the breadcrumbs and shake off any excess. Brush the underneath edges of each small pastry pear shape with some of the glaze, then place a stuffed pear half on top, flat side down. Cover each one with a large pastry pear shape, and tuck the edges well under. Place the pastry-wrapped pears on a baking sheet.

Brush the pastry with the glaze and attach the stalks and leaves. Make a few diagonal slashes on each shape, just cutting through the pastry. Cover with plastic film and chill in the refrigerator for 15 minutes.

Bake the pastry-wrapped pears in the oven for about 25 minutes, until the surface of the pastry is golden-brown. Watch the pastry carefully during this time and cover with foil any parts likely to burn.

To serve, place two pastry-wrapped pear halves on each plate, and garnish them with the oakleaf lettuce leaves and walnut halves.

Mushroom Coulibiaca

COULIBIACA IS A TRADITIONAL RUSSIAN PASTY OF FLAKED
SALMON, CABBAGE AND KASHA, BAKED IN AN EGG AND BUTTER-
RICH YEAST DOUGH. THIS VEGETARIAN VERSION USES A
LIGHTER PASTRY AND REPLACES THE CUSTOMARY HARD-
BOILED EGGS AND SOURED CREAM IN THE FILLING WITH AN
ABUNDANCE OF FRESH MUSHROOMS AND HERBS.

Serves 8
Working time: about 1 hour and 30 minutes
Total time: about 4 hours and 30 minutes (includes rising)

Calories **355**
Protein **13g**
Cholesterol **70mg**
Total fat **12g**
Saturated fat **6g**
Sodium **240mg**

750 g	Savoy cabbage, shredded	1 ½ lb
15 g	unsalted butter	½ oz
2	small onions, finely chopped	2
350 g	field or flat mushrooms, wiped clean and sliced	12 oz
75 g	buckwheat groats (kasha)	2 ½ oz
¼ litre	unsalted vegetable stock (recipe, page 9)	8 fl oz
1 tbsp	finely chopped parsley	1 tbsp
1 tbsp	finely chopped fresh dill	1 tbsp
	freshly ground black pepper	
¼ tsp	salt	¼ tsp
60 g	Brie, rind removed, finely diced	2 oz
½	beaten egg, for glazing	½
Yeast dough		
300 g	strong plain flour	10 oz
100 g	barley flour	3 ½ oz
15 g	fresh yeast, or ½ tsp dried yeast	½ oz
15 cl	skimmed milk, tepid	¼ pint
1	egg, beaten	1
60 g	unsalted butter, melted	2 oz

First make the yeast dough: Sift the strong plain flour and the barley flour into a large bowl and make a well in the centre. Crumble the fresh yeast into the tepid milk and set it aside until its surface becomes frothy — 5 to 10 minutes; if using dried yeast, activate it according to the manufacturer's instructions. Pour the yeast liquid into the well in the flour, add the beaten egg and the butter, and mix well. Turn the dough out on to a floured surface and knead it for about 10 minutes, or until it is no longer sticky but pliable and elastic. Return the dough to the bowl, cover it with plastic film and leave it in a warm place to rise until it has doubled in volume — about 1 ½ hours.

While the dough is rising, prepare the filling. Cook the cabbage in a saucepan of boiling water for 5 minutes. Drain it well, and squeeze out as much liquid as possible. Set the cabbage aside.

Melt the butter in a large, heavy-bottomed saucepan over medium heat. Add the onions and cook them until they are soft and transparent — about 3 minutes. Add the mushrooms, cover the pan, and sweat the vegetables gently until the mushrooms are cooked — 7 to 10 minutes. Remove the lid and continue cooking until all the moisture has evaporated. Add the cooked cabbage and stir it well to coat it in butter. Cover the pan and cook the cabbage over very low heat until it is soft — 10 to 15 minutes.

To prepare the kasha, warm the grains of buckwheat gently in a heavy-bottomed saucepan while you bring the unsalted vegetable stock to the boil in another pan. Pour the stock over the buckwheat, stir it, then cover the pan and simmer gently for 10 minutes. Remove the pan from the heat and leave it, covered, for a further 5 to 10 minutes, until all the stock has been absorbed and the buckwheat grains are soft. Set the buckwheat aside to cool a little.

When the dough has doubled in size, knock it back and knead it again briefly. Cut off and reserve about 45 g (1 ½ oz), then divide the remaining dough into two equal portions. Roll out one portion into a rectangle about 35 by 25 cm (14 by 10 inches) and transfer it to a lightly greased baking sheet. Using your fingertips, build up the edges a little, to make a wall to contain the filling. Spread the buckwheat evenly over the dough, leaving 1 to 2 cm (½ to ¾ inch) clear at the edges. Spoon the vegetable mixture evenly on top of the buckwheat, and sprinkle over the parsley, dill, plenty of black pepper and the salt. Finally, distribute the diced cheese evenly over the filling.

Roll out the second piece of dough into a rectangle about 40 by 30 cm (16 by 12 inches) and place it over the filling. Trim the edges, adding the scraps to the

reserved dough. Press the edges of the upper and lower rectangles of dough firmly together, twisting them a little between your fingertips to form a crimped edge. Knead the reserved dough until smooth, then divide it into six and roll out six long, thin strands. Plait the strands together to form two braids long enough to join two diagonally opposite corners of the rectangle. Lay the braids across the pastry, then cut a 2.5 cm (1 inch) slit in the centre of each of the four triangles formed by the crossed braids. Brush the pastry with the beaten egg, and leave the coulibiaca in a warm place to rise a little more while you preheat the oven to 200°C (400°F or Mark 6).

Bake the coulibiaca in the centre of the oven for 40 to 45 minutes, until the pastry is golden-brown. Protect the edges with strips of foil if they appear to be browning too rapidly. Remove the coulibiaca from the oven and wrap it in a clean, dry tea towel for 15 minutes, to soften the pastry. Transfer it to a serving platter and slice it into chunks at the table.

SUGGESTED ACCOMPANIMENTS: *grated raw carrot; salad of mixed leaves; hot consommé.*

Broccoli and Pecorino Pasties

Serves 8
Working time: about 1 hour
Total time: about 2 hours and 15 minutes

Calories **320**
Protein **12g**
Cholesterol **60mg**
Total fat **13g**
Saturated fat **5g**
Sodium **150mg**

1 tsp	virgin olive oil	1 tsp
1	red onion, finely chopped	1
300 g	purple-sprouting broccoli, divided into florets, stalks and leaves finely chopped	10 oz
100 g	kale, washed, stemmed and chopped	3½ oz
200 g	tomatoes, skinned, seeded (page 14) and finely chopped	7 oz
¼	fresh hot chili pepper, seeded and finely chopped (caution, page 25), or ¼ tsp chili powder	¼
1 tbsp	pine-nuts, toasted	1 tbsp
100 g	low-fat ricotta cheese	3½ oz
45 g	pecorino cheese, finely grated	1½ oz
¼ tsp	salt	¼ tsp
Lemon shortcrust pastry		
400 g	plain flour	14 oz
2 tbsp	virgin olive oil	2 tbsp
30 g	unsalted butter	1 oz
2	eggs, beaten	2
½	lemon, juice only, made up to 14 cl (4½ fl oz) with warm water	½

First make the pastry. Sift the flour into a mixing bowl and rub in the olive oil and butter until the mixture resembles fine breadcrumbs. Make a well in the centre and pour in three quarters of the beaten eggs, together with diluted the lemon juice. Stir the ingredients together with a wooden spoon, then gather the dough into a ball and knead it on a lightly floured surface until smooth. Cover the dough with a tea towel and leave it to rest in a cool place for at least an hour.

Meanwhile, prepare the filling. Heat the oil in a heavy-bottomed saucepan over low heat. Add the onion, cover the pan and cook until the onion is soft and transparent — about 5 minutes. Steam the broccoli and kale together over a saucepan of rapidly boiling water, until they are no longer tough but still very crisp — about 5 minutes. Drain well, then toss them with the onion and leave the mixture to cool a little. Stir in the tomatoes, chili, pine-nuts, cheeses and salt.

Divide the dough into two equal pieces, for ease of rolling. Roll out each piece on a floured work surface into a rectangle measuring approximately 90 by 22 cm (36 by 9 inches). Using a round plate or a cake tin as a guide, cut out four 18 to 20 cm (7 to 8 inch) circles from each piece of dough.

Preheat the oven to 200°C (400°F or Mark 6). Place one eighth of the filling slightly off-centre on each round of dough, then fold the rounds in half over the filling. Pinch the edges of the dough together, sealing the filling inside and creating a decorative border; a little water may be used to help seal the edges. Brush each pasty lightly with a little of the remaining beaten egg and place them on a baking sheet.

Bake the pasties for about 25 minutes, until they are a light golden colour. Serve them hot.

EDITOR'S NOTE: *To toast pine-nuts, place them in a small, heavy frying pan over medium-high heat, and cook them for 1 to 2 minutes, stirring constantly, until golden-brown.*

Smoked Cheese Gougère with a Lemon and Fennel Filling

Serves 6
Working time: about 40 minutes
Total time: about 1 hour and 15 minutes

Calories **240**
Protein **7g**
Cholesterol **80mg**
Total fat **15g**
Saturated fat **5g**
Sodium **260mg**

3	fennel bulbs (about 600 g/1 ¼ lb), cleaned and quartered lengthwise	3
2	lemon balm sprigs (optional)	2
1	stick celery, trimmed and roughly chopped	1
⅛ tsp	salt	⅛ tsp
	freshly ground black pepper	
1	lemon, grated rind and juice	1
1 ½ tbsp	cornflour	1 ½ tbsp
30 g	shelled walnuts, roughly chopped	1 oz
	finely chopped fennel leaves, for garnish	
Choux dough		
125 g	plain flour	4 oz
⅛ tsp	salt	⅛ tsp
⅛ tsp	cayenne pepper	⅛ tsp
75 g	polyunsaturated margarine	2 ½ oz
2	eggs	2
1	egg white	1
30 g	smoked cheese, grated	1 oz

Preheat the oven to 220°C (425°F or Mark 7).

First make the choux dough for the gougère. Sift the flour, salt and cayenne pepper on to a sheet of greaseproof paper. Put the margarine and ¼ litre (8 fl oz) of water into a heavy-bottomed saucepan and heat them gently until the margarine melts. Increase the heat to medium high and bring the water and margarine to the boil. Remove the pan from the heat and slide all the dry ingredients off the paper into the liquid, beating vigorously with a wooden spoon. Return the saucepan to the heat and continue to beat the mixture until it forms a ball in the centre of the pan. Remove the pan from the heat and allow the mixture to cool for a few minutes.

Lightly beat the eggs and egg white together. Using an electric hand-held mixer, or beating vigorously with a wooden spoon, gradually incorporate the eggs, a little at a time, into the cooled mixture, beating well after each addition. Beat in the cheese and continue to beat until the mixture forms a smooth, shiny paste. Pipe or spoon the choux dough round the edge of a greased 28 cm (11 inch) ovenproof flan dish, making small mounds of dough that just touch one another.

Bake the gougère in the oven for 10 minutes. Reduce the oven temperature to 190°C (375°F or Mark 5) and continue baking for another 35 to 40 minutes, until the gougère is golden-brown and well risen.

Meanwhile, prepare the filling. Bring 60 cl (1 pint) of water to the boil in a heavy-bottomed saucepan. Add the fennel, lemon balm, if you are using it, celery, salt

and some black pepper to the pan. Reduce the heat and simmer the fennel for 5 minutes, or until it is tender but still crisp. Drain the contents of the pan, reserving the liquid; keep the fennel and celery warm until required. Discard the lemon balm. Return the liquid to the pan and add the lemon rind and juice. Bring the liquid to the boil and boil it rapidly until it has reduced to half its original quantity.

In a small bowl, blend the cornflour with 3 tablespoons of water, to form a smooth paste. Add the paste to the lemon-flavoured stock and cook it for a further 2 minutes, stirring frequently, until the sauce thickens. Remove the pan from the heat.

Place the fennel and celery in the centre of the gougère and pour the lemon sauce over the top. Sprinkle the walnuts over the gougère and garnish it with a few finely chopped fennel leaves.

Steamed Leek and Celeriac Pudding

Serves 6
Working time: about 1 hour
Total time: about 4 hours and 45 minutes

Calories **300**
Protein **7g**
Cholesterol **0mg**
Total fat **15g**
Saturated fat **5g**
Sodium **330mg**

1 tbsp	virgin olive oil	1 tbsp
1 kg	leeks, trimmed, washed thoroughly to remove all grit and thinly sliced	2 lb
2	garlic cloves, crushed	2
1	aubergine (about 250 g/8 oz), cut into small dice	1
350 g	celeriac, peeled and grated	12 oz
2 tbsp	cornflour	2 tbsp
400 g	canned tomatoes, sieved	14 oz
½ tsp	salt	½ tsp
	freshly ground black pepper	
Vegetable suet pastry		
250 g	plain flour	8 oz
1 tsp	baking powder	1 tsp
⅛ tsp	salt	⅛ tsp
2 tsp	mixed dried herbs	2 tsp
1 tbsp	chopped parsley	1 tbsp
125 g	vegetable suet	4 oz

Thoroughly grease a 2 litre (3½ pint) pudding basin. Line the bottom of the basin with a small circle of non-stick parchment paper.

For the filling, heat the oil in a large, heavy frying pan over medium heat. Add the leeks and cook them gently for 10 to 15 minutes, until they are soft. Add the garlic, aubergine and celeriac and continue cooking for another 5 minutes. Remove the pan from the heat. In a bowl, blend the cornflour with a little of the sieved tomatoes until smooth, then stir in the rest of the tomatoes. Add the tomato mixture to the vegetables, with the salt and some black pepper. Stir the mixture well, then set it aside.

To make the pastry, sift the flour, baking powder and salt into a mixing bowl. Add the dried herbs, parsley and suet, and mix them in thoroughly. Make a well in the centre of the ingredients. Add 15 cl (¼ pint) of cold water and stir to form a soft dough. Knead the dough lightly on a floured surface until it is smooth.

Cut off and reserve one third of the dough. Roll out the rest on a floured surface into a large circle about 40 cm (16 inches) in diameter. Carefully lift the circle of dough into the prepared pudding basin, pressing it gently into the base and against the sides; allow a little to overhang the rim of the basin. Fill the lined basin with the vegetable mixture. Roll out the reserved piece of dough into a circle large enough to cover the pudding. Brush the edges of the pastry in the basin with cold water, then place the lid in position. Press the edges of the dough together well to seal them.

Cover the pudding with a circle of non-stick parchment paper, then cover the top completely with a large piece of foil pleated in the centre to allow for expansion. Pleat and press the foil tightly under the rim of the basin, to seal it.

Place the pudding in a large saucepan, then pour boiling water into the saucepan to come half way up the side of the basin. Cover the pan with a tightly fitting lid and cook the pudding over low heat for 3½ hours, ensuring that the water in the pan maintains a steady boil. Top up with boiling water as required.

Remove the foil and parchment paper from the pudding and carefully turn it out on to a large, hot plate. Serve the pudding hot, cut into wedges.

SUGGESTED ACCOMPANIMENTS: *tomato sauce; new potatoes; spring cabbage.*

Asparagus Strudel

Serves 4
Working time: about 40 minutes
Total time: about 1 hour and 10 minutes

Calories **225**
Protein **10g**
Cholesterol **60mg**
Total fat **13g**
Saturated fat **5g**
Sodium **380mg**

350 g	asparagus, trimmed, peeled and sliced diagonally into 5 mm (¼ inch) thick pieces	12 oz
175 g	low-fat soft cheese	6 oz
2 tbsp	finely cut chives	2 tbsp
2 tbsp	chopped fresh marjoram	2 tbsp
1 tbsp	chopped parsley	1 tbsp
1	egg, separated	1
¼ tsp	salt	¼ tsp
	freshly ground black pepper	
5	sheets phyllo pastry, each about 45 by 30 cm (18 by 12 inches)	5
30 g	polyunsaturated margarine, melted	1 oz
30 g	fresh wholemeal breadcrumbs	1 oz

Place the asparagus pieces in a steamer set over a saucepan of boiling water and steam them for 5 to 6 minutes, until they are tender. Refresh them under cold running water and drain them well. Pat the asparagus pieces dry on paper towels.

Put the soft cheese into a mixing bowl with the herbs, egg yolk, salt and some black pepper. Beat the ingredients together well and stir in the drained asparagus. In a clean bowl, whisk the egg white until it is stiff, then fold it carefully into the asparagus mixture using a metal spoon.

Preheat the oven to 200°C (400°F or Mark 6). Lightly grease a baking sheet.

Lay one phyllo sheet out flat on the work surface, with a long side towards you. Cover the other sheets with a clean, damp cloth to prevent them from drying out. Brush a little of the melted margarine over the sheet on the work surface and sprinkle it with one fifth of the breadcrumbs. Lay another phyllo sheet on top of the first; brush it with margarine and sprinkle it with crumbs in the same way. Repeat this process with the remaining phyllo sheets.

Spoon the asparagus mixture on to the top sheet of phyllo, mounding it in a neat line about 2.5 cm (1 inch) in from the edge nearest to you, and leaving about 2.5 cm (1 inch) clear at each end.

Fold the sides of the pastry in, over the asparagus mixture, then loosely roll the pastry up to enclose the filling. Place the strudel, with the join underneath, on the prepared baking sheet. Brush the remaining margarine over the top of the pastry.

Bake the strudel for 25 to 30 minutes, until it is golden-brown and puffed up. Serve it either warm or cold, cut into slices.

SUGGESTED ACCOMPANIMENT: *salad of curly endive mixed with red onion rings.*

Spinach and Chinese Cabbage Pie

Serves 6
Working time: about 30 minutes
Total time: about 1 hour and 20 minutes

Calories **170**
Protein **12g**
Cholesterol **90mg**
Total fat **10g**
Saturated fat **5g**
Sodium **430mg**

500 g	Chinese cabbage, leaves separated and washed	1 lb
500 g	spinach, washed, stems removed	1 lb
2	eggs	2
1	egg white	1
175 g	low-fat cottage cheese	6 oz
3 tbsp	cut chives	3 tbsp
2 tbsp	chopped fresh marjoram	2 tbsp
¼ tsp	salt	¼ tsp
	freshly ground black pepper	
6	sheets phyllo pastry, each about 45 by 30 cm (18 by 12 inches)	6
45 g	unsalted butter, melted	1 ½ oz

Bring a large saucepan of water to the boil, add the Chinese cabbage leaves and cook them for 1 minute, until they wilt. Using a slotted spoon, lift the leaves out of the water into a colander and drain them well. Blanch the spinach leaves in the same water for 1 minute, then pour them into a colander and refresh them under cold running water. Squeeze the spinach dry in a piece of muslin. Roughly chop the Chinese cabbage and the spinach.

Put the eggs and egg white into a large mixing bowl and whisk them lightly together. Add the chopped Chinese cabbage and spinach, the cottage cheese, chives, marjoram, salt and some black pepper. Mix the ingredients together well. Set the bowl aside, while you prepare the phyllo pastry

Preheat the oven to 190°C (375°F or Mark 5). Grease a 30 by 22 cm (12 by 9 inch) ovenproof dish.

Cut the sheets of phyllo pastry in half crosswise. Place one piece of phyllo in the bottom of the prepared dish and brush it with a little of the melted butter. Add another three pieces of phyllo, brushing each one lightly with melted butter. Pour the Chinese cabbage and spinach mixture into the dish and level the surface. Cover the filling with the remaining eight pieces of phyllo pastry, brushing each piece with melted butter as before. Using a small sharp knife, mark the top layer of phyllo with a diamond pattern.

Put the pie in the oven and bake it for 50 to 55 minutes, until the top is golden-brown.

SUGGESTED ACCOMPANIMENT: *fresh mushroom salad with a yogurt and dill dressing.*

Fennel, Chicory and Blue Cheese Parcels

Serves 4
Working (and total) time: about 1 hour and 20 minutes

Calories **180**
Protein **7g**
Cholesterol **15mg**
Total fat **11g**
Saturated fat **4g**
Sodium **270mg**

1 ½ tbsp	safflower oil	1 ½ tbsp
400 g	bulb fennel, stalks discarded, finely chopped	14 oz
40 cl	unsalted vegetable stock (recipe, page 9), or water	14 fl oz
250 g	chicory, ends trimmed, thinly sliced	8 oz
60 g	Gorgonzola cheese, cut into small cubes	2 oz
½ tsp	salt	½ tsp
	freshly ground black pepper	
6	sheets phyllo pastry, each about 45 by 30 cm (18 by 12 inches)	6
¼ tsp	ground turmeric	¼ tsp
1 tsp	anise-flavoured spirit	1 tsp
45 g	low-fat fromage frais	1 ½ oz

Heat 1 teaspoon of the oil in a heavy-bottomed saucepan over medium heat. Add 175 g (6 oz) of the chopped fennel and sauté it for 5 minutes, without allowing it to brown. Pour in 12.5 cl (4 fl oz) of the stock, increase the heat to high, and cook for a further 2 minutes, until the fennel is soft and the liquid has evaporated. Add the chicory, stir lightly, and cook for 2 minutes until the chicory has wilted. Remove from the heat. When the vegetable mixture has cooled, add the cubed Gorgonzola, season with ¼ teaspoon of the salt and some pepper, and mix lightly.

Preheat the oven to 180°C (350°F or Mark 4). Cut the sheets of phyllo pastry in half lengthwise, then fold each piece in half, again lengthwise, to obtain 12 double-thickness strips measuring about 45 by 7.5 cm (18 by 3 inches). Place one strip on a dry work surface, keeping the others covered with a damp cloth to prevent them from drying out.

Brush the phyllo strip very lightly with a little of the remaining oil, and place 1 tablespoon of the fennel mixture on the bottom left-hand corner of the strip. Fold this corner of pastry and filling over to form a neat triangle, then fold the stuffed portion away from you, keeping its three-cornered shape. Continue folding — first to the left, then away from you, then to the right, and so on — until you reach the end of the strip. Tuck under the loose end of the phyllo. Fill and fold the remaining phyllo strips in the same way, then brush the bottom of each triangle with a little of the oil and place them on a baking sheet. Brush the tops of the triangles with a little more oil, and set them aside while you start preparing the sauce.

Heat the remaining oil — about a teaspoonful — in a small, heavy-bottomed pan. Add the remaining chopped fennel and sauté for 2 minutes without browning. Add the turmeric and the remaining salt. Pour in the anise-flavoured spirit, and cook over high heat until it has evaporated. Pour in the remaining stock, bring to the boil, then reduce the heat to a simmer. Cover the pan and cook for a further 15 minutes, until the fennel is tender.

Meanwhile, bake the triangles for 10 to 15 minutes, until they are crisp and golden. As soon as they are cooked, bring the softened fennel to the boil over high heat and boil hard to reduce the liquid to about 2 tablespoons in volume. Remove from the heat and cool slightly before stirring in the *fromage frais*.

Serve the fennel sauce with the triangles, allowing three triangles per serving.

SUGGESTED ACCOMPANIMENTS: *baked potatoes; steamed baby sweetcorn.*

Burghul-Stuffed Phyllo Packages

Serves 4
Working time: about 35 minutes
Total time: about 1 hour amd 45 minutes (includes soaking)

Calories **315**
Protein **10g**
Cholesterol **0mg**
Total fat **10g**
Saturated fat **2g**
Sodium **115mg**

125 g	burghul, soaked in 60 cl (1 pint) hot water for 1 hour	4 oz
175 g	carrots, grated	6 oz
6	dried apricots, chopped	6
1 tbsp	currants	1 tbsp
60 g	unsalted cashew nuts, coarsely chopped, or pine-nuts	2 oz
½ tsp	ground cumin	½ tsp
½ tsp	ground coriander	½ tsp
2 tbsp	finely chopped parsley	2 tbsp
⅛ tsp	salt	⅛ tsp
	freshly ground black pepper	
5	sheets phyllo pastry, each about 45 by 30 cm (18 by 12 inches)	5
2 tsp	safflower oil	2 tsp

Preheat the oven to 200°C (400°F or Mark 6). Lightly grease a baking sheet.

Drain the burghul well, pressing out as much moisture as possible. Place the burghul in a large bowl and add the carrots, apricots, currants, cashew nuts, cumin, coriander, parsley, salt and some black pepper. Mix all the ingredients together thoroughly.

Lay out one sheet of phyllo pastry on the work surface; keep the other sheets covered by a clean, damp cloth while you work, to prevent them from drying out. Brush a little oil over the sheet on the work surface. Place a quarter of the burghul mixture near one end of the sheet, half way between the two longer sides, and flatten it down gently. Fold the shorter edge of the pastry over the filling, fold in the two longer side edges, then roll the stuffed section up to the other end, to form a package. Place the package on the baking sheet, with the join underneath. Roll up another three phyllo packages in the same way.

Cut the remaining sheet of phyllo pastry into strips. Crumple the strips loosely in your hand, and use some to decorate the top of each package. Brush the remaining oil or a little skimmed milk over the packages, and bake them in the oven for 20 to 25 minutes, until they are golden-brown.

SUGGESTED ACCOMPANIMENT: *mixed bean salad with a vinaigrette dressing.*

Mushrooms and Asparagus in Phyllo Cases

Serves 6
Working (and total) time: about 1 hour

Calories **105**
Protein **5g**
Cholesterol **0mg**
Total fat **4g**
Saturated fat **1g**
Sodium **90mg**

4 tsp	safflower oil	4 tsp
6	sheets phyllo pastry, each about 45 by 30 cm (18 by 12 inches)	6
250 g	asparagus, trimmed and peeled	8 oz
2	large carrots, julienned, parboiled for 5 minutes and drained	2
4	large spring onions, trimmed and sliced	4
1	garlic clove, crushed	1
350 g	button mushrooms, wiped and sliced	12 oz
¼ litre	skimmed milk	8 fl oz
2 tsp	cornflour	2 tsp
1 tbsp	chopped fresh tarragon	1 tbsp
1 tsp	fresh lemon juice	1 tsp
⅛ tsp	salt	⅛ tsp
	freshly ground black pepper	
	tarragon sprigs, for garnish (optional)	

Preheat the oven to 190°C (375°F or Mark 5). Use 2 teaspoons of the oil to brush the bases of six 15 cl (¼ pint) ramekins.

Fold each sheet of phyllo pastry in half lengthwise, then in three crosswise, to make six 15 cm (6 inch) squares. Trim the three folded edges of each pile of squares, to give six stacks of pastry each containing six squares. Take one stack of squares and rearrange the positions of the pieces of pastry so that the corners are offset, to resemble the petals of a flower. Repeat with the other stacks. Place a stack of squares in each ramekin, pressing them into the contours of the dish. Bake the pastry-lined ramekins in the oven for 15 to 20 minutes, until the cases are evenly browned: take care not to let the edges burn.

Meanwhile, make the filling. Steam the asparagus in a steamer basket over a pan of gently simmering water for about 10 minutes, until tender but still crisp. Cut off and reserve twelve 5 cm (2 inch) long tips, for garnish. Coarsely chop the remaining asparagus.

Heat the remaining 2 teaspoons of oil in a small, heavy-bottomed pan and add the spring onions, garlic and mushrooms. Cook them gently over medium heat, stirring frequently, until the mushrooms soften and begin to exude their juices — about 5 minutes. Add the milk and bring the mixture to the boil. In a small bowl, blend the cornflour to a smooth paste with 2 tablespoons of water. Add the cornflour paste to the sauce and bring it back to the boil to thicken it, stirring constantly. Gently mix in the chopped tarragon, lemon juice, chopped asparagus, carrots, salt and some black pepper. Simmer the sauce for 1 minute, to heat all the ingredients through.

Carefully remove the cooked phyllo cases from the ramekins, and place each one on a warmed serving plate. Spoon the vegetable mixture into and around the cases, and garnish each serving with two of the reserved asparagus tips and a sprig of tarragon, if you are using it.

SUGGESTED ACCOMPANIMENTS: *baked tomatoes; steamed new potatoes.*

Baguette and Brie Bake

Serves 4
Working time: about 10 minutes
Total time: about 40 minutes

Calories			

Calories **220**
Protein **14g**
Cholesterol **80mg**
Total fat **8g**
Saturated fat **1g**
Sodium **460mg**

100 g	Brie or Camembert cheese, chilled	3½ oz
1	small baguette (about 175 g/6 oz)	1
1	egg	1
2	egg whites	2
20 cl	semi-skimmed milk	7 fl oz
	freshly ground black pepper	

Preheat the oven to 180°C (350°F or Mark 4). Lightly grease a large, shallow ovenproof dish.

Using a sharp knife, slice the cheese lengthwise into 5 mm (¼ inch) thick slices, then cut each slice into pieces about 3 cm (1¼ inch) wide, to give 16 small slices. Cut the baguette into 16 slices.

Fit the slices of bread and cheese alternately into the prepared dish. Beat the egg and egg whites in a bowl, add the milk and some black pepper, then carefully pour the mixture over the bread and cheese, ensuring that all the bread is thoroughly soaked.

Place the dish in the oven and bake for 30 minutes, until the surface is golden-brown and crisp, and the custard is just firm in the centre. Serve at once.

SUGGESTED ACCOMPANIMENTS: *salad of mixed leaves; tomato, cucumber and onion salad.*

Scorzonera and Asparagus Muffins

Serves 4
Working (and total) time: about 30 minutes

Calories **240**	4	scorzonera (about 250 g/8 oz), topped, tailed and scrubbed well	4
Protein **20g**			
Cholesterol **20mg**	12	asparagus spears, trimmed and peeled	12
Total fat **7g**	4	wholemeal muffins, halved horizontally	4
Saturated fat **4g**	4 tsp	low-fat fromage frais	4 tsp
Sodium **520mg**		freshly ground black pepper	
	1 tbsp	finely chopped mixed fresh herbs (tarragon, chervil, dill, parsley)	1 tbsp
	125 g	low-fat mozzarella cheese, thinly sliced	4 oz
	1 tsp	paprika	1 tsp
	2 tsp	finely cut chives	2 tsp

Cook the scorzonera in a saucepan of lightly boiling water, covered, for 10 to 15 minutes, until it is tender when pierced with a sharp knife. Drain the scorzonera and, using the back of a knife, scrape each root gently under cold running water until all the black skin has been removed. Cut each scorzonera root into three pieces of equal length.

Meanwhile, steam the asparagus in a steamer basket over a pan of gently simmering water for about 10 minutes, until it is tender but still crisp. Remove the asparagus from the steamer and place the spears on paper towels to dry.

Preheat the grill to medium. Toast the muffins on their uncut side only. Spread the untoasted side of the warm muffins with the *fromage frais*, and season them with some black pepper and the chopped mixed fresh herbs. Put three asparagus spears on each of four of the halves, and three pieces of scorzonera on each of the other four halves. Lay the mozzarella slices on top of the vegetables. Place the muffins under the grill until the mozzarella has melted and is beginning to bubble and brown slightly — 3 to 5 minutes. Garnish the scorzonera muffins with the paprika and the asparagus muffins with the chives. Serve at once.

SUGGESTED ACCOMPANIMENTS: *salad of mixed leaves with a vinaigrette dressing; grilled tomatoes.*

EDITOR'S NOTE: *Scorzonera is similar to the lighter-skinned salsify, which may be used instead in this recipe.*

Italian Poor Man's Salad

THIS ADAPTATION OF A TUSCAN PEASANT DISH USES TWO
TYPES OF BREAD: WHOLEMEAL AND RYE.

Serves 4
Working time: about 30 minutes
Total time: about 2 hours and 30 minutes (includes chilling)

Calories **245**
Protein **10g**
Cholesterol **0mg**
Total fat **10g**
Saturated fat **1g**
Sodium **255mg**

125 g	slightly stale wholemeal bread, crusts removed	4 oz
125 g	slightly stale black rye bread, crusts removed	4 oz
250 g	ripe tomatoes, skinned, seeded (page 14) and diced, seeds and juice reserved	8 oz
	canned or bottled tomato juice (optional)	
4	small black olives, stoned and finely chopped	4
125 g	cucumber, cut into 2.5 cm (1 inch) long bâtonnets	4 oz
4	small green olives, stoned and finely chopped	4
6	large basil leaves, shredded	6
6	large rocket leaves, shredded	6
1 tbsp	chopped fresh chervil leaves	1 tbsp
1 tbsp	finely chopped fresh tarragon	1 tbsp
1 tbsp	finely chopped flat-leaf parsley	1 tbsp
2 tbsp	virgin olive oil	2 tbsp
2 tbsp	white wine	2 tbsp
3 tbsp	red wine	3 tbsp
	freshly ground black pepper	
	basil sprigs, for garnish	

Grate or process the wholemeal bread and the rye bread to make breadcrumbs, placing the two types of bread in separate mixing bowls. Sieve the reserved seeds and juice from the tomatoes. This should yield about 10 cl (3½ fl oz); make up the quantity with some canned or bottled tomato juice, if necessary. Divide the tomato juice equally between the two bowls of breadcrumbs and mix it in thoroughly.

Add the tomatoes and black olives to the wholemeal breadcrumbs, and the cucumber and green olives to the rye breadcrumbs. Divide the basil, rocket, chervil, tarragon and parsley equally between the two bowls. Pour 1 tablespoon of olive oil into each bowl and mix the ingredients well. Finally, add as much of the wine as the mixture in each bowl will readily absorb, using the white wine with the wholemeal breadcrumbs and the red wine with the rye breadcrumbs. (The rye bread-crumbs will probably require a little more wine than the wholemeal to make a pleasantly moist mixture.) Season each bowl with black pepper. Cover the bowls with damp cloths to prevent the salads from drying out, and place them in the refrigerator for 2 hours, for the flavours to infuse.

Serve the bread salads cool or chilled, garnished with basil sprigs.

SUGGESTED ACCOMPANIMENT: *chicory and radicchio leaves.*

Bread, Cheese and Onion Pudding

Serves 8
Working time: about 40 minutes
Total time: about 2 hours and 30 minutes

Calories **300**
Protein **12g**
Cholesterol **60mg**
Total fat **14g**
Saturated fat **4g**
Sodium **485mg**

75 g	polyunsaturated margarine	2½ oz
2	large onions, thinly sliced	2
500 g	courgettes, julienned	1 lb
2 tsp	Dijon mustard	2 tsp
2	garlic cloves, crushed	2
24	thin slices white bread, crusts removed	24
2	eggs	2
2	egg whites	2
60 cl	skimmed milk	1 pint
	freshly ground black pepper	
90 g	Cheddar cheese, grated	3 oz

Heat 15 g (½ oz) of the margarine in a large, non-stick frying pan over medium heat. Add the onions and cook them gently for about 5 minutes, until they are soft but not brown. Add the courgette julienne and cook for another 6 minutes, stirring occasionally. Remove the pan from the heat and allow the courgettes and onions to cool for about 15 minutes.

Meanwhile, put the remaining 60 g (2 oz) of mar-garine in a small bowl with the mustard and garlic, and blend the ingredients together until smooth. Spread the mixture thinly over the sliced bread. Cut each slice of bread into four triangles.

Put the eggs, egg whites and milk into a mixing bowl, add some black pepper, and whisk the eggs and milk together lightly.

Grease a 30 by 22 cm (12 by 9 inch) ovenproof dish. Place one third of the bread triangles in a layer in the bottom of the dish, and spread half of the onion and courgette mixture over the top. Sprinkle on one third of the grated cheese. Add another third of the bread tri-angles, the remaining onion and courgette mixture, and another third of the cheese. Arrange the remain-ing triangles of bread decoratively on the top, overlap-ping them slightly. Pour the whisked eggs and milk over the bread. Scatter the remaining grated cheese evenly over the top. Set the pudding aside in a cool place for 1 hour, to allow the bread to soften and soak up the eggs and milk.

Preheat the oven to 190°C (375°F or Mark 5). Cook the pudding for 45 to 50 minutes, until it is well puffed up, set and golden-brown. Serve immediately.

SUGGESTED ACCOMPANIMENT: *red cabbage salad.*

Fennel, Broccoli and Okra Croustades

Serves 4
Working time: about 40 minutes
Total time: about 1 hour

Calories **270**
Protein **15g**
Cholesterol **10mg**
Total fat **11g**
Saturated fat **4g**
Sodium **465mg**

1	square brown tin loaf, at least 22 cm (9 inches) long	1
1 tsp	safflower oil	1 tsp
1	fennel bulb (about 250 g/8 oz), trimmed and chopped	1
250 g	broccoli florets	8 oz
20 g	unsalted butter	¾ oz
4	spring onions, trimmed and sliced diagonally	4
60 g	okra, trimmed and thinly sliced	2 oz
15 cl	plain low-fat yogurt	¼ pint
¼ tsp	salt	¼ tsp
⅛ tsp	ground allspice	⅛ tsp
	freshly ground black pepper	
30 g	pine-nuts, toasted	1 oz

Prepare four croustade cases from the loaf of bread, paint them with the oil, and bake them, as described below. While the croustade cases are baking, prepare the filling.

Place the fennel in a saucepan with water to cover, and cook it until it is just tender — 5 to 8 minutes. Add the broccoli florets and cook for a further 2 to 3 minutes, until they, too, are just tender. Drain the vegetables and keep them warm.

Melt the butter in a heavy-bottomed saucepan and add the spring onions and okra. Stir-fry them over medium-low heat for 4 to 5 minutes, until the okra be-gins to soften and looks slightly sticky. Add the yogurt, salt, allspice and some black pepper, and bring the mixture to the boil. Reduce the heat and simmer gently for 2 to 3 minutes, until the liquid has thickened a little. Add the fennel, broccoli and most of the pine-nuts, and heat them through.

Divide the mixture among the croustades, piling it up well in the centre. Sprinkle with the remaining pine-nuts, and serve the croustades immediately.

SUGGESTED ACCOMPANIMENT: *tomato salad.*

EDITOR'S NOTE: *To toast pine-nuts, place them in a small, heavy frying pan over medium-high heat and cook them for 1 to 2 minutes, stirring constantly, until they are golden-brown and release their aroma.*

Making Croustades

1 *CUTTING THE CASES. Trim the crust off a sandwich loaf. If the bread is soft, put it in the freezer for a few minutes. Cut 5 cm (2 inch) slices. Using a small, sharp knife, carefully cut a square in the top of each slice, 5 mm (¼ inch) in from each edge and within 5 mm (¼ inch) of the base.*

2 *LOOSENING THE CENTRES. Insert the knife horizontally 5 mm (¼ inch) above the base of one corner and swivel it; the knife point should penetrate beyond the centre of the square. Withdraw it and insert it into the corner diagonally opposite. Swivel the knife again to loosen the centre.*

3 *HOLLOWING OUT THE CASES. Use the tip of the knife to lever out the centre section of each square. Turn the cases upside down, and gently shake out any remaining crumbs. Place the cases on a lightly greased baking sheet.*

4 *BAKING THE CASES. Pour the oil into a small bowl and, with a pastry brush, apply a scant coating to the rims round each hollow. Place the cases in a preheated 170°C (325°F or Mark 3) oven and bake until crisp and golden — about 40 minutes; turn occasionally so they colour evenly.*

4 *Red pepper strips and watercress sprigs adorn this reinterpretation of a vegetarian classic — cauliflower cheese (recipe, opposite).*

Microwaving Vegetarian Dishes

A microwave oven offers far more than just a quick and clean alternative to conventional cooking. Meatless meals prepared in a microwave retain all their colours and fresh flavours. More important, few of the valuable vitamins and minerals are lost in the process, since vegetables cook in their own juices, or with only a few spoonfuls of added liquid. Also, because cooking times are generally so short, heat-sensitive vitamins are less likely to be destroyed by microwaving than by traditional techniques. Microwave ovens are ideal for low-fat cooking too; very little oil is required for the preparation of most vegetarian dishes.

The recipes on the following pages suggest the enticing variety of vegetarian meals that can be produced in a microwave oven. These range in style from a hearty layered bake of Jerusalem artichokes and potatoes *(page 126)* to a sophisticated presentation of stuffed vine leaves, burghul and hot tomatoes *(page 128)* — a complete meal that takes only about 30 minutes to prepare. Several of the recipes are inspired by far-flung traditional cuisines not normally associated with the space-age technology of microwave cooking. Sweet-and-sour tumbled vegetables *(page 133)* recreates the crisp and varied textures of a Chinese stir-fry — but without the stirring. Light and fluffy scrambled eggs, which cook to perfection in a microwave oven, assume a Basque accent with the addition of garlic and sweet peppers in the mixed vegetable pipérade on page 125.

A few simple techniques help ensure successful results in these and other microwave recipes. When covering a container with plastic film, make sure that steam can escape by folding back one corner. Use only film that is recommended for microwave cooking; the plasticizer present in ordinary plastic film may melt and drip into the food. Stirring the ingredients from time to time, and rotating the container, encourages even cooking, although if your oven has a turntable, turning the dish is unnecessary. And because food continues to cook after the oven has been switched off, observe any "standing time" called for by a recipe. The batter in the courgette and tomato clafoutis *(page 124)*, for instance, only sets completely after its 3 minutes' standing time. Rather than risk overdone food, it is advisable to use the shortest cooking time specified in a recipe. If a dish is not entirely cooked after standing, it can be returned to the oven.

All the recipes in this section have been tested in 650-watt and 700-watt ovens. Although power settings may vary among different ovens, the recipes use "high" to indicate 100 per cent power, "medium" for 50 per cent power and "low" for 10 per cent power.

Cauliflower Cheese Mould

Serves 6
Working (and total) time: about 50 minutes

Calories **185**
Protein **11g**
Cholesterol **100mg**
Total fat **11g**
Saturated fat **6g**
Sodium **270mg**

1 kg	cauliflower florets	2 lb
45 g	unsalted butter	1½ oz
45 g	plain flour	1½ oz
30 cl	skimmed milk	½ pint
60 g	Parmesan cheese, grated	2 oz
2	eggs, beaten	2
½ tsp	salt	½ tsp
	freshly ground black pepper	
¼ tsp	grated nutmeg	¼ tsp
	strips of peeled sweet red pepper, for garnish	
	watercress sprigs, for garnish	

Put the cauliflower florets into a very large bowl, add 6 tablespoons of cold water, then cover the bowl with plastic film, pulling it back at one corner. Cook on high for 15 to 20 minutes, stirring every 5 minutes, until the cauliflower is cooked but still slightly firm. Meanwhile, grease a 20 cm (8 inch) round dish. Line the bottom with greased non-stick parchment paper.

Drain any excess water from the cauliflower florets, then process them briefly in a food processor until they are finely broken up but not puréed. Set aside.

Put the butter into a large bowl and microwave it on high for 30 seconds, until melted. Mix in the flour, then gradually stir in the milk. Cook on high for 4 minutes, stirring every minute with a wire whisk, until thick. Remove from the microwave and beat in the Parmesan, eggs, salt, pepper, nutmeg and cauliflower.

Carefully spoon the cauliflower mixture into the prepared dish and level the surface. Cover the dish with plastic film, leaving a corner open. Cook on high for 12 to 15 minutes, until set, giving the dish a quarter turn every 3 minutes.

Remove the cauliflower mould from the oven and allow it to stand for 5 minutes, then carefully turn it out on to a flat serving dish. Garnish with the sweet pepper strips and watercress sprigs. Serve cut into wedges.

SUGGESTED ACCOMPANIMENTS: *new potatoes; mixed salad.*

EDITOR'S NOTE: *To peel a sweet red pepper using the microwave, prick the pepper several times with a fork or skewer and place it on a double layer of paper towels in the oven. Microwave on high for 5 minutes, until soft, turning once. Transfer the pepper to a bowl and cover it with plastic film. Leave it to sweat for 5 to 10 minutes, then peel it. Alternatively, follow the instructions on page 21.*

Courgette and Tomato Clafoutis

CLAFOUTIS, TRADITIONALLY BLACK CHERRIES BAKED IN A
SWEET PANCAKE BATTER, IS A SPECIALITY OF THE LIMOUSIN
DISTRICT OF FRANCE. IN THIS SAVOURY ADAPTATION,
VEGETABLES AND HERBS REPLACE THE FRUIT.

Serves 4
Working (and total) time: about 45 minutes

Calories **120**
Protein **9g**
Cholesterol **110mg**
Total fat **4g**
Saturated fat **1g**
Sodium **270mg**

2	eggs	2
30 g	wholemeal flour	1 oz
30 g	plain flour	1 oz
2 tbsp	wheat germ	2 tbsp
30 cl	skimmed milk	½ pint
½ tsp	salt	½ tsp
200 g	cherry tomatoes, pierced with a fine skewer	7 oz
250 g	courgettes, sliced into 1 cm (½ inch) rounds	8 oz
2	fresh thyme sprigs, leaves only, chopped if large	2
8	large basil leaves, torn into strips	8
½ tsp	bottled peppercorns, drained and rinsed	½ tsp
	freshly ground green pepper (optional)	

In a bowl, combine the eggs with the plain and
wholemeal flours and 1 tablespoon of the wheat germ.
Whisk in the milk and salt. Set the batter aside to rest
for 20 to 30 minutes.

Brush the base and sides of a 25 cm (10 inch)
diameter shallow microwave dish with a little olive oil
and sprinkle evenly with the remaining wheat germ.
Arrange the tomatoes and courgettes in the dish.

Stir the batter well, then mix in the herbs and peppercorns. Pour the mixture over the vegetables. Cover
the dish with plastic film, leaving one corner open. Microwave on medium, stirring the contents of the dish
from time to time, until the edges of the batter begin to
set — 3 to 5 minutes. Then microwave for a further 10
minutes, giving the dish a quarter turn every 3
minutes. Remove the plastic film, place a layer of ab-
sorbent paper towel lightly over the surface of the
clafoutis and cover it with a fresh piece of plastic film.
Allow the *clafoutis* to stand, covered, for 3 minutes.

The *clafoutis* should now be set in the centre. If it is
not, microwave it on medium for a further 2 to 3
minutes, then allow it to rest for 2 more minutes.

Serve the *clafoutis* warm, cut into wedges. Grind a
little green pepper over each portion if you like.

SUGGESTED ACCOMPANIMENTS: *sourdough rye bread; salad of
lamb's lettuce.*

Mixed Vegetable Pipérade

PIPÉRADE, A SPECIALITY OF THE BASQUE COUNTRY, IS A
SAVOURY DISH OF VEGETABLES AND SCRAMBLED EGGS. HERE,
BROCCOLI AND POTATO ARE INCLUDED IN ADDITION TO THE
TRADITIONAL SWEET PEPPERS.

Serves 4
Working (and total) time: about 20 minutes

Calories **120**
Protein **5g**
Cholesterol **110mg**
Total fat **7g**
Saturated fat **1g**
Sodium **250mg**

1 tbsp	virgin olive oil	1 tbsp
1	garlic clove, halved	1
¼ tsp	cayenne pepper	¼ tsp
125 g	potatoes, cut into 1 cm (½ inch) cubes	4 oz
125 g	broccoli, cut into small florets, stems peeled and finely sliced	4 oz
1	sweet yellow pepper, seeded, deribbed and cut into 2.5 cm (1 inch) squares	1
1	sweet red pepper, seeded, deribbed and cut into 2.5 cm (1 inch) squares	1
½ tsp	cornflour, mixed with 1 tsp cold water	½ tsp
½ tsp	salt	½ tsp
2	eggs, beaten	2
	crushed hot red pepper flakes (optional)	

Place the oil and garlic in a wide, shallow dish. Microwave on medium for about 1½ minutes, or until the oil is hot and infused with garlic. Discard the garlic and sprinkle the cayenne pepper over the oil. Add the potato cubes, stir them to coat them in oil and spice, then cook them on high, covered with plastic film pulled back at one corner, for 1 minute.

Stir the potato cubes again, then add the broccoli and yellow and red peppers. Cover as before and microwave on high for 5 minutes. Stir the contents of the dish twice during this time, replacing the plastic film each time. After cooking, stir once more and allow the vegetables to rest, covered, for 2 minutes.

Stir the cornflour mixture and the salt into the beaten eggs, then pour the egg mixture over the vegetables. Stir the contents of the dish, and microwave on medium for 3 minutes. Keep the dish covered during cooking as before, but stir the contents after every minute. The egg mixture and the juices should be almost set at the end of this time.

Remove the dish from the oven and rest the contents, covered, for a further minute. Serve the pipérade immediately, sprinkled with the crushed red pepper flakes, if you are using them.

SUGGESTED ACCOMPANIMENT: *warm crusty bread rolls.*

Jerusalem Artichoke Gratin

Serves 4
Working (and total) time: about 30 minutes

Calories **200**
Protein **9g**
Cholesterol **20mg**
Total fat **5g**
Saturated fat **3g**
Sodium **410mg**

500 g	new potatoes, scrubbed	1 lb
500 g	firm Jerusalem artichokes, scrubbed	1 lb
1 tbsp	fresh lemon juice	1 tbsp
1 tbsp	potato flour	1 tbsp
2 tbsp	dry white wine	2 tbsp
½ to 1 tbsp	Dijon mustard	½ to 1 tbsp
2 tbsp	soured cream	2 tbsp
2 tbsp	plain low-fat yogurt	2 tbsp
½ tsp	salt	½ tsp
250 g	tomatoes, sliced, slices halved	8 oz
	freshly ground black pepper (optional)	
	grated nutmeg	
60 g	Gruyère cheese, finely grated	2 oz
1 tbsp	finely chopped parsley	1 tbsp

Halve the potatoes and place them in a shallow dish with 3 tablespoons of cold water. Cover them with plastic film, leaving a corner open, and microwave on high for 8 minutes, stirring once or twice during this time. Leave the potatoes to rest, covered, for a further 2 minutes, then immediately drain them. Peel the potatoes and slice them into thin rounds.

Halve the artichokes, or quarter them if they are large, then place them in a shallow dish with the lemon juice and 2 tablespoons of cold water. Cover with plastic film, leaving a corner open, and cook on high for about 6 minutes, stirring three or four times during cooking. Leave the artichokes to rest, covered, for 2 minutes, then immediately drain them. Peel the artichokes, then slice them into rounds a little thicker than the potatoes. (Any artichokes that are too soft to slice can be placed under slices, or piled into the centre, when you assemble the gratin.)

In a mixing bowl, mix together the potato flour and white wine, then stir in the mustard according to taste, the soured cream, yogurt and ¼ teaspoon of the salt. Place the bowl in the microwave and cook on low for 1½ minutes, or until the sauce thickens, stirring every 30 seconds. Remove the bowl from the oven, whisk the sauce vigorously, and set it aside.

In a 22 cm (9 inch) round gratin dish, arrange concentric rings of slices of potato, artichoke and tomato, then arrange a few more artichoke slices in the centre. Sprinkle the tomato with the remaining salt, and with some black pepper if desired. Pour the mustard sauce over the artichokes and sprinkle with a little grated nutmeg. Sprinkle the cheese over the potato. Scatter the parsley over the top of the gratin.

Cook, loosely covered, on high for 7 to 10 minutes, turning the dish once or twice, until the gratin is hot in the centre. Rest it for 2 to 3 minutes before serving.

SUGGESTED ACCOMPANIMENT: *crisp green salad with a few toasted flaked nuts, or steamed broccoli.*

Salad-Filled Potato Pie

Serves 6
Working time: about 30 minutes
Total time: about 40 minutes

Calories **190**
Protein **5g**
Cholesterol **45mg**
Total fat **4g**
Saturated fat **1g**
Sodium **230mg**

1 kg	large potatoes, scrubbed	2 lb
1 tbsp	potato flour	1 tbsp
2 tbsp	skimmed milk	2 tbsp
1	egg	1
3 cl	plain low-fat yogurt	1 fl oz
45 g	crème fraîche	1½ oz
2 tbsp	finely chopped fresh dill	2 tbsp
¾ tsp	salt	¾ tsp
	freshly grated nutmeg	
1 tsp	safflower oil	1 tsp
60 g	watercress leaves, roughly chopped	2 oz
100 g	cucumber, peeled and cut into 2.5 cm (1 inch) long bâtonnets	3½ oz
200 g	tomatoes, skinned, seeded and chopped	7 oz
	freshly ground black pepper	
½ tsp	mild paprika	½ tsp

Prick each of the potatoes all over with a fork and arrange them in a circle, on a double layer of paper towels, in the microwave. Microwave on high for 12 to 15 minutes, rotating the paper towels every 3 minutes, until the potatoes are cooked through. Leave the potatoes to rest for a further 3 minutes, then peel them and mash them.

In a bowl, blend the potato flour with the milk, then beat in the egg, yogurt, crème fraîche, dill, ½ teaspoon of the salt and some grated nutmeg. Beat this mixture into the mashed potato.

Brush a 25 by 16 cm (10 by 6½ inch) baking dish with the safflower oil. Spread half of the potato mixture over the base and sides of the dish. Scatter the watercress over the potato to within 1 cm (½ inch) of the sides. Arrange the cucumber and the chopped tomatoes on top of the watercress. Sprinkle the filling with the remaining ¼ teaspoon of salt and a generous grinding of black pepper.

Carefully spread the remaining potato over the filling to enclose it completely. Mark the surface with a fork and sift the paprika evenly over the top.

Cover the dish with plastic film, leaving two opposite corners open. Microwave on high for 7 to 10 minutes, giving the dish a quarter turn every 2 minutes, until heated through. Remove the pie from the oven and allow it to rest for a further 3 minutes. Serve the potato pie cut into squares.

SUGGESTED ACCOMPANIMENT: *curly endive and red lollo lettuce salad, with a fromage frais and mustard dressing.*

EDITOR'S NOTE: *To skin tomatoes in the microwave, pierce the skin once or twice, then microwave on high for about 45 seconds, until the skin starts to peel away. Alternatively, follow the instructions on page 14.*

Stuffed Vine Leaves with Burghul and Tomatoes

Serves 4
Working (and total) time: about 30 minutes

Calories **290**	200 g	burghul, rinsed and drained	7 oz
Protein **15g**	½ litre	unsalted vegetable stock (recipe, page 9)	16 fl oz
Cholesterol **25mg**			
Total fat **7g**	12	vine leaves, fresh or preserved	12
Saturated fat **1g**	1 tsp	cumin seeds	1 tsp
Sodium **350mg**	2 tbsp	finely chopped fresh mint	2 tbsp
	½ tsp	ground cinnamon	½ tsp
	75 g	feta cheese, cubed and rinsed	2½ oz
	75 g	fresh breadcrumbs	2½ oz
	100 g	sheep's milk yogurt	3½ oz
	½ to 1 tbsp	lemon juice	½ to 1 tbsp
	½ tsp	virgin olive oil	½ tsp
	400 g	beef tomatoes, sliced	14 oz
	12	large basil leaves, torn	12
		freshly ground black pepper	

Place the burghul in a 1 litre (1 ¾ pint) bowl. Bring the stock to the boil and pour it over the burghul. Stir, cover the burghul with plastic film, and set it aside while you prepare the vine leaves.

Rinse the leaves and place them in a bowl; if you are using preserved leaves, rinse very thoroughly. Cover the leaves with a generous quantity of boiling water, cover the bowl with plastic film, leaving a corner open, and microwave on high for 5 minutes, to soften the leaves. Drain them in a colander, refresh them under cold running water and spread them out on paper towels or a tea towel to dry.

Place the cumin seeds in a small dish, cover them and microwave them on high for 2 minutes, until they are warm and aromatic.

Set the bowl containing the burghul in the microwave oven, pull back a corner of the plastic film and microwave on high for 5 minutes. Stir in the mint and cinnamon, cover the bowl completely, and set it aside until the rest of the meal is ready to serve, by which time all the stock will have been absorbed.

Mash the cheese with a fork and blend it with the breadcrumbs, yogurt and cumin seeds, adding the lemon juice, according to taste. Place a vine leaf, veined side up, on the work surface. Place a heaped teaspoon of the cheese mixture above the base of the leaf, fold the stalk end over the stuffing, then fold both long edges over to enclose the stuffing completely. Gently roll the stuffing mound towards the leaf tip, tucking in the edges if they loosen, to form a compact roll. Stuff the remaining vine leaves in the same way.

In a round dish, arrange the stuffed leaves to resemble the spokes of a wheel. Brush the leaves with the olive oil, cover the dish with plastic film, again leaving one corner open, and microwave on high for 3 to 4 minutes, until the stuffed leaves are heated through; rotate the dish once or twice during this time. Remove the vine leaves from the oven and let them rest in their dish for 2 minutes while you warm the tomatoes.

Arrange the tomatoes evenly over the base of a wide, shallow dish, overlapping the slices slightly if necessary. Sprinkle on the torn basil leaves and some black pepper, cover the dish loosely and heat the tomatoes on high for 2 minutes, until hot and aromatic.

Fluff up the burghul mixture with a fork and arrange it on four warmed individual plates together with three vine-leaf packages per serving, and a portion of the hot tomato salad.

Warm Camembert and Fruit Salad

Serves 4
Working (and total) time: about 20 minutes

Calories **150**
Protein **5g**
Cholesterol **10mg**
Total fat **12g**
Saturated fat **1g**
Sodium **380mg**

60 g	Camembert, rind removed, cut into 12 cubes	2 oz
1 tsp	crushed mixed white, black, green and pink peppercorns	1 tsp
100 g	broccoli, cut into tiny florets, stalks peeled and finely sliced	3 ½ oz
½ tbsp	sesame oil	½ tbsp
½ tbsp	safflower oil	½ tbsp
1	garlic clove, lightly crushed	1
2.5 cm	piece fresh ginger root, sliced	1 inch
1	large ripe peach, peeled, halved, stoned and sliced, slices halved if too large	1
½	avocado (about 75 g/2 ½ oz), peeled and stoned, flesh cut into cubes	½
1 tbsp	balsamic vinegar, or 2 ½ tsp red wine vinegar mixed with ¼ tsp clear honey	1 tbsp
½ tsp	salt	½ tsp
60 g	radicchio leaves, washed and dried, torn into pieces	2 oz
100 g	mixed lettuce leaves, washed and dried	3 ½ oz

Roll the cubes of Camembert in the peppercorns and chill them in the refrigerator while preparing the salad.

Place the broccoli in a bowl with 2 tablespoons of cold water, cover with plastic film, leaving a corner open, and microwave on high for 1 ½ to 2 minutes, until no longer tough but still very firm. Drain the broccoli, return it to the bowl, cover it and set it aside.

Put the oils in a dish with the garlic and ginger, and cook on medium for 2 to 3 minutes until hot, stirring once or twice during this time. Remove the garlic and ginger with a slotted spoon and discard them. Place the peach slices in the dish with the flavoured oil. Cover the dish as before and microwave on high for 1 minute. Stir the peach slices, add the avocado, cover again and cook on high for another minute. Then add the vinegar, salt and broccoli. Cover and cook on high for a further minute. Finally, toss the radicchio in the dish, stir well, cover the dish and set it aside.

Arrange the mixed lettuce leaves round the edge of a large serving platter, or on four individual plates. Place the Camembert cubes, evenly spaced, on a plate and microwave them on medium for 20 seconds, until just warm. Quickly arrange the warm salad in the centre of the lettuce and sprinkle the Camembert cubes on top. Serve at once.

SUGGESTED ACCOMPANIMENT: *white and granary bread.*

EDITOR'S NOTE: *A nectarine may be substituted for the peach; there is no need to peel a nectarine before use.*

Potato, Carrot and Cauliflower Curry

Serves 6
Working time: about 30 minutes
Total time: about 1 hour

Calories **230**
Protein **6g**
Cholesterol **0mg**
Total fat **11g**
Saturated fat **5g**
Sodium **230mg**

2 tbsp	virgin olive oil	2 tbsp
2	onions, finely chopped	2
60 g	fresh ginger root, peeled and grated	2 oz
3	garlic cloves, crushed	3
2	fresh hot green chili peppers, seeded and finely chopped (caution, page 25)	2
2 tsp	paprika	2 tsp
½ tsp	ground turmeric	½ tsp
1 tsp	ground cumin	1 tsp
45 cl	unsalted vegetable stock (recipe, page 9)	¾ pint
500 g	potatoes, cut into 1 cm (½ inch) dice	1 lb
250 g	carrots, cut into 1 cm (½ inch) dice	8 oz
250 g	cauliflower florets	8 oz
175 g	French beans, trimmed and cut into 2.5 cm (1 inch) lengths	6 oz
175 g	shelled peas, or frozen peas, thawed	6 oz
90 g	coconut milk powder or creamed coconut, blended with 12.5 cl (4 fl oz) warm water	3 oz
1 tbsp	cornflour, blended with 3 tbsp cold water	1 tbsp
½ tsp	salt	½ tsp
	freshly ground black pepper	

Put the olive oil and onions into a large bowl. Microwave on high, uncovered, for 5 to 6 minutes, until the onions are softened, stirring half way through the cooking time. Stir in the ginger, garlic, chilies, paprika, turmeric and cumin and cook on high, uncovered, for 2 minutes. Add the stock, potatoes, carrots and cauliflower and stir well, then cover the bowl with plastic film, pulling back one corner to allow steam to escape. Cook on high for 20 minutes, stirring every 5 minutes. Then stir in the beans and peas and cook, covered as before, for a further 10 minutes, until the vegetables are tender.

Stir the coconut milk and cornflour mixtures into the vegetables and cook, uncovered, on high for 5 minutes, stirring half way through. Season with the salt and some black pepper. Allow the curry to stand for 5 minutes before serving.

SUGGESTED ACCOMPANIMENTS: *pasta tossed in chopped parsley; lemon wedges; thinly sliced onion rings.*

Spiced Bean Medley

BEANS COOKED IN THE MICROWAVE TAKE ALMOST AS LONG AS WHEN COOKED CONVENTIONALLY, BUT HAVE THE ADVANTAGE THAT HOWEVER LONG THEY COOK THEY DO NOT GO MUSHY.

Serves 6
Working time: about 20 minutes
Total time: about 2 hours and 40 minutes (includes soaking)

Calories **220**
Protein **12g**
Cholesterol **0mg**
Total fat **4g**
Saturated fat **0g**
Sodium **25mg**

125 g	dried red kidney beans, picked over	4 oz
90 g	dried pinto beans, picked over	3 oz
60 g	dried black kidney beans, picked over	2 oz
30 g	dried aduki beans, picked over	1 oz
1 tbsp	safflower oil	1 tbsp
2	garlic cloves, sliced	2
1	onion, diced	1
1	small fresh red chili pepper, seeded and finely chopped (caution, page 25)	1
1	small fresh green chili pepper, seeded and finely chopped (caution, page 25)	1
1	sweet red pepper, seeded, deribbed and cut into strips	1
⅛ tsp	salt	⅛ tsp
500 g	tomatoes, skinned, seeded and chopped	1 lb

Put all the beans into a large casserole, pour in about 2 litres (3½ pints) of boiling water and microwave, uncovered, on high for 15 minutes. Stir the beans, then set them aside to soak for 1 hour.

Put the oil, garlic, onion, chili peppers and sweet red pepper into a casserole and cook, uncovered, on high for 3 minutes. Stir in the salt and the tomatoes, then set the sauce aside until needed.

After the beans have soaked, drain them and rinse them well in cold water. Return them to the casserole and cover them with fresh boiling water. Cook the beans, uncovered, on high for 30 minutes, then cook them on medium for a further 50 minutes. At the end of cooking, drain the beans and return them to the casserole, together with the sauce. Cook on high for 3 to 5 minutes, until thoroughly heated through. Stir the medley before serving it.

SUGGESTED ACCOMPANIMENT: *steamed broccoli spears.*

EDITOR'S NOTE: *To skin tomatoes in the microwave, pierce the skin once or twice, then microwave on high for about 45 seconds, until the skin starts to peel away. Alternatively, follow the instructions on page 14. The spiced bean medley may also be served cold, in which case a crisp green salad makes a good accompaniment.*

Oriental Parchment Parcels

Serves 4
Working (and total) time: about 20 minutes

Calories **100**
Protein **5g**
Cholesterol **0mg**
Total fat **8g**
Saturated fat **0g**
Sodium **10mg**

4 tsp	sesame oil	4 tsp
200 g	firm tofu, cut into 2 cm (¾ inch) cubes	7 oz
100 g	fresh shiitake mushrooms, finely sliced	3½ oz
75 g	baby sweetcorn, cut into 2.5 cm (1 inch) lengths	2½ oz
75 g	courgettes, sliced	2½ oz
60 g	young carrots, cut into thin ribbons with a vegetable peeler	2 oz
4 tsp	low-sodium soy sauce or shoyu	4 tsp
2	large garlic cloves, halved, or four small garlic cloves	2
5 cm	piece fresh ginger root, cut in half	2 inch

Take four sheets of greaseproof or non-stick parchment paper, each about 25 cm (10 inches) square, and brush the centres with 1 teaspoon of the oil.

Divide the tofu cubes and vegetables equally among the four pieces of paper, piling the ingredients on to the oiled section. In a small bowl, mix the remaining oil with the soy sauce. Using a garlic press, crush the garlic and ginger and add the pulp and juices to the bowl, discarding any coarse fibres that may have been pushed through the press. Sprinkle a quarter of this mixture over each pile of vegetables.

Bring two facing edges of one of the paper sheets together above the vegetables, and make a double fold in the edges, to seal and join them. Then make a double fold in each of the two open ends, to seal the parcel completely. Prepare the other three parcels in the same way, and place all four in a wide shallow dish, arranging them towards the outside edges of the dish so that they will cook evenly.

Microwave on high for 4 to 5 minutes, until the vegetables are tender, giving the dish a quarter turn after each minute. Serve as soon as possible, keeping the parcels closed until the moment of serving.

SUGGESTED ACCOMPANIMENT: *Oriental noodles sprinkled with finely sliced spring onion.*

Sweet-and-Sour Tumbled Vegetables

Serves 4
Working time: about 30 minutes
Total time: about 45 minutes

Calories **150**
Protein **5g**
Cholesterol **0mg**
Total fat **5g**
Saturated fat **0g**
Sodium **25mg**

1 tbsp	safflower oil	1 tbsp
2	garlic cloves, crushed	2
1 tbsp	finely chopped fresh ginger root	1 tbsp
250 g	courgettes, ends trimmed, sliced diagonally into 5 mm (¼ inch) thick slices	8 oz
125 g	okra, stalk ends trimmed	4 oz
1	bunch spring onions, roots trimmed, all but 5 cm (2 inches) of green top cut off, sliced diagonally into 2.5 cm (1 inch) lengths	1
1	sweet red pepper, seeded, deribbed and cut into strips	1
1	sweet green pepper, seeded, deribbed and cut into strips	1
1	sweet yellow pepper, seeded, deribbed and cut into strips	1
1	sweet orange pepper, seeded, deribbed and cut into strips	1
125 g	bean sprouts, picked over	4 oz
125 g	baby sweetcorn, stalks trimmed if necessary	4 oz
1 tsp	clear honey	1 tsp
2 tbsp	low-sodium soy sauce or shoyu	2 tbsp
15 cl	unsweetened pineapple juice	¼ pint
350 g	fresh pineapple, diced	12 oz

Put the oil, garlic and ginger into a large casserole and microwave on high for 2 minutes. Add all the vegetables, stirring well. Stir the honey, soy sauce and pineapple juice together in a jug or bowl. Pour this sauce over the vegetables and stir in the pineapple.

Cover the casserole with plastic film, leaving one corner open. Microwave on high for 10 to 12 minutes, until the vegetables are cooked but still crisp; during this time, give the casserole a quarter turn every 3 minutes, and stir the contents after 5 minutes' cooking.

Remove the casserole from the oven and allow the vegetables to stand, covered, for 5 minutes. Then stir them once more and serve.

SUGGESTED ACCOMPANIMENT: *steamed rice.*

EDITOR'S NOTE: *For best results, select tender young vegetables for this dish. If older vegetables are used, increase the cooking time by 1 to 2 minutes.*

Savoy Timbale with Tomato Sauce

Serves 4
Working time: about 40 minutes
Total time: about 1 hour and 15 minutes

Calories **380**
Protein **18g**
Cholesterol **20mg**
Total fat **12g**
Saturated fat **5g**
Sodium **485mg**

12	large savoy or other dark green cabbage leaves, protruding ribs trimmed away	12
1	onion, sliced	1
1	leek, trimmed, split, washed thoroughly to remove all grit and sliced	1
175 g	carrots, diced	6 oz
175 g	shelled fresh broad beans, skins removed	6 oz
1 tbsp	safflower oil	1 tbsp
175 g	brown rice	6 oz
20 cl	unsalted vegetable stock (recipe, page 9)	7 fl oz
⅛ tsp	salt	⅛ tsp
250 g	tomatoes, halved	8 oz
1 tbsp	chopped fresh basil	1 tbsp
1 tbsp	Worcester sauce	1 tbsp
125 g	low-fat smoked cheese, grated	4 oz
	freshly ground black pepper	
Tomato sauce		
6	tomatoes, halved	6
⅛ tsp	salt	⅛ tsp
	freshly ground black pepper	
1 tsp	cornflour, mixed with 1 tbsp water	1 tsp
1 tsp	tomato paste	1 tsp

First, make the tomato sauce. Place the tomatoes, cut side down, on a plate and microwave them on high for 4 to 5 minutes. Remove the skins as soon as the tomatoes are cool enough to handle. Mash the flesh in a bowl, or press it through a sieve for a smoother sauce, and season the mixture with the salt and some black pepper. Stir in the cornflour mixture and the tomato paste. Cover the bowl with plastic film pulled back at one corner, and microwave the sauce on high for 2 to 3 minutes, until it is thick. Stir it and set it aside.

Arrange the cabbage leaves in a large casserole, keeping them as flat as possible. Add 6 tablespoons of cold water, cover with plastic film left open at one corner, and microwave on high for 6 minutes. Drain the leaves well on paper towels and set them aside.

Put the onion, leek, carrots, broad beans and oil in a large casserole and cook them, uncovered, on high for 5 minutes, stirring half way through the cooking time. Stir in the rice, stock and salt, cover as before, and microwave on medium for 12 to 15 minutes, until the rice is almost cooked. Remove the rice mixture from the oven and leave it to stand for 5 minutes.

Meanwhile, place the tomatoes cut side down on a plate. Cook on high for 3 minutes, then remove and discard the skins and seeds. Roughly chop the flesh.

Drain off any excess water from the rice mixture, and stir in the tomatoes, basil, Worcester sauce, grated cheese and some black pepper.

Line the base and sides of an 18 cm (7 inch) soufflé dish with eight of the cabbage leaves, overlapping them and allowing the top part of each leaf to overhang the top of the dish. Tip the rice mixture into the centre of the dish. Place the remaining cabbage leaves on top of the filling and bring the overhanging leaves in over the top, pressing down firmly. Cover the dish with plastic film, leaving one corner open. Microwave on high for 8 minutes, giving the dish a quarter turn after every 2 minutes. Remove the timbale from the oven and drain off any excess water.

Reheat the tomato sauce on high for 2 to 3 minutes, then stir it and pour it into a serving bowl. Invert the timbale on to a serving plate and serve it hot, cut into wedges, accompanied by the tomato sauce.

Mushroom Quiche

Serves 4
Working (and total) time: about 40 minutes

Calories **265**
Protein **10g**
Cholesterol **30mg**
Total fat **14g**
Saturated fat **6g**
Sodium **120mg**

125 g	wholemeal flour	4 oz
30 g	unsalted peanut butter	1 oz
30 g	unsalted butter, chilled	1 oz
Mushroom filling		
175 g	fresh shiitake mushrooms	6 oz
175 g	oyster mushrooms	6 oz
15 g	unsalted butter	½ oz
15 g	wholemeal flour	½ oz
15 cl	skimmed milk	¼ pint
1 tbsp	chopped parsley	1 tbsp
¼ tsp	salt	¼ tsp
	freshly ground black pepper	

To make the pastry, put the flour into a mixing bowl and lightly rub in the peanut butter and butter, until the mixture resembles fine breadcrumbs. Using a round-bladed knife to mix, add enough cold water to the flour mixture to form a fairly firm dough — about 3 to 4 tablespoons. Turn the dough out on to a work surface dusted with a little flour, and roll it out to line an 18 cm (7 inch) fluted flan dish. This kind of dough is quite crumbly, so use any trimmings to fill in the cracks. Chill the pastry case in the refrigerator for 5 minutes, then line it with a paper towel. Press the towel gently into the contours of the case. Microwave on high for 4 to 5 minutes, until the pastry looks dry.

For the filling, put the mushrooms into a bowl with 2 tablespoons of cold water. Cover with plastic film, leaving one corner open, and cook on high for 2 minutes. Remove from the oven and set aside. In a separate bowl, heat the butter on high for 15 to 20 seconds, or until melted. Stir in the flour and then whisk in the milk. Add the parsley and cook on high for 3 minutes, stirring every minute with a wire whisk. Season with the salt and some pepper, then add the mushrooms and cook on high, covered as before, for a further 3 minutes, stirring after the first minute.

Remove the paper towel from the pastry case, pour in the mushroom filling and serve immediately.

SUGGESTED ACCOMPANIMENT: *rice salad or green salad.*

EDITOR'S NOTE: *If shiitake and oyster mushrooms are not available, you can use a mixture of small open cup mushrooms and button mushrooms instead.*

Nutritional Values

The figures refer to 100 g (3½ oz) of raw ingredient, the edible part only, fresh unless stated.

A dash indicates that no information was available.

tr indicates that a trace is known to be present.

The figures given should be taken as a guide only; the composition of many foods can vary.

rda = recommended daily amount.

*contains oxalic acid, which may inhibit absorption of the vegetable's calcium.

**measured in retinol equivalents.

	CALORIES 1900-2900 rda	PROTEIN 47-72 rda	CARBOHYDRATES 230-360 rda	FOLIC ACID 200 rda	VITAMIN A ACTIVITY** 750 rda	VITAMIN C 30 rda	CALCIUM 400-500 rda	SODIUM 2000 max. rda	POTASSIUM 1875 min. rda	DIETARY FIBRE 25-30 rda
		g	g	mcg	mcg	mg	mg	mg	mg	g
Fruits and Vegetables: Apples	45	tr	12	5	5	3	5	tr	120	2
Apricots	30	tr	7	5	250	7	15	0	320	2
Artichoke, globe (1)	30	3	11	90	50	15	50	45	43	2
Artichokes, Jerusalem	40	2	15	—	15	4	15	—	—	1
Asparagus	25	3	5	—	270	35	20	2	280	1
Aubergines	15	1	3	20	tr	5	10	3	240	3
Avocados	225	4	2	65	15	15	15	tr	400	2
Bamboo shoots	25	3	5	—	tr	5	15	tr	535	1
Banana	80	1	20	20	35	10	10	tr	350	4
Beans, French	10	tr	1	30	65	5	40	tr	100	3
Beans, broad	105	8	20	—	65	30	25	4	471	2
Beans, runner	25	2	4	60	65	20	25	tr	280	3
Bean sprouts	30	4	5	15	0	20	15	tr	35	3
Beetroot	30	1	6	90	tr	6	25	85	300	3
Broccoli	25	3	3	130	415	110	100	12	340	4
Brussels sprouts	25	4	3	110	65	90	100	10	340	4
Cabbage, Chinese	15	2	3	75	45	30	45	25	255	1
Cabbage, green	20	3	3	90	50	55	55	7	390	3
Cabbage, red	20	2	3	90	3	55	55	30	300	3
Cabbage, Savoy	25	3	3	90	50	60	75	25	260	3
Carrots	25	1	5	15	2000	6	50	95	220	3
Cauliflower	15	2	2	40	5	60	20	8	350	2
Celeriac	40	2	9	—	0	8	45	100	300	1
Celery	10	1	1	12	tr	7	50	140	280	2
Chicory	10	2	1	50	0	5	15	7	180	—
Courgettes	20	1	4	50	95	20	30	1	200	1
Cucumber	10	1	2	16	tr	8	23	13	140	tr
Fennel bulbs	50	4	10	—	—	—	—	—	—	2
Garlic (1 clove)	4	tr	1	tr	0	1	5	1	12	tr
Kale	55	6	9	—	3000	185	250	75	380	1
Kohlrabi	30	2	6	0	6	66	40	8	370	1
Leeks	30	2	6	30	6	20	60	10	310	3
Lemons	15	tr	3	7	0	80	110	5	160	5

	CALORIES 1900-2900 rda	PROTEIN 47-72 rda	CARBOHYDRATES 230-360 rda	FOLIC ACID 200 rda	VITAMIN A ACTIVITY** 750 rda	VITAMIN C 30 rda	CALCIUM 400-500 rda	SODIUM 2000 max. rda	POTASSIUM 1875 min. rda	DIETARY FIBRE 25-30 rda
		g	g	mcg	mcg	mg	mg	mg	mg	g
Fruits and Vegetables: Lettuce	10	1	1	34	165	15	25	9	240	2
Mango	60	tr	15	—	200	30	10	5	190	2
Mushrooms, dried	290	10	60	—	0	0	75	40	1480	—
Mushrooms, fresh	15	2	0	25	0	3	3	9	470	3
Nectarines	50	tr	12	5	85	10	tr	10	270	2
Okra	20	2	2	100	15	25	70	7	190	3
Onions	25	1	5	15	0	10	30	10	140	1
Oranges	35	tr	9	40	10	50	40	tr	200	2
Parsley (5 tbsp chopped)	5	1	tr	—	1165	40	85	8	270	2
Parsnips	50	2	11	65	0	15	55	17	340	4
Peaches	35	tr	10	tr	85	10	5	tr	260	1
Pears	40	tr	10	10	tr	tr	10	tr	130	2
Peas (shelled)	65	6	10	—	50	25	15	1	340	5
Peas, mange-tout	50	3	12	—	65	50	60	6	170	4
Peppers, chili, green	20	1	5	—	250	130	9	13	215	1
Peppers, chili, red	116	6	10	—	1100	95	85	25	1285	—
Peppers, sweet	15	1	2	11	90	100	9	2	210	1
Pineapple	45	tr	12	10	10	25	10	tr	250	1
Potatoes	90	2	20	15	tr	15	8	7	570	2
Pumpkin	15	1	4	13	250	5	40	1	310	1
Radishes	15	1	3	24	tr	25	45	60	240	1
Spinach, cooked	30	5	1	140	2000	25	600	120	490	6
Spinach*, raw	25	3	4	—	2430	30	95	70	470	1
Spring onions (green part included)	35	1	9	40	600	10	140	13	230	3
Swedes	20	1	4	27	0	25	55	50	140	3
Sweet potatoes	90	1	20	50	665	25	20	20	320	3
Sweetcorn	125	4	25	50	40	9	4	1	300	4
Tomatoes	14	1	3	30	100	20	13	3	290	2
Turnips	20	1	4	20	0	25	60	60	240	3
Vine leaves	15	4	tr	—	380	15	390	—	45	5
Water chestnuts	50	1	13	—	0	6	20	14	155	—
Watercress	14	3	1	200	500	60	220	60	310	4
Yam	130	2	32	—	tr	10	10	—	500	4

The figures refer to 100g (3½oz) of raw ingredient, the edible part only, fresh unless stated.

A dash indicates that no information was available.

tr indicates that a trace is known to be present.

The figures given should be taken as a guide only; the composition of many foods can vary.

rda = recommended daily amount.

		CALORIES 1900-2900 rda	PROTEIN 47-72 rda	TOTAL FAT 72-109 rda	SATURATED FAT 32-48 max. rda	CARBOHYDRATES 230-360 rda	CALCIUM 400-500 rda	SODIUM 2000 max. rda	POTASSIUM 1875 min. rda	IRON 10-12 rda	DIETARY FIBRE 25-30 rda
			g	g	g	g	mg	mg	mg	mg	g
Grains:	Barley, whole grain	325	10	2	—	70	50	5	560	6	15
	Buckwheat groats, (kasha)	335	10	2	—	75	45	—	445	3	7
	Burghul	350	13	2	—	70	40	50	315	4	10
	Cornmeal	370	9	3	—	75	20	tr	285	3	4
	Couscous	225	6	1	—	50	20	—	—	5	—
	Flour, plain	350	10	1	—	80	150	tr	140	2	3
	Flour, wholemeal	320	13	2	—	65	35	tr	360	4	10
	Millet	355	6	2	—	75	40	20	365	—	—
	Oats	400	12	9	2	70	55	35	370	4	7
	Rice, brown	350	8	2	—	80	30	10	215	2	4
	Rice, white	360	7	1	—	85	5	5	110	tr	2
	Semolina	350	10	2	—	75	20	10	170	1	3
	Wheatgerm	365	28	10	—	50	65	10	825	7	2
Pulses:	Lentils	305	24	1	—	53	40	35	670	8	12
	Chick-peas	320	20	6	—	50	140	40	800	6	15
	Aduki beans	325	21	1	—	59	80	15	1500	6	4
	Black-eyed peas	345	23	2	—	62	75	30	1025	6	—
	Broad beans, boiled	50	4	1	—	7	20	20	230	1	4
	Butter beans	275	19	1	—	50	85	60	1700	6	22
	Haricot beans	270	21	2	—	45	180	40	1160	7	25
	Kidney beans, red or black	270	22	2	—	45	140	40.	1160	7	25
	Mung beans	230	22	1	—	36	100	30	850	8	22
	Pinto beans	350	23	1	—	64	135	10	985	6	—
	Soya beans	400	35	32	5	32	225	5	1505	9	—
Nuts and Seeds:	Almonds	565	17	54	4	4	250	5	860	4	14
	Cashew nuts	560	17	46	5	29	40	15	—	4	—
	Chestnuts	170	2	3	tr	37	45	10	500	1	7
	Hazlenuts	380	8	36	3	7	45	tr	350	1	6
	Peanuts	570	24	49	9	9	60	5	680	2	8
	Pine-nuts	620	35	51	—	2	515	50	890	2	—
	Pistachio nuts	625	20	54	—	15	140	tr	—	14	—
	Walnuts	525	11	52	6	5	60	tr	690	2	5
	Pumpkin seeds	600	30	47	—	11	40	—	—	9	—
	Sesame seeds	580	17	53	7	14	750	60	375	12	—
	Sunflower seeds	490	17	33	—	15	90	30	—	6	—

	CALORIES 1900-2900 rda	PROTEIN 47-72 rda	TOTAL FAT 72-109 max. rda	SATURATED FAT 32-48 max. rda	CHOLESTEROL 300 max. rda	CARBOHYDRATES 230-360 rda	CALCIUM 400-500 rda	SODIUM 2000 max. rda	IRON 10-12 rda
		g	g	g	mg	g	mg	mg	mg
Dairy Products: Whole milk	65	3	4	2	14	5	120	50	tr
Skimmed milk	33	3	tr	tr	tr	5	130	50	tr
Single cream	210	2	21	13	65	3	80	40	tr
Double cream	450	2	48	29	140	2	50	25	tr
Plain yogurt, low-fat	50	5	1	tr	10	6	180	75	tr
Thick Greek yogurt	135	6	10	6	10	8	130	75	tr
Fromage frais, low-fat	90	17	1	tr	tr	—	110	35	tr
Brie	335	21	28	17	100	tr	185	630	tr
Camembert	300	23	24	15	70	tr	380	1410	1
Cheddar	405	26	34	20	70	tr	800	610	tr
Cottage cheese, low-fat	95	14	4	2	15	1	60	450	tr
Edam	305	24	23	14	70	tr	740	980	tr
Feta	265	14	21	15	90	4	490	1115	1
Gruyère	410	30	32	19	110	tr	1010	335	tr
Mozzarella, low-fat	280	27	17	11	55	3	730	530	tr
Parmesan	405	35	30	18	90	tr	1220	760	tr
Ricotta, low-fat	140	11	8	5	30	5	270	125	tr
Roquefort	370	22	31	19	90	2	660	1810	tr
Stilton	460	26	40	24	120	tr	360	1150	tr
Fat and Eggs: Butter, unsalted	740	tr	82	49	230	tr	15	10	tr
Polyunsaturated margarine	730	tr	81	20	tr	0	5	800	0
Hard white vegetable fat	730	tr	81	30	0	0	0	0	0
Safflower oil	900	0	100	10	0	0	0	0	tr
Sunflower oil	900	0	100	13	0	0	0	0	tr
Virgin olive oil	900	0	100	14	0	0	0	0	tr
Eggs	150	12	11	3	450	tr	50	140	2
Egg yolks	340	16	31	10	1260	tr	130	50	6
Egg whites	35	9	tr	0	0	tr	5	190	tr
Miscellaneous: Bread, white	235	8	2	tr	0	50	100	540	2
Bread, wholemeal	215	9	3	tr	0	42	25	540	3
Pasta, dried	380	14	1	tr	0	84	25	5	1
Tofu	70	7	4	—	0	tr	505	5	1
Currants	245	2	0	0	0	63	95	20	2
Raisins	245	1	0	0	0	65	60	50	2
Sultanas	250	2	0	0	0	65	50	50	2
Honey	280	tr	0	0	0	76	5	10	tr
Salt (1 tsp)	0	0	0	0	0	0	tr	2132	0
Sugar, white	395	tr	0	0	0	100	tr	0	0

Glossary

Agar: a setting agent prepared from red seaweed, most easily available as flakes or powder, which is used as a vegetarian alternative to gelatine.

Balsamic vinegar: a mild, extremely fragrant wine-based vinegar made in northern Italy. Traditionally, it is aged in wooden casks.

Bamboo shoots: sold canned in the West, the best-quality bamboo shoots are known as winter bamboo. Ordinary bamboo is less tender.

Bâtonnet (also called bâton): a vegetable piece that has been cut in the shape of a stick; bâtonnets are slightly larger than julienne.

Bean curd: see Tofu.

Bean sprouts: the germinated and sprouted seeds of a wide selection of grains, pulses and other plants. Bean sprouts are rich in protein, iron and vitamins A, C, E, and those in the B group.

Buckwheat: the seed of the flowering buckwheat plant. Buckwheat groats (also called kasha) are hulled, steamed, dried and sometimes toasted to intensify flavour. Buckwheat flour is unrelated to wheat flour and lacks the proteins required to form gluten.

Burghul (also called bulgur): a type of cracked wheat, where the kernels are steamed and dried before being crushed.

Calorie (kilocalorie): a precise measure of the energy food supplies when broken down for use in the body.

Caraway seeds: the pungent seed of the herb caraway, often used to flavour rye bread.

Cardamom: the bittersweet aromatic dried seeds or whole pods of a plant in the ginger family.

Cayenne pepper: a fiery powder ground from the seeds and pods of various red chili peppers.

Celeriac (also called celery root): the knobby, tuberous root of a plant in the celery family.

Ceps (also called porcini): wild mushrooms with a pungent earthy flavour that survives drying or long cooking. Dried ceps should be soaked in hot water before they are used.

Chestnut mushroom: a cultivated mushroom with a dark skin and firm flesh. Its taste is stronger than that of button mushrooms.

Chili peppers: a variety of hot red or green peppers. Serranos and jalepeños are small fresh green chilies that are extremely hot. Anchos are dried poblano chilies that are mildly hot and dark red in colour. Fresh or dried, chili peppers contain volatile oils that can irritate the skin and eyes; they must be handled with extreme care *(caution, page 25)*.

Chinese cabbage (also called Chinese leaves): an elongated cabbage resembling cos lettuce, with long broad ribs and crinkled, light green to white leaves.

Chinese five-spice powder: a pungent blend of ground Sichuan pepper, star anise, cassia, cloves and fennel seeds; available in Asian food shops.

Cholesterol: a waxlike substance manufactured in the human body and also found in foods of animal origin. Although a certain amount of cholesterol is necessary for proper body functioning, an excess can accumulate in the arteries, contributing to heart disease. See also Monounsaturated fats; Polyunsaturated fats; Saturated fats.

Cloud-ear mushrooms (also called tree ears, tree fungus, mo-er and wood ears): flavourless fungus used primarily for their crunchy texture and dark colour. Cloud ears expand more than other mushrooms when soaked.

Coriander (also called cilantro): the pungent peppery leaves of the coriander plant or its earthy tasting dried seeds. It is a common seasoning in Middle Eastern, Oriental and Latin-American cookery.

Cornmeal: finely ground dried maize, often used in combination with wheat flour.

Cottage cheese: a low-fat soft cheese with a mild flavour and a non-uniform texture. It is made from skimmed milk but the cottage cheese used in this book has added cream to give it a fat content of 4 per cent.

Couscous: cereal processed from semolina into pellets. A classic North African stew, it is traditionally steamed and served with meat and vegetables.

Creamed coconut: coconut flesh that has been dried and pressed into blocks.

Crème fraîche: a slightly ripened, sharp-tasting French double cream containing about 35 per cent fat.

Crêpe: a paper thin pancake that can accommodate a variety of savoury or sweet fillings.

Cumin: the aromatic seed of an umbelliferous plant similar to fennel used, whole or powdered, as a spice, especially in Indian and Latin-American dishes. Toasting gives it a nutty flavour.

Dietary fibre: a plant-cell material that is undigested or only partially digested in the human body, but which promotes healthy digestion of other food matter.

Dijon mustard: a smooth or grainy hot mustard once manufactured only in Dijon, France.

Fennel: a herb (also called wild fennel) whose feathery leaves and dried seeds have a mild anise flavour. Its vegetable relative, the bulb — or Florence — fennel (also called finocchio) can be cooked, or eaten raw in salads.

Fenugreek: a plant native to Asia. The seeds are highly aromatic with a bitter aftertaste and are normally used as a flavouring in Indian cookery.

Feta cheese: a salty Greek and Middle Eastern cheese made from goat's or sheep's milk.

Fromage frais: a soft cheese made from skimmed milk. The *fromage frais* used in this book has a 0.5 per cent fat content.

Garam masala: an aromatic mixture of ground spices used in Indian cookery. It usually contains coriander, cumin, cloves, ginger and cinnamon.

Ghee: a type of clarified butter much used in Indian cookery. To make ghee, butter is heated until it separates into a clear yellow liquid and milk solids. The solids are allowed to brown, which imparts a nutty flavour to the liquid, and are then skimmed off. The remaining liquid — ghee — has a higher burning point than most oils.

Ginger: the spicy, buff-coloured rhizome, or rootlike stem, of the ginger plant, used as a seasoning either fresh or dried and powdered.

Goat cheese: a pungent soft cheese made with goat's milk.

Jerusalem artichoke: neither an artichoke nor from Jerusalem, this vegetable is the tuberous root of a member of the sunflower family. In texture, colour and flavour, it resembles the water chestnut.

Julienne: the French term for vegetables or other food cut into strips.

Kasha: see Buckwheat.

Kohlrabi: a cruciferous vegetable whose major edible part is an enlarged part of the stem, a light-green or lavender bulb.

Lemon grass (citronella): a long, woody, lemon-flavoured stalk that is shaped like a spring onion. Lemon grass is available in Asian shops.

Mace: the ground aril, or covering, that encases the nutmeg seed.

Mange-tout: flat green pea pods eaten whole, with only stems and strings removed.

Mango: a fruit grown throughout the tropics, with sweet, succulent, yellow-orange flesh, rich in vitamin A. Like papaya, it can cause an allergic reaction.

Millet: a nutritious grain with a nutty, mild taste.

Molasses: a thick, dark, strongly flavoured syrup, rich in iron and a good source of B vitamins. It is a by-product of sugar-cane refining.

Monounsaturated fats: one of the three types of fats found in foods. Monounsaturated fats are believed not to raise the level of cholesterol in the blood.

Mozzarella: soft kneaded cheese from southern Italy, traditionally made from buffalo's milk, but now also made from cow's milk. Full-fat mozzarella has a fat content of 40 to 50 per cent, but lower-fat versions are available. The low-fat mozzarella used in the recipes in this book has a fat content of only about 16 per cent.

Non-reactive pan: a cooking vessel whose surface does not chemically react with food. Materials used include stainless steel, enamel, glass and some alloys. Untreated cast iron and aluminium may react with acids, producing discoloration or a peculiar taste.

Nori: paper-like dark green or black sheets of dried seaweed, often used in Japanese cuisine as a flavouring or as wrappers for rice and vegetables.

Okra: the green pods of a plant indigenous to Africa where it is called gumbo.

Olive oil: any of various grades of oil extracted from olives. Extra virgin olive oil has a full, fruity flavour and very low acidity. Virgin olive oil is lighter in flavour and slightly higher in acidity. Pure olive oil, a processed blend of olive oils has the lightest taste and highest acidity. For salad dressings, virgin and extra virgin olive oils are preferred. Store in a cool, dark place.

Oyster mushroom: a variety of wild mushroom, now cultivated. They are stronger tasting than button mushrooms and are usually pale brown.

Phyllo (also spelt "filo"): a paper-thin flour and water pastry popular in Greece and the Middle East. It can be made at home or bought, fresh or frozen, from delicatessens and shops specializing in Middle Eastern food.

Pine-nuts (also called *pignoli*): seeds from the cone of the stone pine, a tree native to the Mediterranean. Toasting brings out their buttery flavour.

Pistachio nuts: green, with a pleasant flavour, pistachio nuts must be shelled and boiled for a few minutes before their skins can be removed.

Polenta: cooked cornmeal, traditionally eaten in northern Italy.

Polyunsaturated fats: one of the three types of fats found in foods. They exist in abundance in such vegetable oils as safflower, sunflower, corn and soya bean. Polyunsaturated fats lower the level of cholesterol in the blood.

Pot barley: a nutritious whole grain that has had just

the hard, outer husk removed, thus retaining the vitamins and minerals present in the outer layers. When the grain is polished it is known as pearl barley; this process reduces the vitamin B$_1$ present by 60%.

Quark: a type of soft cheese with a mild, clean, slightly acid flavour. The quark used in the recipes in this book is very low in fat, but smoother varieties which contain added cream are also available.

Recommended Daily Amount (RDA): the average daily amount of an essential nutrient recommended for healthy people by the UK Department of Health and Social Security.

Rice wine: wine made from fermented rice. The best imported Chinese rice wine is shao-hsing. Japanese rice wine, sake, has a different flavour, but it may be used as a substitute for the Chinese variety. If rice wine is unavailable, use dry sherry.

Ricotta: soft, mild, white Italian cheese, made from cow's or sheep's milk. Full-fat ricotta has a fat content of 20 to 30 per cent, but the low-fat ricotta used in this book has a fat content of only about 8 per cent.

Rocket (also called arugula): a peppery-flavoured salad plant with long, leafy stems, popular in Italy.

Safflower oil: a vegetable oil that contains the highest proportion of polyunsaturated fats.

Saffron: the dried, yellowish-red stigmas (or threads) of the saffron crocus, which yield a powerful yellow colour as well as a pungent flavour. Powdered saffron may be used instead, but it has less flavour.

Saturated fats: one of the three types of fats found in food. They exist in abundance in animal products and coconut and palm oils; they raise the level of cholesterol in the blood. Because high blood-cholesterol levels may cause heart disease, saturated fat consumption should be restricted to less than 15 per cent of the calories provided by the daily diet.

Savoy cabbage: a variety of head cabbage with a mild flavour and crisp, crinkly leaves.

Scorzonera: a thin, long, cylindrical root with brown or blackish skin, similar in shape and taste to salsify.

Semolina: the ground endosperm of kernels of durum wheat. Fine semolina makes a pasta of excellent resilience and body.

Sesame oil: an oil from the the sesame plant seed that has a nutty, smoky aroma. It is frequently used as a flavouring, especially in Chinese cooking.

Sesame seeds: small, nutty-tasting seeds used frequently, either raw or roasted in Middle Eastern and Indian cookery. They are used to make sesame oil.

Shiitake mushroom: a variety of mushroom, originally grown only in Japan, sold fresh or dried. The dried form should be soaked and stemmed before use.

Skimmed milk: milk from which almost all the fat has been removed.

Sodium: a nutrient essential to maintaining the proper balance of fluids in the body. In most diets, a major source of the element is table salt, which contains 40 per cent sodium. Excess sodium may contribute to high blood pressure, which increases the risk of heart disease. One teaspoon (5.5 g) of salt, with 2,132 milligrams of sodium, contains just over the maximum daily amount recommended by the World Health Organization.

Soft cheese: any soft, spreadable cheese with a high moisture content and a mild, slightly acidic flavour. The low-fat soft cheese used in this book has a fat content of 8 per cent.

Soured cream: cream that has been thickened by the addition of acid-producing bacteria which give it a tart taste. It has a 21 per cent fat content.

Soy sauce: a savoury, salty brown liquid made from fermented soya beans, available in light and dark versions. One tablespoon of ordinary soy sauce has 1,030 milligrams of sodium; lower-sodium variations, as used in this book, may contain half that amount.

Strong flour: a white flour milled from strains of wheat with a high protein content. The high proportion of protein, which combines with water to form gluten, produces breads with an even texture.

Sun-dried tomatoes: tomatoes that have been naturally dried in the sun, then preserved in oil and seasoning, usually including herbs. Sold in jars or cans and used to garnish pasta, pizza or salads.

Sweet potato: one of two types of nutritious tuber, one with yellowish mealy flesh, the other with a moist, sweet, orange flesh. The latter is often sold as yam but should not be confused with the true yam (see below).

Tabasco sauce: a hot, unsweetened chili sauce.

Tahini (also called sesame paste): a nutty-tasting paste made from ground sesame seeds that are usually roasted.

Tamarind (also called Indian date): the pulp surrounding the seeds of the tamarind plant, yielding a juice considerably more sour than lemon juice. Grown and used throughout Asia, tamarind is available fresh in pod form, in bricks or as a concentrated paste.

Tofu (also called bean curd): a dense, unfermented soya bean product with a mild flavour. Tofu is rich in protein, relatively low in calories and free of cholesterol. (See also box, page 85.)

Tomato paste: a concentrated tomato purée, available in cans and tubes, used in sauces and soups.

Total fat: an individual's daily intake of polyunsaturated, monounsaturated and saturated fats. Nutritionists recommend that fats provide no more than 35 per cent of the energy in the diet. The term as used in this book refers to the combined fats in a given dish or food.

Turmeric: a yellow spice from a plant related to ginger, used as a colouring agent and occasionally as a substitute for saffron. Turmeric has a musty odour and a slightly bitter flavour.

Vine leaves: the tender, lightly flavoured leaves of the grapevine, used in many ethnic cuisines as wrappers for savoury mixtures. The leaves are usually packed in brine and should be rinsed before use.

Virgin olive oil: see Olive oil.

Water chestnut: the walnut-sized tuber of an aquatic Asian plant, with rough brown skin and sweet, crisp white flesh.

Wheat germ: the embryo of the wheat kernel, usually separated out in milling. Wheat germ is high in protein and fat. It should be refrigerated after opening because it can quickly turn rancid.

Wild rice: the seeds of a water grass native to the Great Lakes region of the United States. Wild rice is appreciated for its robust flavour.

Yam: a number of varieties of hairy tuber, rich in vitamin A and similar in taste, when cooked, to the potato. Sometimes known as the Indian potato, it should not be confused with the sweet potato, which is sometimes also sold as yam. The yam is less sweet and less widely available than the sweet potato.

Yeast, easy-blend: a recently developed strain of yeast that reduces the time necessary for rising.

Index

Picture Credits

Cover: James Murphy. 4: top, Martin Brigdale; left, Andrew Whittuck; right, Simon Butcher. 5: left and right, Martin Brigdale; bottom, Chris Knaggs. 6: John Elliott. 10-11: John Elliott. 12: Simon Butcher. 13: Martin Brigdale. 14: top, Simon Butcher; right, Taran Z Photography. 15: John Elliott. 16: Chris Knaggs. 17: David Johnson. 18-19: John Elliot. 20: Chris Knaggs. 21: top, Taran Z Photography; bottom, Martin Brigdale. 22: James Jackson. 23: David Johnson. 24: John Elliott. 25: Andrew Whittuck. 26: John Elliott. 27: Chris Knaggs. 28: Simon Butcher. 29: Andrew Whittuck. 30: Martin Brigdale. 31-33: John Elliott. 34: Andrew Whittuck. 35: John Elliott. 36: Simon Butcher. 37: John Elliott. 38: Chris Knaggs. 39-40: John Elliott. 41-42: James Jackson. 43: Martin Brigdale. 44: John Elliott. 45: Martin Brigdale. 47: John Elliott. 48-49: David Johnson. 50-53: John Elliott. 54: David Johnson. 55-56: Simon Butcher. 57: David Johnson. 59: Andrew Whittuck. 60: David Johnson. 61: Martin Brigdale. 62-63: John Elliott. 64: James Jackson. 65-67: Andrew Whittuck. 68: Simon Butcher. 69: Chris Knaggs. 70: John Elliott. 71: Martin Brigdale. 72: Chris Knaggs. 73: Simon Butcher. 74: James Jackson. 75: Martin Brigdale. 76: John Elliott. 77: Martin Brigdale. 78: Chris Knaggs. 79: top, David Johnson; bottom, John Elliott. 80: Chris Knaggs. 81: Andrew Whittuck. 82: James Jackson. 83: top, Steve Ashton; bottom, John Elliott. 84: John Elliott. 85: Andrew Whittuck. 86: Chris Knaggs. 87-91: John Elliott. 92: Simon Butcher. 93-95: John Elliott. 96: Chris Knaggs. 97: top, John Elliott;

bottom, Simon Butcher. 98: John Elliott. 99: Martin Brigdale. 100: Andrew Whittuck. 101-102: John Elliott. 103: Simon Butcher. 104: John Elliott. 105-106: Andrew Whittuck. 107: John Elliott. 108-109: Simon Butcher. 110: Andrew Whittuck. 111-113: John Elliott. 114: David Johnson. 115: John Elliott. 116: Martin Brigdale. 117-118: John Elliott. 119: David Johnson. 120: John Elliott. 121: top, Martin Brigdale; bottom, John Elliott. 122-126: John Elliott. 127: David Johnson. 128: Simon Butcher. 129-130: Chris Knaggs. 131: John Elliott. 132: Simon Butcher. 133: David Johnson. 134-135: John Elliott.

Props: the editors wish to thank the following outlets and manufacturers; all are based in London unless otherwise stated. Cover: plate, Rosenthal (London) Ltd. 4: *(top)* plates and cutlery, Mappin & Webb Silversmiths; cloth and napkin, Ewart Liddell; *(left)* platter, Hutschenreuther (UK) Ltd; cloth, Ewart Liddell. 5: *(left)* china, Rosenthal (London) Ltd; *(bottom)* plate, Inshop. 14: platter, Villeroy & Boch. 15: oblong platter, Rosenthal (London) Ltd. 17: marble, W.E. Grant & Co. (Marble) Ltd. 20: plate, Hutschenreuther (UK) Ltd. 21: plates and cutlery, Mappin & Webb Silversmiths; cloth and napkin, Ewart Liddell. 24: plate, Hutschenreuther (UK) Ltd. 25: plate, Villeroy & Boch. 28: plate, Inshop. 29: platter, Hutschenreuther (UK) Ltd; cloth, Ewart Liddell. 30: fork, Mappin & Webb Silversmiths. 31: pie

dish, Winchcombe Pottery, The Craftsmen Potters Shop. 32: plate, Royal Worcester, Worcester. 51: marble, W.E. Grant & Co. (Marble) Ltd. 57: plates, Royal Worcester, Worcester. 59: two dishes, Clive Bowen, The Craftsmen Potters Shop. 66: plate, Royal Worcester, Worcester. 71: china, Hutschenreuther (UK) Ltd. 74: plate, Villeroy & Boch. 75: china, Rosenthal (London) Ltd. 77: platter, John Leach, The Craftsmen Potters Shop. 78: plate, Rosenthal (London) Ltd. 79: plate, Royal Worcester, Worcester. 81: platter, Royal Worcester, Worcester. 84: plate, Hutschenreuther (UK) Ltd. 87: platter, Rosenthal (London) Ltd. 90-91: white marble, W.E. Grant & Co. (Marble) Ltd. 94: plates, Line of Scandinavia. 96: plate, Inshop. 98: marble, W.E. Grant & Co. (Marble) Ltd. 99: plate, Royal Worcester, Worcester. 100: marble, W.E. Grant & Co. (Marble) Ltd. 101: plate, Royal Worcester, Worcester. 102: plate, Villeroy & Boch. 105: napkin, Ewart Liddell. 106: pizza pan, Chicago Pizza Pie Factory. 107: plate, Rosenthal (London) Ltd. 108: plates, Villeroy & Boch. 111: large plate, Line of Scandinavia. 112: marble, W.E. Grant & Co. (Marble) Ltd. 113: plate, Inshop. 116: plate, Hutschenreuther (UK) Ltd; cutlery, Mappin & Webb Silversmiths. 123: marble, W.E. Grant & Co. (Marble) Ltd. 126: napkin, W.E. Grant & Co. (Marble) Ltd. 127: plates, Inshop; platter, Rosenthal (London) Ltd. 129: platter, Royal Copenhagen Porcelain and Georg Jensen Silversmiths Ltd. 132: plate, Rosenthal (London) Ltd. 133: plates, Rosenthal (London) Ltd.

Acknowledgements

The index for this book was prepared by Myra Clark, London. The editors also wish to thank the following: René Bloom, London; Sara Brown, London; Maureen Burrows, London; Jonathan Driver, London; Neil Fairbairn, Wivenhoe, Essex; Ellen Galford, Edinburgh; Wendy Gibbons, London; Hyams and Cockerton Ltd, London; Bridget Jones, Guildford, Surrey; Perstorp Warerite Ltd, London; Sharp Electronics (UK) Ltd, London; Jane Stevenson, London; Toshiba (UK) Ltd, London.

Colour separations by Fotolitomec, S.N.C., Milan, Italy
Typesetting by G. Beard and Son Ltd, Brighton, Sussex, England
Printed and bound by Oriental Press, Dubai